Doing Business in Emerging Europe

Doing Business in Emerging Europe

Y. Zoubir and F.S. Lhabitant

palgrave
macmillan

First published 2003 by
PALGRAVE MACMILLAN
Houndmills, Basingstoke, Hampshire RG21 6XS and
175 Fifth Avenue, New York, N.Y. 10010
Companies and representatives throughout the world

PALGRAVE MACMILLAN is the global academic imprint of the Palgrave Macmillan division of St. Martin's Press, LLC and of Palgrave Macmillan Ltd. Macmillan® is a registered trademark in the United States, United Kingdom and other countries. Palgrave is a registered trademark in the European Union and other countries.

ISBN 0–333–99301–2

This book is printed on paper suitable for recycling and made from fully managed and sustained forest sources.

A catalogue record for this book is available from the British Library.

Library of Congress Cataloging-in-Publication Data
Zoubir, Yahia H.
    Doing business in emerging Europe/Y. Zoubir & F.S. Lhabitant.
        p.   cm.
    Includes bibliographical references and index.
    ISBN 0–333–99301–2
    1. Europe, Eastern—Commerce—Handbooks, manuals, etc.   2. Europe, Central—Commerce—Handbooks, manuals, etc.   3. Former Soviet republics—Commerce—Handbooks, manuals, etc.   4. Turkey—Commerce—Handbooks, manuals, etc.   I. Lhabitant, François-Serge. II. Title.
HF1532.7 .Z368 2002
330.947—dc21

2002029317

10   9   8   7   6   5   4   3   2   1
12   11   10   09   08   07   06   05   04   03

Printed and bound in Great Britain by
Antony Rowe Ltd, Chippenham and Eastbourne

To my father, to the memory of my mother, my life-long inspiration, and to the memory of my father-in-law, Harold 'Bud' Penningroth, a true friend whose continuous encouragement will never be forgotten.

Yahia H. Zoubir

To my mother, to my wife, and to the memory of my father.

François-Serge Lhabitant

Contents

Foreword

Dr Yusaf Akbar

The term 'emerging markets' has many different connotations for many different people. It conjures up notions of niche, entrepreneurial opportunities for those managers prepared to take risks. It also implies a degree of dynamism in changing market opportunities for the brave.

On a less positive note, emerging markets imply a significant number of impediments to doing business in the time-honoured way in developed, mature markets. A lack of transparency, an absence of predictable institutions, clientelism and underdeveloped consumer demand are the negative benchmarks for managers in these countries. Indeed, trying to be successful in these kinds of markets normally implies a mixture of frustration, optimism and patience. Linguistic barriers also play a significant role in slowing down business transactions. Local market knowledge, so intrinsically linked to cultural-linguistic barriers is arguably one of the most difficult and intangible barriers to overcome in emerging markets. Countless anecdotes of cultural miscomprehension abound in trying to sign a contract or develop relationships with key suppliers and customers.

In many senses, this is precisely the aim of this book: to help managers get more business intelligence on emerging markets; to help prepare business people for the challenges they will face in future business endeavours. By taking such a broad range of countries in Eastern and Central Europe, this book provides an in-depth and comprehensive analysis of the institutional, environmental and structural issues facing entrepreneurs and managers in the diverse and challenging Eastern and Central European (ECE) region. The remainder of this foreword is devoted to giving the reader a brief summary of the structure of the book and offering some personal reflections on doing business in ECE – one of the most exciting regions of the world economy.

The concept of the 'PEST' analysis: evaluating Political, Economic, Social and Technological environments facing companies is a well-established and robust taxonomic approach. Indeed, a grasp of each of these factors enables managers to get an idea of 'country political risk' involved in doing business and especially foreign direct investment (FDI) decisions. The ratings agencies themselves have developed models for country risk, which help inform decision-makers on market entry strategies. All of these factors are also intrinsically linked – it would not be possible to get an understanding of the current investment climate in a particular emerging market without an understanding of the political situation. Each of the chapters in this book does an excellent job of opening up an understanding of the current business environment with reference to the current political situation.

In this context, it is important to realize that the majority of the countries surveyed in this book have made joining the European Union (EU) a central aim of foreign policy. Seen in this light, it is clear that we should expect an increasingly friendly approach towards foreign direct investment (FDI). This is because EU rules will require significant liberalization of the regulatory systems in place in these countries. Indeed, countries such as the Czech Republic and Poland have fully harmonized their domestic regulations on FDI with EU regulations making the legislative basis identical as that of the EU.

The political situation in these countries is also intrinsically linked to the economic development of these nations – as incomes rise in these ECE emerging markets, political stability is bound to increase as a broad based middle class will be expected to favour more business-friendly legislation in the fields of fiscal policy. This is likely to further encourage more liberal and business-minded politics and may well undermine nationalistic forces in the parliaments of these countries.

Notable among the countries covered by this volume is Belarus. The Belarus leadership under Lukashenko has decided that its economic future, rather than being based on inclusion within a wider EU, is to be based around a confusing mix of rapprochement with Russia and economic self-sufficiency. As the chapter notes, this creates specific problems for foreign business interests in this country.

Turkey is also an 'outlier' in the countries covered. First, this is because despite the official position that it would eventually become a member of the EU, its cultural background being seen as a link between Asia and Europe makes it unique. Second, despite the existence of a dynamic entrepreneurial class, Turkey is suffering from severe macroeconomic problems. The continuing disagreement over the future of Cyprus is also likely to hinder Turkey's entry into the EU.

Social changes are also closely linked to technological forces in these societies. The growth in the use of the Internet in these emerging markets has opened a youth demographic to international influences, thus increased demand for 'cosmopolitan' products and services continues. This is buttressed by increasing incomes and leisure time for the younger generation of citizens in these rapidly evolving societies.

Each of the chapters in this book has a section devoted to cultural issues. This is probably one of the most valuable aspects of this reference guidebook since despite the increased internationalization of these economies, cultural specificities remain important in all of the countries concerned. The difference between an Estonian and a Hungarian conducting contractual negotiations is huge and is largely a function of the indigenous cultural–linguistic map in each of the countries surveyed.

Indeed, the experience of many observers in ECE emerging markets is that an understanding and appreciation for the negotiating styles of different ethnicities in the region can liberate managers from being lost in seemingly endless barriers to successful business.

One of the most tangible aspects of ECE emerging markets is the rapid rate of change of attitudes to service provision. Whereas less than a decade ago, it would have been difficult to find late-opening convenience stores in many of these states, they are now commonplace and cater to both local and foreign citizens. Indeed, the growth of the service sector is probably the single biggest market opportunity for entrepreneurs in these societies.

With increased cosmopolitanism comes increased crime. One of the negative consequences of the changes since 1989 has been the growth in theft, violent crime and illegal drug-related activities. This has spawned a growth in 'protection' companies linked to aspects of Mafia and organized crime. On the positive side, future EU membership is forcing governments to clamp down on state corruption. Increased transparency in the fields of public procurement has a considerable way to go but it has improved manifestly since the early years of post-1989 transition.

Thus on balance, doing business in Eastern and Central Europe is likely to be easier, more exciting and hopefully more profitable for those managers and entrepreneurs who are seeking a challenge. Rising incomes, and increased access to the EU augur well for the future of these emerging markets. Indeed, there may come a time in which we no longer refer to these economies as 'emerging' markets. In the meantime, opportunities abound!

Dr Yusaf Akbar teaches International Political Economy at IMC Graduate School of Management, Central European University, Budapest, Hungary. He is author of *The Multinational Enterprise, Regulatory Convergence and EU Enlargement* (Palgrave Macmillan, 2002).

Introduction

The fall of the Berlin Wall in 1989 undoubtedly ranks as one of the most important events of the end of the twentieth century. The downfall of the symbol that stifled the hopes and dreams of several nations and their people was the predictable result of the half-hidden decrepitude of the Soviet empire and the centrifugal forces that cohabited within it. The fall of the wall marked the disappearance of what Winston Churchill called the 'Iron Curtain' and, more importantly, it signified the end of the Cold War. Despite all of Mikhail Gorbachev and of Boris Yeltsin's efforts, the formal disintegration of the Soviet Union was only a matter of time. After two attempted coups within the space of a year, the USSR finally acknowledged the independence of its former republics in 1991, thus closing a chapter of almost half a century of communist domination and downtrodden liberties in Eastern and Central Europe. The economic, political, social, and cultural transformation that ensued and unfolded was an extraordinary historic event.

Several 'new' states rose from the ashes of the Soviet empire and immediately engaged in the construction of viable market economies. From the perspective of the new leaderships in that region, the fall of the Soviet Union in 1991 meant that the wealth and prosperity of Western countries was finally within reach. But the initial euphoria rapidly gave way to tough budget constraints and discipline, privatization, and the arduous establishment of the working institutions of representative democracy.

A decade later, specialists of Eastern and Central Europe have reported important developmental disparities. A handful of countries, most noticeably those that were geographically closer to the West (e.g. Poland, Hungary, the Czech Republic, Slovenia, and to a lesser degree the Baltic States and Slovakia) have made significant progress towards free markets and democracy, and are even patiently queuing for a slice of the action within the European Union. However, a much longer list of other states, such as Albania, Bosnia-Herzegovina, Bulgaria, Macedonia, Romania, Yugoslavia, and the former non-Baltic Soviet republics, have made little or no progress. Finally, certain middle-of-the-road countries such as Belarus, Croatia, Slovakia, and Ukraine, are still struggling between the two categories at the whim of their political leaders.

Surprisingly, Eastern and Central Europe itself remains a relatively untapped market. Most investors prefer Russia, although not without risk, as evidenced by the events of 1998. Nevertheless, in most of these countries, the overall transition has been quite positive, and most observers forecast continued real growth in the coming years. Access to mid- to long-term capital, Western technology and management skills will be the key factors shaping the future development and success of the countries of that region. However, while opportunities abound, doing business there may prove to be quite convoluted. Building a business relationship in general depends in part upon obtaining reliable information not only about a partner, but also about the country's business, legal, political, cultural, and regulatory environment. In an emerging market, information is not readily available; often it is out of date or unreliable.

Our book, *Doing Business in Emerging Europe*, aims at filling this information gap. It provides the first user-friendly source of practical information for executives doing or planning on doing business in that region. For obvious reasons, we decided to focus on the subset of most promising countries, namely the Czech Republic, Estonia, Hungary, Latvia, Lithuania, Poland, Slovakia, Slovenia, and Turkey. We also decided to include an overview of Belarus and Ukraine, as they have the potential of becoming major emerging markets.

Since the objective of our book is to serve as a reference guide to business practitioners, we decided to avoid cumbersome footnotes and lengthy macroeconomic statistics that usually plague academic books. Using a common structure, each chapter provides detailed information on a broad range of important topics specific to each country. These include vital geographic and demographic data, a general overview of history and politics, various industry sectors, the investment climate, taxation, the types of business organizations, the banking system and services, the financial market, accounting and business practices, the legal and regulatory environment (including dispute-resolution options), as well as each country's etiquette, and cultural and business behaviour. We limited each chapter to no more than 8,000 words and switched all additional useful references, including on-line websites, contact addresses and a bibliography to a separate section. Our book draws primarily from public sources, which are listed in "References and Contacts".

In writing this book, every effort has been made to collect the most up-to-date information and present it in a clear manner. Of course, the information in the text is intended merely as general guidelines. Businesspeople should consult professional advisers for more detailed information on specific topics (for example, taxes, regulation, and legal issues) before making important decisions.

Writing this book was a great learning experience. However, we could not have completed it without those who have provided valuable suggestions and insights along the way. We would like to thank in particular our Editor, Caitlin Cornish, for allowing us to pursue this undertaking. Most sincere thanks go to Tanja Maffei, who served as Zoubir's research assistant in 1997 and 1998 at Thunderbird, The American Graduate School of International Management in Arizona, USA. In close collaboration with Zoubir, she developed a template, which all successive research assistants have used for every country under study. Zoubir would also like to thank Andrea Banes, his research assistant in 1999 at Thunderbird Europe in France, who did considerable research on Hungary and Poland. We would also like to thank our research assistants at Thunderbird Europe, namely, Shelby Kardas, Dipali Murti, Yvett Rebelo, Lucinda Gilbert, Brian Wozniak, and Yan Yanovskiy, for their assistance during the research process. We would also like to express our appreciation to Jill Monney for proofreading and checking over the manuscript. Last but by no means least, our gratitude go to our families for their support. This book was written during hours literally stolen from them. We hope that their patience will prove worthwhile.

1
Belarus

1.1 Basic facts

The Republic of Belarus is a small territory (207,600 sq km) situated in the heart of Europe, at the crossroads of trade routes from West to East and from North to South. It shares a border with Russia (959 km) in the northeast, Ukraine (891 km) in the south, Poland (605 km) in the east and the Baltic States in the northwest, that is Lithuania (502 km) and Latvia (141 km). The name 'Belarus' means 'white Rus' and there is still no exact version of its origin. Some historians believe that 'white' in old Slavic languages meant 'free', pointing to the fact that Belarus was never invaded by the Tartars, unlike the other principalities in the thirteenth to fifteenth centuries.

The Republic of Belarus is divided into six administrative provinces (Brest, Gomel, Grodno, Minsk, Mogilev and Vitebsk) that are subdivided into 120 administrative districts. The capital is Minsk (1.7 million inhabitants), an ancient city known as a major trade and craft centre. Other important cities are Gomel (0.5 million), Vitebsk (0.37 million), and Mogilev (0.37 million).

The Belarusian population consists of 10 million people, composed of pure Belarusians (77.9%), Russians (13%), Poles (4.1%), Ukrainians (2.9%) and other ethnic groups. The official language is Belarusian, a Slavic language closely related to Ukrainian and Russian. The latter was also retained in the 1994 Constitution as the language of inter-ethnic communication. English and German are also widely used for business purposes. Most of the population (71%) is urban and has a high level of education. The dominant religion is Eastern Orthodox (80%) followed by Roman Catholic, Protestant, Jewish and Muslim.

The Belarusian climate is characterized by cold winters and cool, humid summers. It represents a transition between a continental and maritime climate. The average daily temperature in the capital city, Minsk, ranges from 6 °C in January to 18 °C in July. The annual rainfall is around 558.8 to 711.2 mm.

The Belarusian terrain is generally flat and contains much marshland and agricultural land occupies almost half of the territory. Favourable natural conditions enable it to produce highly profitable commodities, such as milk, beef, pork, poultry meat, eggs, grain, potatoes, fibre flax, sugar beet, etc. The potential for cattle breeding represents the dominant commodity branch of agriculture. Rye, wheat, barley and oats are the main crops in the grain sector.

The official currency is the Belarusian rouble (official symbol BYR), as distinct from the Russian rouble.

Means of communication

Official statistics list 740 newspapers, 294 magazines, four information agencies and 145 television and radio stations in Belarus. Technically, these figures are correct. However, state-controlled newspapers dominate political information due to their wide circulation. In addition, there is only one domestic nationwide television channel, Belarusian Television (BT) and the leading television channels are Russian.

1.2 Historical background

It is hard to define precisely the origins of Belarus. Prior to the ninth century, its territory was occupied by several tribes that lived in small communities located in forests or near rivers and lakes. Then, some of these tribes – who had much in common in their language, customs and beliefs – decided to merge to create Kyivan Rus', the first East Slavic state, and adopted Christianity. When its Prince Yaroslav the Wise died in 1054, the state split into several principalities, including Polatsk and Turau, the nucleus of the future Belarus.

In 1240, the principalities of Belarus came under the control of Lithuania. In 1569, Poland and the Grand Duchy of Lithuania united under the name of the Polish–Lithuanian Commonwealth. Belarus remained part of this union until 1795, when Russia, Prussia and Austria dismantled the Polish territory. Belarus was transferred to the Russian Empire, with the exception of a few Western lands, which were given to Prussia. In 1839, Tsar Nicholas I adopted a policy of Russification, banned the Belarusian language and imposed Orthodox religion, heavy taxes, and military service lasting 25 years. This resulted in several anti-Russian uprisings and large-scale migrations (1.5 million people in 50 years) to the United States and Siberia.

During World War I, Belarus was the theatre of fierce battles between the German and Russian armies. In 1917, the Russian Revolution caused Tsar Nicholas II to abdicate and leave power to Lenin's Bolsheviks. In December, the Belarusian Congress proclaimed a republican government in Belarus and separated the country from the Bolshevik Russian Empire. Nevertheless, the result of the 1919–21 war between Russia and Poland was again the partitioning of Belarus between the Byelorussian Soviet Socialist Republic (BSSR) and Poland. The short renaissance of Belarusian culture in 1920–28 was thus brought to a halt by Stalin's mass deportations to Siberia and executions in the 1930s, as well as by Polish persecutions in western Belarus.

Belarus was also heavily affected during World War II. When Germany attacked Poland in 1939, Soviet troops occupied the Western part of Belarus and deported anyone not strictly following communist ideology. In June 1941, when German troops invaded Belarus on their way to Moscow, they imposed a policy of Germanization on Belarus and started mass execution of the Jewish population. During the three years of Nazi occupation, more than two million people died and most cities were devastated. To make matters worse, when the Red Army liberated Belarus from the Nazis, Stalin deported those who had collaborated with the Nazis in any way, including German prisoners of war, since they were 'ideologically contaminated', and those who were suspected of 'bourgeois nationalism'. Both Stalin and Khrushchev imposed a policy of heavy Russification, banned the Belarusian language and suppressed Belarusian national culture.

In 1986, Belarus was severely affected by the explosion of the Chernobyl nuclear reactor. It is estimated that Belarus absorbed around 70% of the radioactive contaminants spewed out by the accident. Several intellectuals also sent a petition to Gorbachev expressing their concerns about the future of the Belarus culture (the 'cultural Chernobyl'). Several groups started to publicly demand reforms. Nevertheless, in the 1990 elections, the Communist Party of Byelorussia won 86% of the seats in the republic's Supreme Soviet.

It was only in 1991 that a wave of major strikes put an end to the country's political apathy and ideological inertia. Following Estonia, Latvia and Ukraine, the Supreme Soviet in Minsk declared the independence of Belarus. After extensive negotiations, the Supreme Soviet adopted a new constitution that declared Belarus a democracy, granted freedom of religion, established Belarusian as the official language and proclaimed the Belarus' goal to become a neutral non-nuclear state. Nevertheless, the winner of the 1994 presidential election was Aleksandr Lukashenko, who is known for his intention to bind Belarus to Russia politically, economically and militarily.

1.3 Political environment

Belarus is a presidential republic. The constitution that came into force in March 1994 created the office of president and a constitutional court, with a clear separation of powers. The bicameral National Assembly (*Natsionalnoye Sobranie*) is a representative and legislative body that was established by the November 1996 constitutional referendum. In theory, it consists of 260 members. It is divided into a Council of the Republic and a House of Representatives. The Council of the Republic has 64 members, who serve a four-year term; the president appoints eight members and local council deputies elect the other 56. The House of Representatives has 110 members, all of whom came from the defunct Supreme Soviet. In practice, since the November 1996 constitutional referendum, the Belarusian parliament has a merely ceremonial function. This explains why (a) 40 members of the Supreme Soviet refused to join the House of Representatives on the grounds that the referendum was unconstitutional; and (b) the opposition withdrew its delegates and created a shadow government, called the opposition Supreme Soviet as a successor to the dissolved Supreme Soviet.

The president is the head of state as well as the head of the security police and the army. His powers have been significantly extended by the November 1996 constitutional referendum. Among these powers are the appointment of the prime minister, the nomination of candidates for six key ministries and the appointment of half of the members and the head of the Constitutional Court, as well as the head of the Supreme Court. Furthermore, the president may dissolve parliament in the event that it infringes upon the constitution. Therefore, in practice, president Lukashenko exercises complete control over most aspects of government.

According to the Ministry of Justice, there are 18 political parties in Belarus. The major parties are the Belarusian Communist Party (KPB) and the Agrarian Party (APB). The former models itself on the USSR, opposes reforms and privatization and supports Lukashenko, while the latter was founded by agrarian specialists and has a left wing pro-European orientation. In practice, many parliamentarians are registered as independents, and the opposition parties to president Lukashenko assemble in the Consultative Council of Parties. The latter comprises the Belarusian Popular Front (BNF), the United Civic Party (OGP), the Belarusian Social Democratic Party (BSDP), the Labour Party (BRP) and the Party of Communists of Belarus (PKB).

Since the 1996 referendum, there have been numerous tensions between the Lukashenko government and the opposition. According to the latter, Lukashenko continues to curtail human rights, limit opposition demonstrations and arrest key dissidents. There are also numerous tensions within the government, due to severe criticism by Lukashenko of government officials for failing to reduce inflation. This has resulted in various cabinet reshuffles.

Nevertheless, the parliamentary elections in October 2000 gave a majority to pro-Lukashenko candidates, which is not surprising given the boycott called by opposition forces. The presidential elections in September 2001 turned out to be non-democratic and meaningless. Officially, Lukashenko was re-elected for another four-year mandate with 75.6% of the votes on the first round in a poll condemned as rigged by Western governments, independent monitors and opposition parties. In their statement, EU officials even declared: 'The European Union regrets that the Belarus authorities have not seized the opportunity afforded by these presidential elections to engage their country fully on the path of democracy'.

1.4 Economic environment and infrastructure

Despite an ideal location, an industrial base superior to that of most of its neighbouring states, a cheap, educated workforce and ready access to the Russian marketplace, the economic environment in Belarus lags behind all of its neighbours due to the lack of economic reforms and concerns about the country's progress towards a market-oriented economy.

Macroeconomic tendencies

Despite the positive impact of Russia's strong recovery, economic growth has slowed down in Belarus, as illustrated by the GDP growth that dropped from 11.4% in 1997 to an estimated 4.8% in 2001. In 2001 (a presidential election year), the government significantly increased all wages following its promise of an average monthly wage equivalent to US$ 100. Consequently, the budgetary wage bill jumped from 6% of GDP in 2000 to an estimated 9% in 2001, while the overall wage share rose from 34% of GDP to 39%. This has put considerable pressure on enterprises, squeezing their profits and limiting their ability to invest and, therefore, their future growth potential. Overall, this resulted in a weakening of economic activity, as suggested by the rising level of inventories, non-cash transactions (in particular export barter arrangements) and domestic arrears. Although CPI inflation declined from 294% in 1999 to an estimated 68% in 2001, monthly inflation picked up in the second half of 2001 due to wage increases, monetary easing and some price liberalization. The unemployment rate remained low at 2.3% in 2001.

The current account deficit narrowed to US$ 162 million (1.3% of GDP) in 2000. This reflects an increase in agricultural exports and lower energy prices rather than any improvement in competitiveness. In reality, Belarus has been losing ground to its main external competitors, and most export increases were limited to sectors where Belarus has a quasi-monopolistic share in Russia.

Nevertheless, some steps were taken to initiate structural reforms in 2001. The Belarusian authorities made major headway in foreign exchange liberalization in 2001 leading to further deepening of the foreign exchange market. In order to achieve a monetary union with Russia in 2005, the National Bank of Belarus (NBB) anchored the Belarusian rouble to the Russian rouble with a band of 2% points around central parity and gave advanced warning of monthly devaluations. This band was later enlarged to 5 percentage points. Several interventions of the NBB were necessary to reduce pressures on the exchange market when demand for dollars increased on account of higher wage incomes. These interventions were facilitated by a stabilization loan of US$ 54 million granted by the Central Bank of Russia (CBR). During 2001, the Belarusian rouble depreciated against the US dollar by 2.5% per month on average, which was less than expected.

In 2001, the government also started to tighten monetary policy, dismantled the extensive system of price controls, reduced budgetary and implicit subsidies and cross-subsidies and announced a new investment code in October 2001. The latter is a single, comprehensive document, which replaced existing multiple regulations on foreign investment. It should provide a better legal framework for domestic and foreign investments and make the business/investment climate in Belarus friendlier.

Industry

During the Soviet era, Belarus' industry was dedicated to defence-related industries and human capital-intensive goods, such as machinery and equipment. Consequently, in comparison with other newly independent states, Belarus has maintained a relatively well-developed and diversified industrial profile, which represented around 34% of GDP in 2001. However, since 1991, Belarusian industrial companies have had to fight to find new markets as well as new suppliers of raw materials (e.g. steel, plastics, resins, etc.) and energy, on which Belarus continues to depend heavily. Moreover, in 2001, a sharp increase in real wages cut back labour productivity, weakened the financial situation of several enterprises and significantly increased barter and arrears. For instance, a large part of industrial production is used as payments in kind to Russia for gas and construction materials arrears. It should be noted that most industrial companies are still state-owned or state-controlled, and that the State also influences industrial companies that were privatized through output and price directives from the line ministries.

Energy

Belarus is highly dependent on energy imports, with 88% of its total energy consumption coming from Russia. Russia's Gazprom supplies gas to Belarus at a discount. The latter implicitly accounts for a transit fee on the transhipment of Russian gas to Europe through Belarusian pipelines. Despite this subsidy, Belarus has built up large debts to Gazprom, essentially because of difficult payment recovery from consumers. In April 2001, the corresponding debt to Gazprom was renegotiated and rescheduled over three years, with payments made by supplies of material resources. The sole natural gas distributor is Beltopgas and its major consumer (60%) is the Ministry of Fuel and Energy, which converts the gas into electricity and thermal energy is sold to enterprises, large industrial plants, households and the agricultural sector. Another major actor is Beltransgas, which operates the 3,780 miles of natural gas pipelines in Belarus and plans to build new pipelines and compressor stations.

Although it lacks significant indigenous oil reserves, Belarus also has a small oil industry and a fairly large refining industry, but the lack of political and economic reform in the past decade has hindered any investment to increase production or improve oil-processing efficiency. Consequently, Belarus needs to import most of its oil consumption from Russia, and about 50% of Russia's net oil exports transits through Belarusian pipelines.

On the electricity side, Belarus has a power-generating capacity of 7.4 GW, almost entirely from oil- and natural gas-fired power plants. This capacity is steadily decreasing due to decaying infrastructure, a lack of investment in maintenance and upgrades, and a decline in domestic demand. Consequently, Belarus needs to import most of its electricity from Lithuania. Large debts have been settled by a tripartite agreement with the Russian company Energiya, which buys electricity generated at Lithuania's Ignalina nuclear plant for subsequent delivery to Belarus. Energiya pays for the electricity with nuclear fuel for the Ignalina plant, while Belarus pays Russia by supplying commodities. This apparently does not contradict the 'nuclear-free' declaration of Belarus.

Agriculture

Agriculture occupies almost half of Belarus territory. It employs 17% of the active population, but only represents around 15% of GDP. Natural conditions favour the production of milk, beef, pork and poultry meat, eggs, rye, wheat, barley and oats, potatoes, sugar beets, fibre flax, vegetables and fruits. The agricultural sector remains largely unreformed, and most farms are of the collective or public type. In 'kolkhozes', production and all the assets are the property of all the members of these farms, while in 'sovhozes', production and all the assets are the property of the state, and the workers are state employees. There are also a few private farms, which have proven to be more productive than collective/ public farms. Nevertheless, the president has stressed that collective farms and state enterprises should remain the foundation of the agricultural sector. The imposition of fixed prices for certain basic agricultural products has created few incentives for private ownership. Furthermore, since the Chernobyl nuclear accident in neighbouring Ukraine, nearly one-third of Belarus agricultural land is unusable, since it was contaminated by fallout.

It should be noted that Belarus also possesses large, high-quality wood resources, particularly pine, fir, birch and oak. The total area of wood stock constitutes about 43% of the territory of the country and supplies timber, berries, mushrooms, medicinal raw material and honey. Despite intensive logging, the forest area is expanding due to well-organized reforestation.

Financial sector

Belarus has a two-tier banking system that consists of the National Bank of Belarus (NBB) and several commercial banks. The NBB is responsible for issuing money, managing the monetary and credit policy, stimulating the development of credit and financial institutions and regulating banking activities. Commercial banks execute all types of operations, including universal credit lending and investments. Six commercial banks (Belarusbank, Agroprombank, Promstroibank, Priorbank, Vnesheconombank, and Belinvestbank) account for more than 90% of the Belarusian banking sector activities. The state owns a majority stake in three of these banks and a significant minority stake in the three others. The financial situation of most banks is delicate, due to the recent increase in bad loans and the lack of financial reserves. Short-term defaults should be avoided due to significant direct and indirect government ownership and involvement in bank management, as well as the regular liquidity support of the NBB for troubled institutions.

However, long-term vulnerabilities will remain until the sector is completely restructured. There are several stock exchanges in Belarus, including the Agro-Industrial Trade and Stock Exchange, the Belarusian Stock Exchange, the Belarusian Universal Stock Exchange and the Minsk Stock Exchange. There are also 61 insurance companies, including the state-owned Belarusian state insurance company, which controls about 40% of total insurance deposits.

Telecommunications

Belarus has begun to renovate and upgrade its telecommunication services with the installation of digital equipment and fibre-optic links. Since 1999, a GSM digital cellular network has been introduced in the major cities of the country. A satellite-based system (INTELSAT, EUTELSAT, and INTERSPUTNIK) covers the national requirements in satellite circuits for telephony, data communications and television. Internet and e-mail services are now widely used in the capital city of Minsk, and on the regular mail side, EMS-BELARUS and the national network of express postal service, EXPRESS, offer one-day mail delivery.

Transportation

Belarus, situated at an important crossroads in Eastern Europe, has a well-developed transportation infrastructure, which plays a crucial role in the development of its economy. Belarus has over 55,000 km of roads and highways, which are in relatively good condition by CIS standards. Among these are major international transport corridors for cargo and passenger traffic (Berlin–Warsaw–Minsk–Moscow and Helsinki–St Petersburg–Pskov–Vitebsk–Gomel), as well as a good network of international bus routes. The railway network covers more than 5,500 km, but its use has been decreasing and now only operates at about 50% of its full capacity. Finally, Belarus has several civil airports, of which five are international – the major airport being Minsk-2. Belarus has no access to the sea and relies upon the use of other countries' ports, such as Klaipeda (Lithuania), Ventspils (Latvia), Kaliningrad (Russia), Kherson and Nikolayev (Ukraine).

1.5 Legal environment and regulations

Crime and corruption

Belarus has a moderate crime rate. However, foreigners tend to be easily targeted by common street crime and should, therefore, be cautious. Although Belarus is not a signatory of the OECD Convention on combating bribery, giving or accepting a bribe in Belarus is a criminal act. Nevertheless, corruption may be encountered, particularly at local level. So far, it has not been identified as a particularly significant obstacle to foreign direct investment.

Judicial system, dispute settlement and bankruptcy procedures

The Belarusian judicial system cannot provide a reliable and impartial mechanism for resolving disputes, since it is not independent of the executive power. In particular, tax authorities have the power to disregard adverse court decisions and seize any assets unilaterally. A bankruptcy law was passed in 1991 and significantly amended in 1998, but bankruptcy proceedings are not often contemplated. As an illustration, many state-controlled enterprises operate at a significant loss and are simply subsidized. Furthermore, there is no comprehensive system of laws regulating everyday business matters and there is often an arbitrary understanding of current legislation. Existing laws are often in contradiction with presidential decrees, which appear unexpectedly and require that investors change their policies overnight.

It should be noted that Belarus is a member of the International Centre for the Settlement of Investment Disputes (ICSID), also known as the Washington Convention. As an affiliate of the New York Convention on the recognition and enforcement of arbitration awards, the Government of Belarus is required to uphold arbitration awards in disputes between Belarusian and foreign parties.

Taxation, accounting, and auditing rules

An income and profit tax is levied on all commercial entities. Income tax is paid on dividends at a rate of 15%. Profit tax is paid on the balance-sheet profit at a rate of 30%. Reduced rates apply to specific sectors (agro-industrial, construction, repair, etc.) and very small companies. Profit tax concessions or exemptions may be granted legislatively to environmental programmes, scientific research and disaster recovery at Chernobyl, or enterprises employing a minimum percentage of disabled workers and retirement-age workers. For individuals, income tax is collected on a progressive rate scale. Taxable income includes cash income in domestic and foreign currencies and in-kind income earned in Belarus as well as abroad. As a general rule, the tax rates are high and are applied to income before deduction of legitimate business expenses. The tax system also includes a real estate tax (1% for legal entities), a land tax, and a tax on use of natural resources.

Laws on establishing and conducting business

In September 1998, president Lukashenko suspended the procedure for business registration on the ground that it was too liberal. His major concern was the profusion of 'one-day' firms that were created to make a fast sale or purchase of hard currencies and then disappear. The new procedure he established in March 1999 is much more stringent and likely to raise concerns among new investors. Among other things, (a) the registering authority has full discretion to refuse an application for a limited liability corporation or to close down an existing corporation without court approval; and (b) limited liability clauses may be waived and the owners of an insolvent business may be held personally liable if a court so decides. In addition, to establish an enterprise with foreign capital in Belarus, it is necessary to apply for state registration at the Ministry of Foreign Economic Relations.

Various forms of business organizations available to foreigners

Foreign investment in Belarus may take several forms. The most widespread is the share participation in enterprises established jointly with Belarusian legal entities and individuals – joint ventures, which are regulated by the law 'On Foreign Investments on the Territory of the Republic of Belarus'. They essentially take the form of joint-stock societies and limited liability companies. The minimum contribution for a foreign investor is US$ 20,000. The law guarantees foreign investors the right to transfer dividends abroad in free convertible currencies. If the foreign investors represent more than 30% of the capital, these joint ventures may also set up prices on their products, works and services and choose their suppliers. An alternative is to set up an enterprise completely owned by foreign investors, a branch enterprise (the founder is not liable for a branch enterprise), or a company's representation (it is not a legal entity and does all its business on behalf of the represented company).

Restrictions on foreign investments

Generally, there is no particular discrimination or screening against foreign investors. However, by law, foreign investment in banking, insurance, and stock exchanges may not exceed 49% of the outstanding shares.

Investment incentives

Foreign investors and foreign enterprises (businesses in which the foreign ownership is at least 30%) are entitled to substantial value added tax (VAT), customs and income tax privileges at the initial stage of their business activities in Belarus, while local investors are denied many of such benefits. The Belarusian government may also provide additional benefits on an ad hoc basis, particularly to major big-name investors. The Belarusian Foreign Investment Promotion Agency (BFIPA) is also a useful source of support in such areas as legislation of business and search for local partners.

Protection of property rights

As a former member of the Soviet system, Belarus did not recognize the intellectual property rights of individuals. In 1994, the Civil Code was amended to define the rights that could be protected, that are patents for inventions, trademarks, service marks, and computer programs. Moreover, Belarus is a member of the World Intellectual Property Organization (WIPO) and a signatory to many other conventions on intellectual property rights.

Entry requirements

Foreign citizens entering Belarus – even in transit – should have a passport valid for three months beyond the intended stay, necessary travel documents for return or onward travel, and a visa. The latter is absolutely necessary, and obtaining one normally requires an official invitation from an organization authorized to invite business visitors to Belarus. Belarus also requires all foreign visitors entering the country to purchase Belarusian medical insurance, regardless of any other insurance one might have. The cost is proportional to the expected length of stay.

1.6 Business environment

Privatization

The Ministry for Managing State Property and Privatization manages and co-ordinates the privatization process in Belarus. Its major aim is to reorganize state-owned and leased enterprises by turning them into open joint-stock companies to increase productivity, while at the same time avoiding social dislocation. The major channels to privatization are the transformation of state-owned enterprises into open joint-stock companies and the sale of state property through auctions and tenders.

Foreign investors may participate in these auctions and tenders, while specific authorization is needed in the case of direct transactions.

So far, privatization in Belarus has been quite slow and limited to small-scale enterprises. Although the government's intention is officially to accelerate the privatization process, the five-year economic development programme presented in May 2000 explicitly mentions that the state should continue to play a dominant role in the economy. Furthermore, according to the existing legislation, sale of stakes over 50% in industrial companies is forbidden, and the difficulty in converting the Belarusian rouble to hard currency is seriously deterring Western investors.

Foreign direct investment (FDI)

Foreign direct investment peeked at US$ 443.2 million in 1999 due to large investments by Russia's Gazprom in the building the Yamal–Western Europe pipeline through Belarus, but fell to US$ 90 million in 2000. This low level is not surprising given the sluggish privatization process, the regular state interventions in private sector operations, the numerous price and wage controls and foreign trade restrictions.

Apart from the Yamal–Western Europe pipeline, most FDI takes the form of joint ventures and wholly foreign-owned businesses. The major investors to date are coming from Germany (12.4%), the Netherlands (10.9%), Cyprus (6.9%), the US (6.6%), the UK (4.2%) and Poland (4.1%). Among the largest Western foreign investors in Belarus are Coca-Cola (US), Fresiniuss (Germany), McDonald's (US) and MAN (Germany).

Free economic and trade areas

To attract foreign investment and promote trade and economic relations, the Belarus government has created free economic zones (FEZ) in the border town of Brest (December 1996), the capital, Minsk (March 1998), Gomel-Raton (March 1998) and Vitebsk (August 1999). FEZ residents enjoy low land rents, as well as several tax privileges, for example five-year tax exemption on profit growth from production, reduced profit taxes from 30% to 15%, VAT exemption for goods imported into and exported from the zone, VAT reduction from 20% to 10% otherwise, etc. In addition, FEZ residents should have the support for their investment from the central and local authorities, and these investments cannot be nationalized, requisitioned or confiscated. Belarus has also free trade agreements with other CIS states providing for zero import tariffs, but the future of these is not clear if some of its members join the World Trade Organization (WTO).

Major trading partners

In year 2000, Belarus imported US$ 8.5 billions' worth of goods and exported US$ 6.1 billion. The major export partners in 2000 were Russia (51%), Ukraine (7.6%), Latvia (6.3%), Lithuania (6.1%), Poland (3.8%) and Germany (3.1%). The major import partners were Russia (65.3%), Germany (6.9%), Ukraine (4%), Poland (2.5%) and Italy (2%).

Although a switch in Russian demand towards higher quality imports remains a concern to Belarusian producers, it is likely that Belarus will still have access to a niche market for low- or middle-quality products as long as regional and income disparities in Russia persist. In the absence of progress in large-scale privatization, restructuring or private sector growth, Belarusian producers will find it much easier to switch from one Russian region to another than to break into more competitive, non-traditional markets.

Foreign trade agreements

Belarus has close economic and commercial ties with Russia. The two countries have signed numerous bilateral agreements and their parliaments even ratified an economic-union treaty in December 1999. The original schedule included the harmonization of price regulations in 2001, a unified tax code in 2002, a harmonized foreign trade and customs regime by 2005, and a monetary union by 2005. Despite this ambitious programme, overall progress in economic and political integration has been limited.

Belarus is also a member of the Commonwealth of Independent States (CIS). According to the free-trade agreement signed in 1992, import duties are in principle not imposed on trade within the CIS. However, the large number of export and foreign exchange controls, combined with the accumulation of arrears and the reliance on barter transactions, has significantly limited the benefits of this free-trade agreement.

It should be noted that Belarus, Russia, Kazakhstan, the Kyrgyzstan, and Tajikistan signed a treaty setting up the Eurasian Economic Community (EAEC) in October 2000. The EAEC is a first step towards NAFTA-style international policy agreements and the Committee on Regional Trade Agreements of the WTO has recognized it. Belarus is also currently engaged in negotiations for its accession to the WTO.

Value added tax (VAT)

Since January 2000, all legal entities are subject to VAT, which is calculated on the total value of the goods, including customs duty and excise tax where applicable. There are several VAT rates in force, varying from 0% (exports and transit via the territory of Belarus of goods and related services) and going up to 20% (most goods). It should be noted that the VAT is collected when goods and services are imported from CIS countries while goods and services exported to CIS countries are not taxed. Exceptions are Russia, Turkmenistan and Georgia, for which Belarus maintains the country of origin principle.

Tariff system

On the import side, Belarus has a widespread and escalating import-tariff structure, with a maximum rate at 150% (for vodka). However, the average rate for imports is 7.43%, which implies a moderate level of protectionism. A few quantitative import restrictions remain, in accordance with Articles XX and XXI of GATT. There are also preferential rates for developing countries (half of the most-favoured-nation rate) and least-developed countries (0%). On the export side, Belarus has tariffs, quotas and licensing requirements for a number of raw materials and intermediate goods. These are required to ensure a sufficient supply of goods for the domestic market, given that domestic prices are regulated and below the world market level.

Foreign trade regulations

Virtually any import contract must be registered within 10 days with the Ministry of Foreign Economic Relations, which issues an import certificate. Failure to register a contract may result in heavy fines, customs problems, and a bank refusal to make the corresponding payment. Importers must also ensure that they receive goods that they have paid for within 60 days of the due date. It should be noted that the state has a monopoly on several types of imports (e.g. pharmaceuticals, etc.).

Any export activity requires permission from the competent authorities. Exporters must ensure they receive payment for the products they have exported within 60 days of the shipment date. Furthermore, all exporters are required to sell 30% of their hard currency earnings.

1.7 Etiquette and cultural issues

Belarus has a strong publishing and musical tradition, which goes back to the bibles printed in Eastern Europe, as well as several Orthodox hymns and sermons. After several years of persecution under Soviet occupation, the Belarusian cultural scene is now undergoing a revival. On the literature side, popular authors are Jakub Kolas and Natalla

Arseneva. In the world of music, Belarusian folk music is well known and the Minsk opera and ballet companies enjoy international reputations. Belarusians tend to be formal in business circumstances and are rarely effusive in public. Greetings are usually limited to a handshake and the pronouncement of one's name, including between men and women. Only close friends or relatives will give a kiss on the cheek in public. Dinner invitations normally take place in restaurants. An invitation at someone's home is a great honour and should always be accepted. In such a case, one should arrive bearing gifts, and eat and drink plentifully. Politics and economics are normally perfectly acceptable topics of conversation. Toasts are common practice at dinner and foreigners are expected to make at least one toast.

2
Croatia

Having recently won its independence, Croatia has largely completed its transition from socialism to a market economy. The new government that took office in early 2000 has strengthened democratic institutions and opened up Croatia to closer integration with Europe.

2.1 Basic facts

Situated at the crossroads between Central Europe and the Mediterranean, the territory of Croatia spreads its 56,538 sq km in an arc, with a long Adriatic coastline forming the Western leg and the land between the rivers Drava and Sava forming the northern leg. Croatia shares a border with Slovenia in the northwest (670 km), Hungary in the north (329 km), Bosnia-Herzegovina in the south (932 km), Serbia (241 km) and Montenegro (25 km) in the southeast and Italy in the west (coastal border). The Danube is the eastern border with Serbia, while the rivers Sava and Drava form the southern and northern borders with Bosnia-Herzegovina and Hungary respectively.

The terrain of Croatia is diverse. The eastern region of Croatia is mostly flatland, which is a part of the Panonian Plain. The northwest is mostly hills and river valleys, while central Croatia is the highest part of the country with Mount Velebit (1757 m) and Mount Dinara (1830 m). The Adriatic coast and its islands, islets and reefs make up the largest region of Croatia. It runs the entire length of the Western border, from the 430 km Istrian peninsula in the north to Dubrovnik in the south. As could be expected, the climate is also quite diverse: northern Croatia has a continental climate, central Croatia has a semi-highland and highland climate, and the Croatian coast has a Mediterranean climate.

The total population is just above 4.3 million inhabitants. The major ethnic group is Croats (78.1%). National minorities include Serbs (12.2%), as well as Muslims, Slovenes, Hungarians, Montenegrins, Albanians, Czechs, Slovaks, Italians, and others. The official language is Croatian, which is a Slavic language based on the Latin alphabet. Over three-quarters of the population is Roman Catholic, but most of the Serb minority follow Orthodox Christianity. The administrative, cultural, academic and communication centre of Croatia is the capital, Zagreb (0.73 million inhabitants). Other major cities are Split (0.2 million) and Rijeka (0.17 million).

The official currency is the kuna (local symbol kn, international symbol HRK), which consists of 100 lipa (lp).

Means of communication

After a decade of repression by the late president Franjo Tudjman and his associates, one could expect that the new political situation would have dramatically changed the media landscape in Croatia. Reality is somehow different: the new government does not want to abandon the idea and practice of controlling the media. After several years of discussions, the telecommunications law is still in draft form, so that potential investors do not want to invest. Almost half of the private television stations and one-third of the private radio stations have expired licences and operate in legal uncertainty. The new government owns and heavily subsidizes one national daily paper as well as the state television (the main source of information for almost two-thirds of the population). It allows them to practice a dumping policy on advertising at the expense of other private media. In addition, since April 2001, the government has imposed a value added tax (VAT) on newspaper returns, which is a new and substantial financial burden on publishers.

2.2 Historical background

Although Greek colonies were established along the Dalmatian coast in the fourth century BC, Croatia's history as a united independent nation started in the ninth century, when Duke Tomislav became ruler of Croatian Dalmatia and united it with Slavonia. After his death, a series of civil wars weakened central authority and the Croats became subjects of the king of Hungary. In 1526, threatened by the Ottoman expansion, the region was added to the Habsburg Empire, where it remained until the end of World War I.

In October 1918, following the collapse of the Austro-Hungarian Empire, the Croatian National Council took power in Zagreb and called for union with the other South Slavic regions of Austria-Hungary. The Kingdom of the Serbs, Croats and Slovenes was created. It regrouped countries with different traditions, religions, nations, languages and alphabets, including those from opposing sides during World War I, namely the Austro-Hungarian side (Slovenia, Croatia, Vojvodina, Bosnia-Herzegovina), Serbia and Montenegro. Its official aim was to organize the new state on a confederal basis and to preserve each country's national identity and sovereignty.

However, despite the stout resistance of the Croatian parliament, Serbian nationalists rapidly centralized the new kingdom under their control in an attempt to create a Greater Serbia. The Serbian police initiated a long period of persecution and terror against Croatian peasants and intellectuals, as well as Muslims. As an illustration, Stjepan Radić, the leader of the opposition Croatian Peasant Party, was assassinated in the Yugoslav parliament in 1928, and in 1929, Belgrade made use of the world economic crisis to destroy the Croatian banking system, which was the strongest in Yugoslavia. The terror continued until the outbreak of World War II.

After the military defeat of the Kingdom of Yugoslavia in 1941, despite security agreements with Britain and France, parts of Croatia were occupied by Nazi Germany and Fascist Italy, which brought about the formation of an independent state of Croatia. With the aim of creating ethnically pure Croatian territories, mass executions of Serbs, Jews, and Gypsies were organized in the infamous Jasenovac concentration camp. Not all Croats agreed with this policy and many joined the communist partisans in proclaiming a new Yugoslavia at Jajce (Bosnia) in 1943. By the time the war ended, about one million people had died in Croatia and Bosnia-Herzegovina.

In 1945, communist partisans re-established a new Yugoslav Federation, substantially restoring the old borders of Bosnia and Croatia, but splitting Macedonia from Serbia and setting up two autonomous regions within Serbia. Yugoslavia's new president was Marshall Josep Tito, a Croat born near Zagreb. In 1948, he rejected the Soviet dictatorship of Stalin, but retained a rigid communist system and tolerated his own personality cult.

During his lifetime, Tito focused on suppressing any sign of ethnic nationalism, with all power to the multi-ethnic (in theory, non-ethnic) Yugoslav Communist Party. Furthermore, to prevent the domination of the country by any one republic, Tito established a rotating presidency, to come into effect on his death. Each of the six republics in turn, plus the two autonomous regions of Serbia, would have its representative as federal president for one year. This system achieved its primary goal, but also seriously weakened the presidency and accelerated the disintegration of the system after Tito's death in 1990.

The impact was not obvious until the leadership of the Serbian Republic adopted an openly nationalist policy in the late 1980s and severely repressed the Albanian majority in Serbia's Kosovo province. This sparked fears that Serbia was trying to impose its rule on the rest of the federation. Croatia, which made by far the greatest contribution to the federal treasury, was the first to react. It virtually eliminated controls on the media before the end of 1988 and consented to multi-party elections won by Tudjman's Croatian Democratic Union (HDZ) in 1990.

As communist governments fell throughout Eastern Europe, Croats began agitating for autonomy. In December 1990, a new Croatian constitution was drawn up. It changed the status of Serbs in Croatia to a 'national minority' rather than a 'constituent nation' and did not guarantee their rights. Many Serbs lost their government jobs. In May 1991, a referendum produced a 93% vote in favour of independence, despite a boycott by the Serb population. In June 1991, Croatia declared its independence from the Yugoslav Federation. Simultaneously, the Serbian enclave of Krajina declared its independence from Croatia. Heavy fighting broke out throughout the country and the federal army, dominated by Serb communists, intervened in support of the Serbs. In a few months, Serb militias and the federal army bombed the presidential palace in Zagreb and seized about one quarter of Croatia, including overland routes to the Dalmatian coast tourist sites, most of Croatia's petroleum resources, and a section cutting the primary access route from Zagreb to Slavonia.

The intervention of United Nations' forces in January 1992 halted most of the fighting, but froze an unacceptable situation in Croatian eyes. Nevertheless, the federal army withdrew from Croatia and in May 1992 Croatia was admitted to the UN, after amending its constitution to protect minority groups and respect human rights. In January 1993, Croatia launched an attack on Krajina, which was still controlled by Serb paramilitary groups. Krajina responded by declaring itself the Republic of Serbian Krajina (RSK) and reducing its Croat population by nearly 98%. In 1994, Krajina signed a ceasefire but in May 1995 violence recurred. However, Krajina lost the support of Belgrade and Croatian forces flooded the area. Some 150,000 Serbs fled, many from towns where their ancestors had lived for centuries. In 1995, the Dayton

Agreement finally put an end to the Yugoslav–Croat war and brought a sense of stability to the country, with Yugoslavia formally recognizing the borders of Croatia and establishing diplomatic relations. Under UN supervision the last Serb-held enclave in eastern Slavonia was returned to Croatia in 1998.

2.3 Political environment

Although the Republic of Croatia was officially established in 1991 as a constitutional parliamentary democracy, it was only in January 2000, after president Tudjman's death, that new elections resulted in the victory of a six-party coalition effectively committed to democracy. Under the new president, Stjepan (Stipe) Mesić, the constitution was significantly amended to reduce the powers of the presidency in favour of the parliament. It now outlines a clear separation of power between executive, legislative and judicial branches.

Executive power is in the hands of the president, who is elected by popular vote for a five-year term and can only hold office twice consecutively. He is the commander-in-chief of the armed forces, promulgates laws validly enacted by parliament and can refer them to the Constitutional Court on grounds of constitutionality. He also has the authority to appoint and dismiss the prime minister, who in turn names a Council of Ministers. Legislative authority is invested in a unicameral parliament (*Hrvatski Sabor*), of which the representatives are elected by popular vote for a four-year term. It has the power to pass laws, amend the constitution, adopt the state budget, exercise certain supervisory powers over the work of government ministries and declare war.

The initial parliament coalition enjoyed a two-thirds' majority in parliament and regrouped the Social Democratic Party (SPD), the Croatia Social Liberal Party (HSLS), the Croatian Peasant Party (HSS), the Istrian Democratic Party (IDS), the Liberal Party (LS) and the Croatian People's Party (HNS). However, several political tensions have severely threatened the stability and effectiveness of the coalition government led by prime minister Ivica Racan (SPD). In particular, the extradition to the Hague Tribunal of two Croatian generals charged with war crimes led to a split in the HSLS, to the IDS leaving the coalition and to discontent among the far right parties. The programme of wage and job cuts at a time of high unemployment also sparked discontent among public sector unions. So far, the government has succeeded in managing the resulting political challenges, but the opposition Croatian Democratic Union (HDZ) has managed to establish itself as the second largest party behind the SPD. As one gets closer to the 2004 parliamentary election and 2005 presidential election, further threats are likely to occur. However, since no party would benefit from an early election, the government's coalition is likely to hold.

2.4 Economic environment and infrastructure

Macroeconomic tendencies

Since independence in 1991, Croatia has faced the typical difficulties of a country in transition, along with the problems associated with regional conflicts. When the new coalition government was elected in early 2000, Croatia's economy was severely affected by the disintegration of the former Yugoslavia, the economic slowdown in Germany (then Croatia's most important trading partner) and the country's situation on the sideline of European and international structures. Since then a deepening reform process has succeeded in stimulating economic growth. Notwithstanding delays in policy implementation and a less favourable market environment, GDP rose 3.7% in 2000 and 3.8% in 2001, and inflation fell to 6.2% in 2000 and 3.6% in 2001. The restrictive monetary policy of the central bank resulted in a relative stability of the Kuna within a narrow range against the Euro. Bank deposits in both domestic and foreign currencies are higher – the introduction of the Euro in the 12 Euro zone countries caused a huge inflow of foreign exchange in Croatian banks and forced the central bank to intervene three times to shore up the Kuna against the Euro. In 2001, international currency reserves reached their highest level in five years at Euro 5,400 million. Consequently, the economy is being remonetized, interest rates have declined, and bank lending is surging.

However, there are still areas of major concern. First, privatization and serious restructuring of companies, together with rigidities in the labour market, have fuelled Croatia's unemployment rate – officially at 23% in early 2002. The government is now under considerable pressure to increase employment, even though this is likely to further delay certain necessary structural reforms. Second, the government still has difficulty in curbing public expenditure. Largely following the advice of the IMF, it has undertaken to slash its budget deficit below 4.25% of GDP in 2002, essentially by reducing subsidies, freezing public sector wages and rationalizing social transfers (e.g. pension funds and health insurance funds). However, the financing of the budget deficit is still heavily dependent on the proceeds from privatization. Third, the overall foreign debt burden is high (US$ 11.05 billion or 54% of GDP), partly inherited from the dissolution of the Socialist Federal Republic of Yugoslavia, the economic mismanagement and excessive spending of the previous government. By means of rigid belt-tightening measures, the government has been able to meet public debt settlement commitments, but the country still relies quite heavily on borrowing to finance its current-account deficit and amortize its arrears. However, insolvency risk is somehow reduced by high foreign-currency reserves, which encourage a rather favourable credit rating. In January 2002, Moody's changed its outlook on Croatia's Baa3/Ba1 foreign currency ceilings for bonds/deposits to stable from negative. On the positive side, between 2000 and 2001, industrial production increased by 6% (including 2% growth in the manufacture of transport vehicles), the manufacture of food and beverages increased by 5.8%, and the annual growth in retail trade turnover reached 9.8% on a seasonally adjusted basis. The IMF professed itself satisfied with Croatia's performance and provided a significant endorsement of the government's economic programme by granting Croatia a SDR 200 million (US$ 260 million) stand-by facility. The country is also one of the World Bank's darlings with US$ 780 million committed and US$ 550 million disbursed (mostly on transportation infrastructure, urban development, and finance-related projects).

Industry

Croatian manufacturing industry employs about 350,000 people, essentially in the textile, clothing and food industries. Other important industries are fabricated metals, chemical products (in particular alkaline and derivatives), wood products, electrical appliances, and shipbuilding.

Energy

Croatia used to be a substantial energy producer, but it has yet to reach its pre-war levels of energy production and is now an energy importer. Liquid fuels (48.5%) and natural gas (26.1%) dominate the country's primary energy consumption.

The state-owned Croatian Oil and Gas Company (Industrija Nafte, INA) controls all activities related to exploration, production and transportation of natural gas as well as oil exploration, production, refining and most of marketing activities. INA supplies around two-thirds of the country's crude oil consumption (including from fields operated in Angola, Egypt and Russia) and one-third of its gas consumption, the balance being imported from Russia and Slovenia. Recently, Croatia also reinforced its role as a transit country for gas and oil. There are major pipelines through Croatia, including the Adria pipeline. The latter belongs to the state-owned Adriatic Pipeline Company (Jadranski Naftovod, JANAF) and runs from the Adriatic port of Omisalji eastward to Sisak, with branches to Hungary and Serbia. Several additional pipelines and extensions are currently being considered, including a connection to Yukos's Druzhba pipeline that feeds Russian oil into Central Europe. Croatia is also attempting to increase its domestic production by developing gas fields in the northern Adriatic, through a joint venture with ENI of Italy.

Founded in July 1990 by consolidating 119 different power entities, the state-owned Croatian Electricity Company (Hrvatska Elektroprivreda, HEP) carries out the activities of generation, transmission and distribution of electricity in the entire territory of Croatia. It also operates the national power system, which is very hydro-dependent. HEP owns a major hydroelectric plant (Varazdin) in the area near the Slovenian–Hungarian border and three others (Senj, Obrova, and Zakucac) in the area along the Adriatic coastline. Since the beginning of 2000, it has stopped utilizing electric power from the Russian designed Krsko nuclear plant in neighbouring Slovenia, although it did provide around 8% of Croatia's power requirements.

In July 2001, the Croatian parliament passed a set of laws liberalizing the energy sector in preparation for privatization, and also in compliance with European Union regulations. Consequently, the three energy monopolies INA, JANAF and HEP are slated to be split up and subsequently privatized in 2003. The privatization process should enable the creation of markets and competition by gradually opening the process of demonopolization. A short-term consequence should be a rise in energy prices but in the long run the open market will increase energy efficiency and, thus, lower energy prices.

Agriculture

Agriculture accounts for about 10% of Croatia's GDP and plays a significant role in the Croatian economy. Approximately 63% of the 3.18 million hectares of agricultural land is cultivated; the remainder is pastureland. Agriculture is varied, reflecting the country's geographical diversity. The main food crops are maize, barley, wheat, sugar beets, soybeans and potatoes. The leading meat products are pork, chicken, beef, turkey and horsemeat. There is also fish and tobacco, as well as olives, citrus fruit and grapes on the Adriatic coast.

Unlike in other formerly communist countries, Croatian farmers were always able to retain private ownership of land, so that today more than 80% of the agricultural land is privately owned. However, there have also been noticeable delays in implementing the necessary structural reforms and financial support has been inadequate. The agricultural sector is, therefore, still undergoing the transition to a market economy. Most of the family-owned farms are inefficient and too small to be economically viable. Consequently, farmers tend to group together to exploit the land. Two-thirds of the farms are operated on a part time basis, and 51% of Croatian farmers are over 50 years of age.

The Croatian government had traditionally set pre-harvest guaranteed prices for agricultural products above world prices, resulting in a lack of competition. However, Croatia's accession to the World Trade Organization (WTO) in autumn 2000 resulted in significant changes. The Croatian agricultural authorities are now committed to reducing customs protection, making significant reductions in tariffs and stopping export subsidies. This is likely to facilitate exports, but also to increase foreign competition in the sector.

Croatia also has two million hectares of forests and woodlands, of which 76% is state-owned. Forestry and timber account for about 3% of GDP, employ 40,000 workers and earn the country US$ 350 million annually.

Financial sector

Croatia has a two-tier banking system, in which the Croatian National Bank (CNB) acts as the central bank. The CNB is an independent institution whose prime goal is to ensure price stability through sound monetary policy. So far, its actions have had the full backing of the international financial institutions.

The commercial banking sector is just emerging from heavy restructuring. In 1998, several banks came under great pressure from monetary tightening, a weakening economy, a depletion of repatriated savings, and a high share of non-performing assets on their balance sheets. This resulted in a lack of confidence among depositors, foreign investors, and ultimately in a liquidity crisis for the whole economy. The restructuring process had to initiate bankruptcy procedures against 12 banks and four savings banks and implied numerous mergers and acquisitions as well as foreign participation (foreign investors now control over 70% of bank assets.). It is now almost completed. As a result, the Croatian banking sector now consists of 44 commercial banks, including eight foreign banks. Given the small size of the economy, this might seem a large enough number for a competitive banking industry, but banking is extremely concentrated and the two largest banks control more than 50% of the total assets.

Dominated by banks and brokerages, the Zagreb Stock Exchange is quite rudimentary, with six companies listed on the official market and 56 on the OTC market. Most companies prefer the OTC market as it has less stringent listing requirements. Settlement takes place on a trade date plus five business days, and that there is no central clearinghouse. The Zagreb Money Market (ZMM) was set up in 1990 as an independent joint-stock company. It acts as a broker for inter-bank transactions.

It should be noted that the Croatian government has embarked on a reform of the pension system, which is broadly based on the World Bank/Chilean model and fairly similar to the system applied in Poland. This reform has a start-up cost of US$ 2 billion and should help to stimulate the Croatian capital market.

Telecommunications

Croatia has a well developed telecommunications system, both in terms of equipment and penetration (35 lines per 100 inhabitants). Hrvatski Telekom (HT, majority owned by Deutsche Telekom) is the owner and operator of the physical network, which is 80% equipped with state-of-the-art main digital switches. Two GSM networks are available. HT introduced its CRONET GSM network in August 1995, while VipNet (majority owned by Mobilkom of Austria), became operational in the summer of 1999. The government might sell a third GSM and two UMTS licences before the end of 2002. There are also a few Internet service providers in Croatia, but HT's Internet service (HINET) has a 95% market share. VipNet has recently entered this market and is expected to become a challenging competitor. Finally, Croatian Post (HP), a wholly owned government enterprise, provides fast and reliable postal services.

Transportation and communications

The war that ended in 1995 and the subsequent limited national budget severely affected Croatia's transport system. The government set as a priority policy area the establishment of an efficient transport system and infrastructure. It targeted a large part of the loans approved so far by the World Bank and the EBRD for the reconstruction of roads, railroads, electricity and water supply network, as well as air-traffic control. Consequently, the Croatian transportation infrastructure is now fairly well developed by Central and Eastern European standards.

The 27,840 km of hard-surfaced road network is extensive, but unevenly distributed. The northern and northwestern regions of the country enjoy a relatively good road network, while the eastern and southern regions are less developed. Furthermore, there are only 330 km of expressways, but an additional 1,600 km should be completed over the next 10 years. Due to the fiscal situation, the government plans to finance these strategic works mainly through foreign loans and concessions. Road traffic safety and reduction of road vehicle emissions are areas of concern.

The Croatian railway network is 2,296 km long (983 km electrified) and is operated by Croatian Railways. Train transportation is usually inexpensive, reliable and safe, but quite slow since track network is mostly single line.

Civil aviation traffic in Croatia is essentially handled by eight airports (Zagreb, Split, Dubrovnik, Zadar, Pula, Osijek, Rijeka, and Brac) and a few seasonal and sports airports. Croatia Airlines, the national company, played a critical role in helping Croatia to establish its international identity. There are plans to expand Zagreb Airport in anticipation of increased passenger traffic with the revival of the tourism sector.

Finally, waterways are becoming an increasingly important mode of transport. About 800 km are perennially navigable, although downed bridges, silt, and debris still block large sections of the Sava River. Major ports in Croatia are Rijeka, Pula, Sibenik, Split, Ploce, Dubrovnik and Vukovar (inland waterways port on the Danube). The government is planning to expand and upgrade the coastal port facilities.

Tourism

Prior to 1990, the tourism industry was one of the most important sectors of the Croatian economy. It accounted for about 6% of GDP, was one of Croatia's main hard currency generators and employed directly or indirectly close to 200,000 people. The war that followed the dissolution of Yugoslavia devastated Croatia's tourism sector and scared away foreign tourists. Direct war damage combined with the general lack of modern management and marketing skills and the use of tourism infrastructure to house refugees has left these facilities in desperate need of repair.

Croatia has started to be recognized again as a desirable tourist destination. Despite capacity constraints, about 7.6 million tourists visited Croatia in 2001, including 6.4 million foreigners (25.3% Germans, 13.3% Slovenes, 12.2% Italians and 9.4% Austrians). In addition to the traditional hotel overnight stays, there has also been a trend towards self-catering and camping accommodation (which are particularly popular with visitors from other transition economies) and a strong growth of the marina sector (which reflects the relatively low cost of berthing pleasure boats in Croat ports). Croatia expects US$ 4.5 billion from tourism in 2002 (against US$ 3.6 billion in 2001) and has started to privatize several hotels and tourism companies and upgrade its tourism infrastructure.

2.5 Legal environment and regulations

In recent years, there have been considerable changes in Croatia's legal environment and regulations. However, most of them were already pointing in the right direction, that is, towards a Western market economy system.

Crime and corruption

Under Tudjman's government, corruption was widespread in Croatia. It ranged from bribes at each and any stage of business transactions to money laundering and large-scale siphoning-off of assets by politically connected cronies. It resulted in higher costs and prices and declining competitiveness. The new coalition government has made serious efforts to eliminate corruption. The implementation of a new legal and institutional framework to deal with corruption, organized crime and money laundering should bring the country closer to European standards in these fields. As a consequence, the Berlin-based Transparency International (TI) has recently upgraded Croatia's ranking on the list of corrupt nations from 74th to 51st. However, bribery and corruption are still frequent in the health system and the judiciary.

Judicial system, dispute settlement, and bankruptcy procedures

The judicial system is still largely inherited from the former Yugoslavia. It consists of three levels of courts: municipal, county and Supreme Court. These courts exercise original jurisdiction over administrative, civil and criminal cases. In parallel, there are also eight commercial tribunals that deal specifically with commercial matters, including bankruptcy and economic crimes. Several reports have described the overall judicial system as cumbersome and inefficient due to bureaucratic inefficiency and political influence. In addition, the effective protection of property is weak, particularly in the case of illegal occupancy.

The 1997 Bankruptcy Law established deadlines that force companies to initiate bankruptcy proceedings within 21 days of insolvency or over-burdening. It also authorizes the initiation of bankruptcy proceedings by creditors and regulates the reorganization procedures. However, in practice, the judicial process for liquidating assets has proven to be extremely slow and commercial tribunals face a heavy backlog of about one million unsolved or pending cases. Measures to strengthen the commercial courts' capacity to settle bankruptcy procedures are now being funded by a World Bank loan.

Taxation, accounting, and auditing rules

The corporate profit tax in Croatia is covered by the Corporate Profit Tax Law, which is currently being updated. The corporate profit-tax rate is 20% of the accounting profit and is applicable to any business entity with a registered office in, or managed from, Croatia. Tax losses may be carried forward for five years. A 15% withholding tax is applied to dividends or interest payments, and a tax-credit system is used to avoid double taxation on foreign-source income. Several double-taxation treaties initially signed by the Socialist Federal Republic of Yugoslavia have been ratified by Croatia.

The personal-tax rate is covered by the Personal Income Tax (PIT) Law, which is also currently being updated. Croatia taxes its residents on their worldwide income and its non-residents on their Croatian-source income only. There are currently three tax brackets with rates of 15%, 25% and 35%.

Croatia also applies a 5% tax on gifts, inheritances, and property transfer. There are also numerous small taxes on selected business activities (e.g. tourism, gambling, motor vehicles, boats, etc.). It should be noted that the Investment Promotion Law promulgated in 2000 and the amended CPT Law passed by the Croatian parliament provide several tax benefits related to foreign investment in Croatia, particularly in (a) free-trade zones, (b) special state care areas and (c) the city of Vukovar.

Croatia's accounting law requires that financial statements (which comprise a profit and loss account, balance sheet, cash flow statement and notes) be prepared for each calendar year in accordance with international accounting standards. Consolidated financial statements are required for groups. The reporting frequency and disclosure requirements depend on whether a company is classified as small, medium or large. All large and medium-sized companies must be audited once a year in accordance with international standards on auditing by an authorized auditing firm. Smaller companies must submit to an abridged audit every three years.

Laws on establishing and conducting business

Provided the condition of reciprocity is met, foreign investors receive national treatment and enjoy the same rights, obligations, and legal status as domestic investors. The constitution guarantees the unrestricted repatriation of both profits and capital for foreigners.

Various forms of business organizations available to foreigners

According to the Croatian Law on Commercial Companies, foreign investors may use a number of different forms of organization to conduct business and business-related activities in Croatia, including general partnerships (j.t.d.), limited partnerships (k.d.), limited liability companies (d.o.o.), joint-stock companies (d.d.), branch offices, and representative offices.

A partnership is an entity through which two or more persons conduct ongoing entrepreneurial activities. In the general partnership, the liability of each of the partners to the creditors of the partnership is unlimited. In the limited partnership, the liability of one or several partners to the creditors is limited, while the responsibility of the remaining partners (at least one in number) is unlimited.

A limited liability company or a joint-stock company is an entity organized to conduct small ongoing business activities. The liability to its creditors is limited to the total value of its property, while the liability of the participants in the company is limited to the value of their ownership interests in the company. Such companies may be founded and owned by a single person. Their ownership interest is divided into shares of stock, which are freely transferred and pledged. The minimum capital requirement is the HRK equivalent of DM 5,000 for the limited liability company and the HRK equivalent of DM 30,000 for the joint-stock company (except for bank and insurance companies). Joint stock companies require the election of a supervisory board.

A branch office must be entered in the commercial register at the commercial tribunal. It may conduct business and should keep account books in accordance with Croatian legislation. However, it is not considered an independent legal entity, but a part of the company that established it.

A representative office must be entered in the Register of Representative Offices at the Ministry of Economy. It may be set up merely to investigate the local market, for advertising and marketing, but not for carrying out commercial activities. It must remain non-profitable and is not permitted to generate income. It does not have a legal personality and has no contractual status in its own right.

Restrictions on foreign investments

There are currently very few restrictions to foreign investments in Croatia. They essentially concern the sectors of military equipment, television and radio stations, as well as fully foreign-owned rail or air transport.

Investment incentives

The amended Corporate Profit Tax (CPT) Law of January 2001 prescribes general and specific incentives for foreign investments, for example partial or total write-off of equipment and business and/or tax reductions or exemptions.

Protection of property rights

Croatia has been a Member of WIPO since 8 October 1991 and is a signatory of the Paris and Berne Conventions. In May 2000, Croatia has ratified the 1996 WIPO 'Internet' treaties, the WIPO Copyright Treaty (WCT) and the WIPO Performances and Phonograms Treaty (WPPT). Industrial Property Registers in Croatia consist of patents, trademarks, models and designs, geographical indications and semiconductor topology. However, in practice, the major threat to intellectual property rights is the inefficiency of the court system.

Entry requirements

Depending on one's country of origin, an entry visa may be necessary to enter Croatia. Entry visas are issued for tourist, transit and business purposes. Foreign nationals willing to work in Croatia must first obtain a residence permit, and then a work permit. The latter is usually granted for one year and only if no Croatian national meeting the requirements of the employer is registered as being unemployed at the Croatian Institute of Employment.

2.6 Business environment

Privatization

When the privatization process started in Croatia in 1991, it was almost considered as a social programme, that is as the free allocation of shares to the social classes that had been most affected by war. During 1991–99, more than 2,500 companies from all sectors were privatized, going mostly into the hands of privileged buyers (including managers and employees) who were granted considerable discounts and credit facilities. However, corruption and lack of controls resulted in large-scale asset stripping and inefficient management, while foreign investors were put off by the constantly changing regulations and the lack of transparency of the privatization process.

In 2000, the new government revised the privatization process completely and affirmed its objectives of attracting foreign investors and improving the effectiveness of operations. In 2001, a 16% stake in the fixed-line telekom operator, Hrvatski Telekom, was sold to Deutsche Telekom for HRK 3.6 billion (US$ 430 m). Despite this, the government failed to achieve its privatization revenue target of HRK 4.5 billion for the year. The target for 2002 is more modest at HRK 2 billion. It should be easily achieved by privatizing the remaining stakes in banks, the dominant insurance company, Hrvatski Osiguranje, as well as several hotels on Croatia's famous Adriatic coast. The government also established a framework for the privatization of key energy related industries (INA, HEP, JANAF).

Foreign direct investment (FDI)

Croatia had a mixed record in attracting foreign direct investment (FDI), essentially because of the political instability of the past decade, as well as the obstructionist policies of the previous regime. The new government enacted active measures to welcome foreign investors, which significantly improved the investment climate. FDI in 2001 exceeded US$ 1.4 billion, which brought the total cumulative FDI to US$ 6.4 billion since 1993.

According to the central bank, most FDI from 1993 through 2001 focused on telecommunications, banking, and manufacturing of pharmaceutical preparations. Over that period, and accounting for privatization stakes, Austria was the leading foreign investor in Croatia (US$ 1.5 billion), followed by Germany (US$ 1.16 billion).

Free economic and trade areas

Croatia currently has seven free-trade zones, located in Zagreb, Rijeka, Ploce, Pula, Split, Zadar and Vukovar. Any goods imported into these zones are free of customs duty. Any export from these zones to Croatia is subject to import customs duty. As a rule, companies that establish operations in a free-trade zone benefit from a 50% deduction on the corporate profit tax. If their investments in infrastructure are in excess of HRK 1 million, they receive a five-year tax exemption.

Major booming sectors

Croatia's principal growth sectors are construction, energy, tourism, transportation and telecommunications. Potential investors can invest in these sectors through the purchase of company shares from the state, from the privatization investment funds (PIFs), banks or other equity holders, or through direct investments in physical facilities.

Major trade partners (imports and exports)

The EU countries are Croatia's main trading partners (54.7% of exports, 56% of imports), with Italy in the lead (22.3% exports, 17% imports), followed by Germany (14.2% exports and 16.4% imports), Slovenia (10.8% exports and 7.9% imports), Austria (6.6% exports and 6.7% imports) and Russia (1.3% exports and 8.5% imports).

Free trade agreements

Croatia is interested in liberalizing trade as much as possible, especially in the area of industrial products. It has free trade agreements with Poland (CEFTA-member), Norway (EFTA and EEA member) and Bosnia-Herzegovina. It is also currently negotiating a free trade agreement with Yugoslavia, as well as bilateral agreements with Bulgaria, the Czech Republic, Poland, Romania, Slovakia and Turkey. At the beginning of 2002, more than three-quarters of the EU's industrial goods exports to Croatia were duty free.

Foreign trade regulations

Special permits need to be obtained for the import or export of certain goods, such as precious metals, military vehicles and weapons, and antiques.

Tariff system

Croatia joined the World Trade Organization (WTO) in December 2000. The Customs Tariff Law prescribes the rates of customs duty applicable to imported products. They are essentially *ad valorem* (percentage of the value), except for some specific agricultural products where a per quantity rule is applied. These rates apply to all countries, with the exception of tariffs that may be agreed upon in bilateral agreements. Excise duties are also levied for oil and oil derivatives, alcoholic beverages, automobiles, tobacco and coffee.

Value added tax (VAT)

Since January 1998, Croatia has replaced its sales tax by a value added tax (VAT) system. The uniform (and comparatively high) VAT rate is 22% and is applicable to all deliveries of goods and services performed in Croatia, as well as to personal consumption, new buildings and the importation of goods. There are a few exempted goods and services, for example medical and banking services, bread, milk, educational literature and social welfare. Exports are zero-rated. Croatia also applies a

30% tax on luxury goods and services (based on the sales price of the good, exclusive of VAT).

2.7 Etiquette and cultural issues

Culture

Croats tend to be quite formal about business protocols. It is customary to shake hands, to address people by their surname and to exchange business cards immediately after formal introductions. Attention should be paid to academic titles, and any political or war related topics should be carefully avoided, since these are particularly sensitive subjects among Croatians. Use of the term 'Serbo-Croatian' to describe the Croatian language should also be avoided. It could be considered as an attack on the identity of the Croatian language, and, by the same token, as an attack on the identity of the Croatian people.

3
Czech Republic

3.1 Basic facts

With a population of more than 10 million, strategically located in Central Europe, the Czech Republic, with its capital, Prague, is bordered by Germany in the west (646 km), Poland in the north (658 km), Slovakia in the east (215 km) and Austria in the south (362 km). This relatively small, landlocked country, with a total of 78,866 sq km, contains some of the most significant land routes in Europe. The country's Moravian Gate is a traditional military corridor between the North European Plains and the Danube in Central Europe.

As of July 2000, the population growth rate was an estimated negative 0.08%. Approximately 70% of the population is between the ages of 15 and 64, and the ratio of male to female within that age group is one to one. Ethnic Czechs make up a large majority of the population (81.2%), while the remainder of ethnic groups consists of Moravians (13.2%), Slovaks, Poles, Germans, Silesians, Romanians, and Hungarians. This does not represent great ethnic diversity, as the once large German minority was expelled after World War II. The main spoken language is Czech.

The Czech population is predominantly of no religious affiliation (39.8%); Roman Catholics number about 39.2%, while Protestants and Orthodox remain a minority. The literacy rate among Czechs over the age of 15 attains an appreciable 99.9%. The population is evenly spread across the country, with little urban concentration. Prague is the only city totalling more than one million inhabitants; approximately 35% of Czechs live in towns of more than 50,000 inhabitants. Population density (131 per sq km) is low compared with most urbanized countries in Western Europe. Prague has a population of 1.8 million, and other large population centres include Brno (379,000), Ostrava (320,000) and Pilsen (166,000).

The Czech Republic has a temperate climate with cool summers and cold, cloudy and humid winters. The country's major agricultural products include grains, potatoes, sugar beets, hops, fruit; pigs, cattle, poultry; forest products. Hard and soft coal, kaolin, clay, graphite and timber constitute the major natural resources of the country.

The currency is the koruna (local symbol: Kč; international symbol: CZK), with 100 haléřu to the koruna.

Means of communication

The nation's major newspaper is *Mlada Fronta dnas*. There are approximately four million main telephone lines in use and approximately one million mobile phones. A large majority of the domestic telephone exchanges are digital. Existing copper-wire systems are enhanced with asymmetric digital subscriber lines (ADSL) to accommodate Internet usage and other digital signals. Satellite stations provide the principal support for international telephone calls. There are more than three million radios and about 3.5 million television sets on the market.

3.2 Historical background

Former Czechoslovakia emerged in 1918 following the collapse of the Habsburg Empire. In March 1939, the Nazis invaded the country and incorporated Czechoslovakia into the Third Reich as the Protectorate of Bohemia and Moravia. Although the Soviet Red Army liberated Czechoslovakia in May 1945, the country was turned into a satellite of the former Soviet Union. The Czechs never accepted their subjugation to the USSR and put up stiff, albeit silent, resistance.

In August 1968, attempts by Communist Party of Czechoslovakia (KSG) to initiate economic reform and establish democratic rule, known as the Prague Spring, were stymied by brutal Soviet intervention. Economic reforms were reversed and the system reverted to the orthodox Soviet model. The KSG's success and continued existence from 1968 onwards was entirely dependent upon Soviet domination. In 1989, political power shifted away from the KSG when the Soviets decided not to intervene against mounting challenges to communist supremacy throughout Eastern Europe. After a two-hour general strike in November 1989, KSG authorities agreed to negotiate with the opposition and finally surrendered their monopoly on political power. This peaceful changeover of power became known as the 'Velvet Revolution'. In June 1990, in the first contested election since 1946, the Civic Forum party prevailed with 51% of the Czech votes for the federal parliament.

Shortly thereafter, a coalition federal government was formed between the Civic Forum and 'Public Against Violence', a Slovak political counterpart. The coalition gave birth to the Civic Democratic Party (ODS), which in the general election of June 1992, campaigned for the preservation of the Czechoslovak state, and won convincingly in the Czech territory. However, the main force in Slovak politics, the Movement for a Democratic Slovakia (HZDS) was opposed, arguing that Slovak issues had been ignored during the reform process and thus change was needed. Although a majority in both republics favoured continued integration, on 25 November 1992, parliament voted to abolish the federation. The Czech Republic ratified its constitution on 16 December 1992, becoming effectively an independent nation on 1 January 1993.

In the 1990s, political attention focused on growing corruption, the deficiency of corporate governance, the build-up of enterprise debt, severe difficulties of the financial system, and a rise in economic insecurity. These factors weakened the ODS, which, as a consequence, lost its overall majority in the parliamentary election of 31 May 1996. This resulted in the rise of the Czech Social Democratic Party (CSSD) as the key influence in a divided parliament.

The Czech Republic began accession negotiations with the European Union (EU) in 1998. In January of that year, an interim government was formed to manage the country until parliamentary elections in June 1998. Opponents within the ODS split to form a new political party called the Freedom Union. The CSSD, which had received the single largest share of the votes in the election, formed a minority government based on an opposition agreement with the ODS. The opposition agreement resulted in a political stalemate, with CSSD initiatives faltering for lack of parliamentary support. This led to long delays in political decision-making, particularly in adopting legislation required for EU accession. Prolonged recession and high unemployment in 1999 eroded support for the CSSD among its core constituency of blue-collar workers. Thus, socially disadvantaged groups began to shift their support to the unreformed Communist Party of Bohemia and Moravia (KSCM). Nonetheless, in March 1999, the Czech Republic joined NATO.

In November 2000, a centre-right coalition called the Quad Coalition, a four-party grouping dominated by the Freedom Union and the CSSD, was created. The Quad Coalition became the dominant party in the Senate (the upper house of parliament). In October 2001, the World Trade Organization (WTO) reported that the Czech government had taken considerable measures to improve the country's economy and pull itself out of recession, by way of both domestic reform and further trade and investment liberalization. The report added that exports and foreign direct investment (FDI) had facilitated the country's economic recovery and improved its standing for EU accession.

3.3 Political environment

The Czech Republic is a parliamentary democracy. The president of the republic is the chief of state and serves as commander-in-chief of the armed forces. He is elected by parliament for a five-year term. The current president is Václav Havel, who was first elected in January 1993 and re-elected in 1998. The prime minister is appointed by the president and serves as head of government. The president, based upon recommendations from the prime minister, also appoints the cabinet members. The parliament is bicameral and comprises the chamber of deputies (*Poslanecká Snemovna*) and the senate (*Senát*). The former has 200 members elected for four years according to a proportional representation formula. The latter has 81 members, elected for a six-year term, with one third re-elected every two years. The two chambers have the authority to initiate legislation and elect the president.

A dozen political parties make up the Czech political landscape: the Assembly for the Republic (SPR-RSC); Christian Democratic Union-Czechoslovak People's Party (KDU-CSL); Civic Democratic Alliance (ODA); Civic Democratic Party (ODS); Communist Party of Bohemia and Moravia (KSCM); Czech Social Democrats (CSSD); Democratic Union (DEU); Freedom Union (US); and the Quad Coalition (which includes, KDU-CSL, US, ODA, DEU).

In February 2000, the Czech Republic had a minority Social Democratic government. The government signed an opposition agreement with the conservative ODS that obliges the ODS to abstain from toppling the government in a vote of no confidence. After much debate, the opposition agreement was broadened in January 2000 to encompass other policy areas. Furthermore, the centre-left CSSD is expected to serve its full term in office under the opposition agreement with the centre-right ODS. With popular support for the CSSD, the ODS and the centre-right Quad Coalition almost equally divided, the outcome of the election in June 2002 remains uncertain.

3.4 Economic environment and infrastructure

In 1997, the country suffered a political and financial crisis. Delays in enterprise restructuring, coupled with failure to develop a smoothly functioning capital market were the major causes of Czech economic troubles, which resulted in a currency crisis. The government cut spending by 2.5% of GDP; subsequently, growth dropped to 0.3% in 1997, –2.3% in 1998, and –0.5% in 1999. However, thanks to the government's domestic reform and further trade and investment liberalization, the country's GDP grew by 2.9% in 2000, with an increased industrial output of nearly 7% that exceeded the most optimistic forecasts.

Improving the country's infrastructure, particularly in the telecommunications and transportation industries, is essential for sustained economic growth and development. Even though a priority for the Czech leadership, the nature of the restructuring will require time and capital. Unfortunately, sharp cuts in government spending in 1997 and 1998 slowed down infrastructure plans. However, accelerated privatization of remaining corporations could entice private investments in telecommunications, energy, and transportation industries.

Macroeconomic trends

The share of the industrial sector's contribution to GDP declined from 47.5% in 1990 to less than 42% in 1998. Likewise, the agricultural sector's share of GDP also declined from 8% in 1993 to 4.2% in 1998. In the 1990s, the service sector developed primarily because of a large increase in tourism. Consumer demand was a major component of GDP growth in the mid-1990s, but has decelerated since. However, the Czech economy began to recover in 2000 due to an increase in exports and a rise in foreign direct investment.

In 1998, consumer price inflation was a much-improved 10.7%, compared to the average annual inflation rate of 56.6% in 1991. Like other Eastern European countries, the fall in world commodity prices, along with a reduction in domestic demand, resulted in a perceptible drop in inflation in 1999 to 2.1%, less than half of the government target. The mounting trade deficit was covered until 1994 by a strong surplus in invisibles, mainly tourism and transportation. Even if the number of tourists fell slightly after 1996, their average spending rose noticeably. Transport proceeds derive from goods crossing the country by road and rail and, of particular importance, from the gas pipeline that links Russia with Germany.

Between 1993 and 1995, the country witnessed a large net surplus on the current and financial accounts, which led in 1995 to a gradual climb in total official foreign reserves to US$ 13.8 billion. By 1996, however, that surplus had ebbed and reserves were on a downward trend until the end of 1997 when they totalled US$ 9.7 billion.

By the end of 1999, foreign reserves had recovered, and rose to US$ 12.9 billion.

Employment in industry fell in line with factory closures and productivity improvements, from around 38% of total employment in 1990 to below 33% in 1998. Unemployment remained practically constant until 1996 due largely to growth in employment in the services sector, but afterwards increased to levels prevalent across Eastern and Central Europe. While employment fell in both agriculture and industry, employment in services witnessed an impressive growth. Overall, the unemployment rate declined to 8.2% in mid-2001, but much of the decline was seasonal. By governmental decree, the minimum monthly wage effective from 1 January 2002 is CZK 5,700 per month.

Industry

The Czech Republic benefits from a diversified industrial structure, with noteworthy assets in engineering. The foremost constituents of the industrial sector comprise fuels, ferrous metallurgy, machinery and equipment, coal, motor vehicles, glass and armaments. In October 1999, the country initiated a 'revitalization' programme to give support to insolvent manufacturing companies. The prime stumbling blocks to industrial production are low levels of productivity (about one-third of the EU average), lack of access to distribution systems, inferior brand image and poorly educated and inexperienced management.

Light industry continues to struggle to defend its domestic market position against competition from abroad, while some branches, especially in the lower value added sectors, have established a stronghold in the EU market. Other Czech-owned enterprises have been thriving with comparatively simple commodities, chiefly in steel and engineering, where they can compete with low prices. However, stable real wage growth in the late 1990s has had a negative effect on the Czech competitive advantage in price-sensitive areas. Like other sectors of the economy, construction was almost entirely state-controlled under communist rule. But, once the communists lost power, it immediately switched to private ownership. Indeed, by 1996, close to 100% of construction firms were under the control of the private sector, which has expanded swiftly since 1990. New and often small firms have mushroomed throughout the country.

Energy

Bedevilled by outdated structures and inefficiencies, the Czech primary energy sector consumes over 12% of GDP and is one of the least efficient in Europe. Primary energy supplies are coal (51.3%), oil (19.9%), natural gas (19.2%) and nuclear (8.1%). The country has moderate coal and lignite reserves. To bring the industry into compliance with EU standards, inefficient mines have been closed down, environmental regulations have been enforced and the mining industry reorganized into six privatized joint-stock companies. Only a small fraction of the country's oil and gas requirements are produced domestically by Moravske Naftove Doly, a state-owned company. Almost all the oil is imported from Russia via the Druzhba pipeline and from Germany via the Mero pipeline. The two major oil refineries in the Czech Republic (the Litvinov and Kralup refineries) are operated by the state-controlled Česká Rafinerska and are due to be privatized in 2002. Almost all natural gas is also imported from Russia's Gazprom subsidiary, Gazexport. A state-owned company, Transgas, is responsible for Czech gas purchases, transport storage, sales, and distribution. Transgas is scheduled to be sold in 2002 to RWE Gas of Germany. Finally, the Czech Republic also has two nuclear power plants, the 1,760 megawatt (MW) Dukovany power plant and the Temelin power plant (planned for two 981 MW reactors of Soviet design). The leading electricity producer is Česke Energeticke Zavody (CEZ), which is also due to be privatized in the near future.

Agriculture

In 1991, the Czech authorities introduced a price-support system following demonstrations by farmers; agricultural subsidies accounted for 5% of the state budget. By 1998, this was reduced to 2%, but some of the allocation has moved into off-budget categories. Overall state support per hectare reached approximately 15% of the EU level, with credit guarantees for agricultural investment the favoured mode of subsidy. In preparation for EU accession, the government intends to institute a price support system analogous to that in existence in the EU's Common Agricultural Policy (CAP), supplemented by production quotas and storage assistance.

Financial sector

Four large banks, whose roots can be found in financial institutions under communism, make up the core of the commercial banking sector. Together, these four banks, Komercni banka (KB), Investicni a Postovni banka (IPB), Česká sporitelna (CS) and Ceskoslovenska obchodni banka (CSOB), account for approximately 72% of all deposits. The government maintains majority jurisdiction over the two largest Czech banks, KB and CS. In March 1999, the country's estimated total assets of the banking sector amounted to US$ 10.7 billion. Ostensibly, the financial sector is reasonably stable. This sector has expanded very rapidly, with a large number of banks competing for clients and credit/GDP ratios that compare with the highly developed market economies in Western Europe. The number of banks rose from five in 1990 to 55 in 1995, when banking sector assets exceeded 150% of GDP. In reality, the health of the domestic banking sector has been rather unsound. Banking as a whole is still burdened with serious debt and liquidity problems and has been operating at a loss since 1997. Corporate bankruptcies have multiplied since 1997, and the necessity to meet the stricter regulatory requirements of the Czech National Bank (CNB, the central bank) has reduced profits in the banking sector. In 1997, the Government's initiative to revive the banking sector cost an estimated Kč 87 billion (5% of GDP), but banks were still burdened in 1999 by Kč 300 billion's worth of credits that are unlikely ever to be repaid. The authorities believe that they could improve the health of the sector through stricter bank oversight, privatization, and better bankruptcy laws.

The highlight of liberalization was the opening on 6 April 1993 of the Prague Stock Exchange (PSE). Two systems, responsible for less than half of the trade in shares, work in tandem with the PSE. People can trade shares more easily on the RM-System, for which there is no need of a broker, or through private transactions, registered after they are concluded. Consequently, most deals are conducted in off-market transactions and there is no mechanism to guarantee a single price for listed shares. The fragmentation of the market, coupled with little regulation, inadequate disclosure requirements, and only minimal protection of minority shareholders, has encouraged insider trading and non-transparent ownership structures.

Only a small number of shares are actively traded on the official market, with the telecom companies and the large banks accounting for two-thirds of all equity turnovers in 1999. The PSE has matured into a dynamic marketplace for government bonds, which account for more than 85% of the PSE's total trading value. The government has sought to stimulate the equity market by improving supervision. In 1997, the authorities set up a new Securities Commission to ensure compliance with an enhanced regulatory structure, but enforcement powers have to be strengthened further if investors are to regain confidence in the PSE. The Commission has made important strides in establishing a regulatory framework for Czech capital markets and enforcing the new rules, but problems remain and confidence has not yet been fully restored. It should be pointed out, however, that Czechs are not only collaborating closely with other Eastern European exchanges, but have also signed a close co-operation agreement with the London Stock Exchange. Furthermore, Czechs have made exceptional efforts towards standard EU rules for foreign equity rights, as well as reporting and transparency regulations.

Telecommunications

Like other Eastern European countries, telephone service in the Czech Republic is lacking. On the whole, telephone lines are outdated, making connections difficult between cities within the country. Nevertheless, serious efforts to modernize the system are underway. The country has made substantial investments in this sector. The European Bank for Reconstruction and Development (EBRD), the European Investment Bank, and large local and foreign banks have provided financing for the country's far-reaching expansion plan for the telecommunications industry.

There are currently roughly 18 lines per 100 people and the aim is to increase this to 35 lines per 100 shortly. Virtually all of the main lines are connected to automatic exchanges. As in other emerging markets, mobile phones are growing in popularity. Unfortunately, their utility is restricted to areas outside major cities. In a number of underserved parts of the country, the authorities have allowed private phone companies to offer basic telephone service. An American cable television joint venture has also provided telephone connections together with television service. The Czech government announced that it would end the SPT Telecom monopoly, as part of the basic WTO telecommunications agreement.

Information technology

Internet penetration has been growing rapidly throughout the Central European region, and the Czech Republic Internet penetration ranks above other countries in the region. There are about 500,000 users with access to Internet, which is approximately 5% of the county's population. Currently, Internet is used for e-business, including business information and advertising, and for e-mail. About two-thirds of e-business consists of business-to-business transactions, and the share is expected to grow. The first Internet bookshop was established in 1996 and now has approximately 8,000 customers who can choose from 80,000 book titles. Travel agencies and real-estate agencies offer their services via the Internet, and the growing interest is noteworthy.

Direct sales to consumers via the Internet are not very well developed. The major problem inhibiting growth in this area is a company's ability to collect payments from consumers. Foreign banks accept credit cards, but not many Czechs are credit card holders. Local banks do not currently accept credit card payments without a physical signature. Payment for purchased goods is possible through delivery services, but this is not a very efficient system.

The Expandia Bank is initiating changes to the payment system for Internet-based purchases. The bank was established in 1997 and has implemented a system for making purchases over the Internet. The new payment system should also help companies allay many of the fears of potential buyers, because it includes security devices that protect customers' credit card numbers. Expandia customers are provided with a form of calculator, which generates individual codes for each bank operation, including Internet purchases. To expand knowledge of Internet services, Expandia launched an interesting virtual project, called E-City. The project was very popular, especially among home users, as it showed all the possibilities for home shopping and banking. Thus far, the most frequent use of Internet for consumer purchases has been for acquiring computers, computer components and software.

About 18 major Internet service providers (ISPs) control approximately 65%–70% of the market. It is expected that the ISP market will grow in terms of users but will consolidate in terms of ISPs. Major ISPs have made several important acquisitions over the last few years and have invested heavily in increased bandwidth, as the high growth of the market is expected along with the liberalization of the telecom sector. The rapid growth of telecommunications infrastructure, in terms of quality and density, has aided the development of the Internet. The country's largest ISP company is Internet Online, which is owned by the country's monopoly voice operator.

Transportation

The Czech Republic aspires to become the crossroads for the new European high-speed rail and highway systems in the next few years. Such achievement would strengthen the country's key position in Central Europe. Hence, renovating the nation's archaic transportation system remains a high priority with the objective of bringing the transportation system up to the standards of advanced EU countries. Decision-makers have decided to upgrade the infrastructure of all transport modes: railway, highway, inland waterway and air. Current projects include a US$ 3.5 billion modernization of the rail system, with priority for the Czech section of the important Berlin–Prague–Vienna Line; a plan to modernize and extend the country's highway network; and a plan to develop the river transport system for intensive usage by the container hauling industry.

With US government assistance, the civilian air traffic control system is being integrated with military systems to provide more advanced methods of air traffic control. This will not only allow better utilization of airspace, but also improve the safety of air traffic. A new terminal at Prague's International Airport has opened, and plans are underway for the privatization and overhaul of several smaller airports, including Karlovy Vary, Brno, and Ostrava.

In 1998, the country counted 9,435 km of railways, an estimated 127,693 km of highways, 677 km of waterways (Elbe/Labe being the principal river), and 53,000 km of natural gas pipelines. Statistical reports show that in 1999, it possessed 114 airports, of which 43 had paved runways and 71 unpaved.

Other economic sectors

Tourism has developed rapidly since 1989, becoming by the mid-1990s one of the country's most important industries. The service sector's growth peaked in 1996 when receipts from tourism accounted for 19% of total exports of goods and services. However, visitor numbers have since fallen, from 103 million in 1998 to 48 million in the first half of 1999, but the sector still accounted for 7% of GDP in 1998. Undoubtedly, Prague, with its rich cultural heritage, remains the main attraction. The Czech authorities have made serious attempts to entice visitors away from the capital to other areas, but the tourism infrastructure outside Prague is less well developed. Only about one-quarter of all visitors travel outside the capital.

In late 1990, the retail industry was privatized, a decision that resulted in the consolidation of several small Czech-owned retail companies into retail chains. In 1998, a stagnant retail market resulted in fierce competition for market share. Consequently, total turnover fell by 7% and recovered only very slowly in 1999. Nevertheless, the Czech retail market is still far less concentrated than Western European sectors, with the top 10 retail stores controlling only one-quarter of the market, compared with the two-thirds typical of developed EU markets.

Since independence, the Czechs have made integration into West European institutions their chief foreign policy objective. Fundamental to this objective is Czech membership of the EU. Thus, in 1996, the government submitted the country's membership application. In July 1997, the EU singled out the Czech Republic as one of five countries (out of 10 Eastern European applicants) to join the 'fast track' to membership. Negotiations began in earnest in 1998, and by October 1999 the government had concluded talks in eight of the 15 policy areas. Unfortunately, delays in economic reform represented a setback for EU accession. Hence, on 13 October 1999, the European Commission published its second annual assessment of the applicant countries' progress in which it judged the Czech Republic's progress 'not satisfactory', with a substantial gap between the government's declared intentions and the results it had achieved. Furthermore, the European Commission voiced alarm about corruption and an inefficient state administration and legal system. Although the Commission praised the progress that Czechs had made in the privatization of the banking sector, it urged them to redouble their efforts in other areas of privatization, price liberalization, and legal and institutional reform. The consequence of slower pace of reforms and only very limited progress in EU accession preparations meant that the country's position slipped on the EU's candidate list.

In March 1993, the Czech Republic joined the General Agreement on Tariffs and Trade (GATT) and in December 1995 became a full member of the OECD. In July 1997, NATO issued a membership invitation and two years later, in March 1999, the Czech Republic became a member of the alliance. The Czech Republic maintains diplomatic relations with more than 85 countries, of which 63 have permanent representation in Prague. The country is also part of the Visegrad group, which also includes Slovakia, Hungary, and Poland.

3.5 Legal environment and regulations

By and large, the Czech Republic has created a free and competitive market. The basic body of legislation that set up the framework for a free market system is the comprehensive commercial code that went into effect in January 1992. The new commercial code replaced roughly 80 assorted codes and regulations, and established the legal framework for most business-to-business activities. This code also brings Czech commercial law into compliance with most EU commercial norms. Furthermore, according to the October 2001 WTO report on the country's trade policies and practices the legal environment for economic and trade activities has substantially improved over the past five years. According to that report, much of the progress can be attributed to the Czech Republic's goal of accession to the EU and that EU-required harmonization has acted as a catalyst to speed up the implementation of reforms.

The government has placed strong emphasis on rooting out corruption. But, as in most former bureaucratic regimes, implementation has been more difficult than anticipated. Most investors complain about the difficulty of protecting their rights by legal means. Investors have been particularly frustrated by the lack of effective recourse to the court system. The slow pace of the courts is often compounded by judges' unfamiliarity with commercial cases.

Crime and corruption

The Czech Republic is a relatively safe country, but observers have reported an alarming increase in street crime, particularly pick-pocketing. According to police statistics, the number of reported crimes in the city has tripled since the 1989 Velvet Revolution and street crime has increased fivefold. Police statistics confirm that Romanian Gypsies commit much of the crimes in Prague. But, contrary to, say, Russia or Poland, violent crimes are rare.

Although it has approved the OECD Anti-Bribery Convention, charges of corruption linked to privatization and procurement have been levelled against the government. Nonetheless, Czech law considers both giving and receiving bribes a criminal act, regardless of the nationality or title of those involved (accordingly, bribes cannot be deducted from taxes). Recently, proposals have been advanced to make changes that would increase jail sentences up to eight years for officials engaging in bribery and corruption. Unfortunately, despite such laws and good intentions, few corruption cases have been brought to justice.

Judicial system, dispute settlement, and bankruptcy procedures

The judiciary consists of the Constitutional Court, Supreme Court, a Supreme Administrative Court, and high regional, and district courts. The Czech commercial and civil codes draw mostly upon the German system. The commercial code details regulations pertaining to legal entities and is analogous to US corporate law. The civil code, for its part, deals primarily with the contractual relationships among parties.

Czech law has great deal of grey area, and due to the late establishment and inexperience of the court system, judicial decisions often vary from court to court. Commercial disputes, particularly those related to bankruptcy proceedings, tend to drag on for years. At the moment, there is a three to four-year backlog in the bankruptcy courts and only a small secondary market for the liquidation of seized assets. The government has sought to amend the law to address these concerns.

As an affiliate of the New York Convention on the recognition and enforcement of arbitration awards, the Czech Republic is required to uphold arbitration awards in disputes between Czech and foreign parties.

However, the arbitration of disputes between two Czech corporations outside the country is not permitted, even if the owners of the corporations are foreign. With respect to judgments of other foreign courts, the rules are less clear.

Taxation, accounting and auditing rules

Generally, Czech tax codes are in line with EU tax policies. In 1995, the government started to provide for tax write-offs of bad debts, although with considerably less generous treatment of pre-1995 debts. The Czech government has carried on its programme of corporate income tax cutbacks. It has undergone a constant decrease from 45% in 1992, 42% in 1994, 41% in 1995, 39% in 1996, 35% in 1998, and is now at 31%. Tax rates for investment, mutual and pension funds are 25%. The tax rate for the highest bracket of personal income tax remains at 40%. Employer and employee social insurance contributions are 35% and 12.5%, respectively.

Laws on establishing and conducting business

In the Czech Republic, the right of foreign and domestic private entities to set up and own businesses is guaranteed by law. However, ownership of real estate by foreign individuals and companies is not permitted. This restriction also applies to Czech branch offices of foreign entities. Czech legal entities, including 100% foreign owned subsidiaries, may own real estate. Moreover, foreign investors can, as individuals or business entities, establish sole proprietorships, joint ventures, and branch offices in the country. The Czech government recognizes joint-stock companies, limited liability companies, general commercial partnerships, limited commercial partnerships, partnerships limited by shares, and associations. But, in 1995, it imposed a Czech language requirement for trade licenses needed for most forms of business. A Czech associate can be used to fulfil this requirement.

Restrictions on foreign investments

Czech procurement law provides a 10% price advantage for domestic firms, including the Czech subsidiary or branch office of a foreign company.

Investment incentives

In 1998, the Czech government approved a six-point package of incentives to attract investment. The incentives are offered to foreign and domestic firms that make a US$ 10 million manufacturing investment through a newly registered company. The package includes tax breaks of up to

10 years offered in two five-year periods, duty-free imports of high-tech equipment and a 90-day deferment of value added tax payments (VAT), potential for the creation of special customs zones, job creation benefits, training grants, opportunities to obtain low-cost land, and the possibility of additional incentives for secondary investments and production expansion.

Protection of property rights

The Czech Republic is bound by the Berne, Paris and Universal Copyright Conventions. The government has brought laws for the protection of intellectual property close to world standards, but, as in many other emerging markets, enforcement has lagged behind. Existing legislation guarantees protection of all forms of property rights, including patents, copyrights, trademarks, and semiconductor chip layout design. The amendments to the trademark and copyright laws have brought Czech legislation into wide-ranging conformity with relevant EU directives and WTO Trade Related Aspects of Intellectual Property Rights (TRIPS).

The Czech parliament will approve an amendment providing 70 years of copyright protection for literary works, up from the present 50 years. There are also two amendments to expand the tools of intellectual property rights (IPR) enforcement: the first, which was pending parliamentary approval in 1999, would enhance the powers of the customs service to seize counterfeit commodities. The other would permit the Czech Commercial Inspection (COI) to act independently in IPR cases. At the present time, the COI can only act in conjunction with the police. The authorities are also preparing a comprehensive amendment to the criminal code that would double sentences in IPR cases to two years. Existing legislation on general protection of private information is likely to be difficult to enforce in the courts. However, confidentiality agreements are becoming more common.

Entry requirements

The employing corporation must secure work permits in the Czech Republic for the individual. The business must acquire the work permits before applying for residency permits. The Czech authorities issue long-term residency permits to foreigners for a maximum period of six months. However, work permits can be renewed after the six-month initial period. In any case, anyone who remains in the country for longer than 30 days must register with the immigration service. People staying in hotels are automatically registered with the authorities. All visas must be obtained in advance of arrival in the country.

3.6 Business environment

The Czech Republic enjoys a modern infrastructure that supports most types of business activities. The country offers a strategic geographical position, expanding communication options, a wide industrial supply base, a skilled and cost-competitive workforce, and is exempt from major health and safety concerns. The Czech Republic's central location makes it an excellent hub for exporting into CEFTA (Central European Free Trade Agreement, including the Czech Republic, Hungary, Poland, Slovakia, Slovenia, Bulgaria, and Romania), Russia, the NIS and the EU.

Most significant business opportunities revolve around the redevelopment of basic infrastructure and restructuring of privatized firms. Additionally, major upgrades of pollution control equipment, telecommunications equipment and services, energy production and distribution, housing/municipal infrastructure, and medical services have been underway for several years.

Privatization

The privatization process has been reasonably speedy, with the private sector accounting for about 75% of GDP by 1998, compared to 5% at the beginning of transition. This led to structural change, opening the way for an expansion in the number of small firms, particularly in services. However, as in most former communist countries, state management of the economy has remained more pervasive than official statistics suggest.

The government has had recourse to diverse privatization methods, including direct sales, international tenders and, most notably, mass privatization by voucher, which was used for about one-third of all privatized state property. Two waves of voucher privatization were completed in May 1993 and March 1995. These schemes allowed the public to purchase vouchers at a nominal price and could then bid for shares in a range of firms. In 1999, except for the sale of Ceskoslovenska obchodni banka (CSOB), privatization was rather sluggish.

Foreign direct investment (FDI)

The relatively stable political and economic environment and highly qualified labour force make the Czech Republic an attractive place for foreign direct investment (FDI). An initial disinclination to put forward an investment incentive package probably lowered the level of potential FDI inflows in the early 1990s, but the government progressively adjusted its policy and approved in 1998 a standard package of incentives for manufacturing investments. Moreover, the government's 1998 FDI incentives, which have since been broadened, appear to have had a positive effect on the economy. This is precisely what led to negotiations regarding accession to the EU.

Foreign direct investment has flowed in at a highly inconsistent pace. Germany is the leading foreign investor followed by the Netherlands and the United States. Other major investors include Austria, the United Kingdom, France, Cyprus, and Italy. The ratio of foreign investment to GDP was 5.3% in 2000 (9% in 1999). In 1998, total FDI amounted to US$ 2.6 billion, up from US$ 1.3 billion in 1997 and US$ 1.4 billion in 1996. Analysis by sector shows that in the period 1990–1998, most FDI was channelled into transport and communications (US$ 1.8 billion, or 16.7%), trade, services and real estate (US$ 1.5 billion, or 13.5%), and banks and insurance companies (US$ 1.3 billion, or 11.5%). Other sectors included engineering, food, electronics, chemicals, consumer goods, energy, tobacco and construction.

Major booming sectors

The major booming sectors are services, telecommunications, transportation and automobiles. Services constitute a thriving services sector, which has evolved from virtually nothing, has emerged as the structure of the economy shifted from industry and agriculture toward services. In the 1990s, analysts attributed the growth within the service sector to the considerable growth of tourism. The government has encouraged competition in the telecom sector by progressively opening up its markets to national and foreign investors. The telecom monopoly company has been partly privatized. Furthermore, additional operators facilitated the provision of international and long-distance services. Progress has been made in liberalizing transport services. While the country has a relatively competitive road haulage industry and a non-subsidized airline company, passenger railway services and, to a lesser extent, bus services require large amounts of financial assistance to cover their losses. Finally, Skoda, once government-owned and operated but now a subsidiary of the Volkswagen Group, is the leading automobile manufacturer in Central and Eastern Europe. Based in Prague, sales for Skoda have increased by about 150% from 1994 to 2000. Furthermore, the Czechs have been successful in attracting FDI from global automotive firms. For example, in December of 2001, Toyota Motor and PSA Peugeot Citroën announced a US$ 1.35 billion joint investment to assemble cars in the Czech Republic.

Major trade partners (imports and exports)

According to the WTO report referred to above, merchandise trade (exports and imports) was the equivalent of 120% of GDP in 2000 (up from 105% in 1994). The distribution of merchandise trade has continued to swing towards Western Europe, thus underscoring the Czech Republic's continued integration with that region. In 2000, the EU accounted for almost 69% of the country's total merchandise exports and 62% of total imports. As of 1999, 42% of exports went to Germany, 8% to Slovakia, 6% to Austria and Poland, respectively, and 4% to France. Export values grew by 16% in 1998 but slowed substantially in 1999 to 7%. The 1998 estimated export figures for the country's major exported products include machinery and transport equipment (41%), other manufactured goods (40%), chemicals (8%), raw materials and fuel (7%). In 1998, net oil exports amounted to 1.2 million tonnes.

Increased tourism spending and greater demand for imports of machinery and components were among the most notable recent import activity. Principal imports include communications equipment, specialized metalworking machinery, chemicals, and transport equipment. The 1998 estimated import figures for the country's major imported products are machinery and transport equipment (39%), other manufactured goods (21%), chemicals (12%), raw materials and fuels (10%), and food (5%).

Free trade agreements

The former Government of Czechoslovakia signed a mutual investment treaty with the United States, which came into effect in December 1992. This treaty was carried over to the Czech Republic after the dismantling of the Federation. Countries that have signed and ratified similar agreements with the Czech Republic include Australia, Austria, Belgium, Luxembourg, Canada, China, Denmark, Finland, France, Germany, Greece, Hungary, Italy, Korea, Norway, Poland, Russia, Slovakia, Spain, Sweden, Switzerland, Thailand, and the United Kingdom. The Czech Republic continues to build up its network of preferential trade agreements and has concluded several free-trade agreements recently with Estonia, Latvia, Lithuania, Israel and Turkey, while continuing liberalization within the framework of previous preferential agreements. The Czech Republic is in the process of signing or ratifying agreements with Bulgaria, Costa Rica, Indonesia, Jordan, Kazakhstan, People's Democratic Republic of Korea, Lebanon, Mauritius, Moldova, Pakistan, Panama, Paraguay, Salvador, South Africa, Uruguay and Yugoslavia. In 1999, 78% of total imports were from free-trade agreement partners.

The impact on net trade creation of the country's anticipated accession to the EU is unknown. Non-tariff barriers on a most favoured nation (MFN) basis are expected to fall. However, EU membership will presumably raise the level of protection on agricultural products, as the current overall MFN tariff on agricultural goods is higher in the EU than in the Czech Republic. Agricultural assistance is also likely to increase considerably.

Tariff system

The average Czech MFN tariff rate decreased to 6% in 2001 from 8% in 2000. With no specific, composite or other non-*ad valorem* rates, the Czech tariff system is transparent. Most agricultural goods, however, are protected by relatively high tariffs. The simple MFN tariff average for agricultural products (WTO definition) in 2001 was 13.4%, compared with an average rate of 4.3% for non-agricultural goods.

Value added tax (VAT)

Czechs introduced the value added tax (VAT) in 1993. The authorities have used VAT as an investment incentive, especially for foreign investors. For example, under certain circumstances the Czech government allows for a 90-day deferment of VAT payments for high-tech equipment imports. The government does not allow VAT refunds or deductions to companies that are unable to collect on merchandise or services sold on credit. VAT contributions are based on sales, not on collections, and are levied on all goods and services that are ordered in the Czech Republic and also on imported goods. Goods exported from the Czech Republic are not taxed. The tax rates are 22% (basic rate) and 5% (most food, fuels, pharmaceutical products, and services).

3.7 Etiquette and cultural issues

Like other Central and Eastern Europeans, Czechs are formal in business circumstances and generally reserved. They smile only when they are amused or pleased. They do not smile as a kind of non-verbal greeting or social lubricant. However, it would be wrong to interpret the scarcity of smiles as a lack of openness or friendliness. Initial business meetings are usually not overly cordial, but rather serious and matter-of-fact. It usually takes several meetings to establish a sense of rapport with a Czech contact and to develop a more informal, relaxed relationship. Czechs appreciate being offered basic refreshments at meetings and will typically offer coffee, tea, water, juice and cookies when they host business visitors. Unlike business meetings, business luncheons are considerably more relaxed. A business lunch, even between just two people, could take more than two hours. Working breakfasts are less common than in other European countries or the United States, probably because the typical workday starts early.

Foreign business people who wish to schedule meetings or events, to which Czech business guests are invited, should avoid doing so on Friday afternoon, since many Czechs go to the countryside for the weekend. Furthermore, unlike Americans, they regard weekends and holidays as family time, and do not allow business to infringe upon it. Czechs resent being called Eastern Europeans, since they think of themselves as Central Europeans. If you make that mistake, someone is likely to point out that Prague is farther west than Vienna.

Greetings, gestures and conversation

As in most European countries, the use of titles is important in both written and verbal address. An appropriate way of addressing a Czech is by means of his or her title and surname ('Mr Novak', 'Dr Novikova'), until, of course, one is on a first name basis. It is considered offensive to use a Czech's first name before being invited to do so.

3.8 Conclusion

After three years of negative growth during 1997–99, the Czech Republic pulled itself out of recession and experienced positive GDP growth in 2000. Much of this growth was attributed to domestic reforms and trade liberalization. Furthermore, the Czech Republic experienced an increase in exports and FDI in 2000, which aided its economic recovery.

A great deal of the country's recent success has been credited to its objective of entering the EU. The goal of EU accession has acted as a catalyst to boost the implementation of reforms. Furthermore, over the past five years, the legal environment for economic and trade activities in the Czech Republic has improved considerably. Moreover, the Czech government has placed strong emphasis on rooting out corruption and although implementation has proven to be challenging, it is not insurmountable.

4
Estonia

4.1 Basic facts

The greatest natural asset of this small (45,226 sq km) Baltic state is its location at the crossroads of east and west. Estonia lies just south of Finland and across the Baltic Sea from Sweden – the EU's newest member. To the east are the huge potential markets of northwest Russia. As members of the former Soviet Union, Estonians are quite familiar with the ways of doing business in Russia and in the Commonwealth of Independent States. Estonia's modern transportation and communication links provide a safe and reliable bridge for trade with the ex-USSR and the Nordic countries.

Estonian, written in the Roman alphabet, is the official language. The Estonian language is part of the Finno-Ugric family of languages, to which Finnish and Hungarian also belong. Many Estonians, especially in the cities, speak English, Russian, and/or German, as well as the other Baltic languages. Estonia's population of approximately 1.5 million people is divided ethnically between Estonians (65.1%), Russians (28.1%), Ukrainians (3%) and Belarusian (2%). Russians are by far the largest minority group. The religion of the majority of Estonians is Lutheranism while that of Russians is the Eastern Orthodox Church.

Water surrounds Estonia on three sides and the country's nearly 4,000 kilometre coastline is characterized by marshy lowlands. It claims 1,520 islands in the Baltic Sea and has more than 1,400 natural and man-made lakes. It has a typical maritime climate: wet, with moderate winters, and cool summers.

The capital is Tallinn with 404,000 inhabitants. The next largest cities are Tartu (101,000 inhabitants), Narva (69,000) and Kohtla-Järve (48,000). The currency is the kroon (EEK); 100 sents make 1 kroon. The kroon is tied to the Euro by a currency board.

4.2 Historical background

The Estonian people belong to the ancient Finno-Ugric tribe that inhabited the region over 5,000 years ago. The name 'Estonia' comes from the word 'Aisti', the name given by the ancient Germans to the people living northeast of the Vistula River. In 1227 the Germans conquered the country and enslaved the people. In 1561, during the Livonian Wars, Estonia came under Swedish control and in 1710 it passed under Russian control. By 1819, serfdom was abolished in the Baltic provinces, giving rise to a national Estonian culture. In 1905, after the Russian Revolution, Estonians demanded national autonomy. Their movement was brutally put down, and it was only in 1917 that Estonia took advantage of the chaos of Russia's Bolshevik Revolution to finally declare its independence on 24 February 1918. The Treaty of Tartu, signed by Soviet Russia in 1920, recognized independence and Soviet Russia renounced in perpetuity all rights to the territory of Estonia.

Despite its policy of neutrality, Estonia did not escape occupation by foreign powers. Indeed, the signing of the Molotov–Ribbentrop Non-Aggression Pact (Soviet–Nazi Pact) on 23 August 1939 signalled a new end to its independence. Under the terms of the agreement, the Soviet Union was allowed to occupy Estonia, Latvia, part of Finland and, later, Lithuania, in exchange for Nazi Germany's control over Poland. Subsequently, Soviet troops invaded Estonia and the Estonian Soviet Socialist Republic (ESSR) was proclaimed on 21 July 1940. The newly created republic was incorporated in the USSR one month after its proclamation. The expropriation of property, the 'Sovietization' of cultural life, and deportations to Siberia immediately marked the installation of Stalinist communism. Thus, when Nazi Germany invaded Estonia, its soldiers were welcomed almost with open arms. Nazi Germany occupied Estonia during 1941–44 and during that period some 5,500 Estonians died in concentration camps. In January 1944, the Soviet Government restored its power, incorporated Estonia back into the USSR and pursued its 'Sovietization' policy. Estonian resistance took the form of a 10-year guerrilla movement called 'Forest Brethren' that operated in the countryside. Nevertheless, the Estonian Communist Party (ECP) grew progressively into the major organization in the country. Dominated by Russians or Russified Estonians, it comprised little more than 3% of the population.

In February 1990, Estonia's Supreme Soviet abolished paragraph 6 of the constitution, which guaranteed the Communist Party's leading role in society. Several parties emerged and a power struggle ensued. Estonia finally proclaimed the restoration of its independence in August 1991, following the weakening and eventual collapse of the Soviet Union. On 31 August 1994, after several years of negotiation, the armed forces of the Russian Federation finally pulled out of Estonia.

4.3 Political environment

The new parliamentary system, with a republican constitution, came into being on 28 June 1992 when Estonians endorsed the constitutional assembly's draft constitution and implementation act. The president, elected for a four-year term by parliament (*Riigikogu*), serves as chief of state. Although the president's role is largely ceremonial, the president can, albeit indirectly, influence policy. The highest organ of state authority is the parliament, a unicameral legislative body. The parliament, with its 101 members, initiates and approves legislation supported by the prime minister, who bears full responsibility for, and power over, his cabinet. The cabinet, or council of ministers, is appointed by the prime minister and approved by parliament. Parliament appoints the prime minister and has the authority to proclaim a state of emergency. Estonians elect the parliament for a four-year term by popular vote on the basis of proportional representation.

Estonia's current government is a coalition of the Fatherland, Reform, and Moderate parties. The current president is Arnold Rüütel elected in September 2001. Although a former communist, he is a respected figure because he negotiated Estonia's independence with Boris Yeltsin. Nevertheless, the 73-year old will have difficulty matching the credibility of his predecessor, Lennart Meri (1992–2001), a competent and highly esteemed statesman. The current prime minister, Siim Kallas, is the former finance minister and leader of the Reform Party. He is also a famous reformist figure in Estonia, who served as the country's first central banker after Estonia gained its independence in 1991.

Estonia is an independent and sovereign democratic republic. Supreme power is vested in the people. Its governance is divided into four branches: the president, the unicameral parliament (*Riigikogu*), the government (cabinet, led by the prime minister), and the courts. There is universal suffrage for Estonian citizens over the age of 18 residing in Estonia or abroad. The party spectrum during election campaigns ranges from single-issue parties to others that provide a complete political, social, and economic programme. Currently, there are about 13 political parties registered in Estonia. There is broad consensus among governments, political parties, and public opinion on pro-European policies and on an open market economy. The major item on the political agenda of Estonians is integration into the European Union (EU). Other issues relate to macroeconomics, such as the pros and cons of participation in the Euro zone, working towards membership in NATO (a government commission was formed for that purpose in 1999), the possibility of adopting direct presidential elections, and citizenship laws.

EU, NATO, and WTO membership

Estonia joined the World Trade Organization (WTO) in November 1999 – the second of the Baltic States to do so. It did so without transition periods. The major policy goal is – and, in fact, Estonia is one of the leading candidates – to conclude EU negotiations this year (2002) and join the EU in 2004, although the accession date may be delayed to 2005 or 2006. Estonia has already achieved 15 of the 31 chapters of the EU 'Acquis Communautaire'/'Community patrimony'.

The country has made important advances in conforming to EU legislation. Because of its smaller economy and free-market enthusiasm, Estonia is perceived as a leader among the countries aspiring to EU membership. In June 2001, the EU and Estonia opened negotiations on the complex agriculture chapter. Monetary policy is underwritten by the currency-board system and the new exchange-rate mechanism, both of which will most likely be maintained after EU accession. Despite the enthusiasm, however, the road is arduous. The government, which faces new elections in 2003, will be careful how it carries out the reforms, some of which risk being quite unpopular.

President Putin of Russia dampened Estonia's chances of early membership of NATO when he restated Boris Yeltsin's position on Russia's perceived sphere of influence. For their part, NATO member governments have been reluctant to complicate matters, and have thus avoided discussing eastward expansion before Estonia joins the EU. In the meantime, the country has backed the Lithuanian-inspired 'big bang' approach, whereby NATO would absorb all nine Eastern European candidates simultaneously. Even with entry to NATO delayed indefinitely, EU membership may create the security zone that Estonia wants through a common European defence strategy.

4.4 Economic environment and infrastructure

Estonia's economic policy will continue to focus on transforming the country into a market economy, with accession to the EU remaining the paramount goal. Ever since independence in 1991, successive

Estonian governments have carried out deep-seated market-oriented reforms. These have helped Estonia, of all the economies of the ex-USSR, to come nearest to a full-fledged market economy. Those reforms have also helped it secure a place on the fast track to EU membership. The remaining hurdles to accession are institutional rather than economic or financial in nature. This small nation has succeeded in outperforming the other two Baltic States, Lithuania and Latvia. Despite the catastrophic impact of the 1998 Russian financial crisis on Estonia, the country was able to bounce back strongly. Indeed, in 2000, the Estonian economy witnessed a robust 6% growth. In addition to the high demand for Estonian exports, Scandinavian and German foreign direct investments played a key role in fuelling the high growth rate.

Estonia's medium- and long-term economic outlook appears excellent and fiscal policy remains sound, although the government will face the challenge of reaching its balanced-budget target in the medium term. The Bank of Estonia (the central bank) is likely to maintain existing policies, including pegging the Estonian currency, the kroon, to the Euro. In March 2000, Estonia signed a precautionary US$ 39 million stand-by credit arrangement with the IMF. It has not used its three earlier arrangements and many analysts regard the stand-by credit as the IMF seal of approval for Estonia's economic management and performance.

Macroeconomics

Estonian economic reforms have been extraordinarily successful in limiting the government's role in the economy. Due to a balanced-budget legal requirement and the use of the currency board system, the government has an extremely restricted range of instruments with which to influence the economy. With the Estonian kroon pegged to the Euro (formerly the Deustch Mark), Estonia's money supply is directly determined by the amount of foreign exchange it can attract through exports, loans, or investments. The Bank of Estonia has initiated a programme to harmonize its framework for monetary policy with that of the European Central Bank. Beyond the constraints imposed by the legally mandated balanced budget, the government has been particularly reluctant to issue sovereign guarantees from international financial institutions, so much so that Estonia has an international public debt burden of about 5% of GDP.

As shown above, largely due to the August 1998 Russian financial crisis, Estonia experienced a sharp economic downturn in 1999. Growth fell from almost 11% in 1997 to 4% in 1998 and 0.5% in 1999. This decline was the country's first experience of the downside of normal economic cycles. Reasonable and sustainable GDP growth of 6% in 2000 and in 2001 backed stronger industrial growth and improved consumer demand. The principal driving force behind the economic revival is external demand, with exports to all major markets rising. Domestic demand is a relatively less important vehicle for growth, although investment-led growth will undoubtedly lead to higher domestic demand.

Estonia's privatization of state assets through the tender process is almost completed. Indeed, the last state-owned bank was privatized in 2000. Estonia will continue to privatize energy, telecommunications, railways, and other state-owned companies in the early 2000s. Telecommunications has become one of the most favoured sectors in Estonia, attracting considerable foreign investment, especially from Finland (Sonera) and Sweden (Telia). Privatization of the remaining utility companies, notably Eesti Raudtee (Estonian Railways), Edelaraudtee (Southwest Railways), and Tallinna Progila (Tallinn Waste Dump) has witnessed an uninterrupted progression. Many view the railways as a valuable asset because they are part of Russia's profitable oil-export logistics. One end result of the maturity of the privatization programme has been the rapid increase in the market capitalization of the Tallinn Stock Exchange, from 10% of GDP at the end of 1998 to around 40% of GDP by the end of 2000. The Helsinki Stock Exchange owns and has maintained close links with the Tallinn Stock Exchange.

The legal requirement for a balanced budget has impelled Estonia to set up an offshore stabilization fund where it has deposited income above its expenditures and much of the revenue from privatizations, including a successful IPO for the telecommunications company. Despite a budget shortfall in the late 1990s, the government was most reluctant to utilize the stabilization reserves. Instead, it decided to deal with the 1999 revenue shortfall by deferring investments, preparing a negative supplementary budget that cuts spending, and by undertaking other measures to restrict expenditures.

Growth in Russia will once again create the demand for Estonian imports, in particular food, which will benefit its producers. The possible resolution of punitive trade restrictions on Estonian imports would further benefit Estonian exports to Russia. The 1998 Russian crisis led Estonian authorities to downsize sectors, such as fisheries and dairy production, that were tied to the Russian market and were non competitive in Western markets. Although trade with Russia may improve, Estonian industry will continue its path of trending away from traditional sectors like food processing, fisheries, and light industry.

Industry

Services contributed the highest proportion to GDP with 65.7% (in 1999), followed by industry (30.7%) and agriculture (3.6%). The performance of the industrial sector confirms the strength of the economic recovery: sales in the first seven months of 2000 were up by 11.4% year on year. Corporate profits for the first quarter surged by 142% year on year. Retail sales in the first quarter of 2000 increased by 9% year on year in real terms, and by 13% in the second.

Estonia's vibrant services sector contributed significantly to offsetting the country's deficit in trade goods. Tourism, especially the millions of Finns who come every year to Tallinn for shopping and leisure, is expected to continue to show steady growth. The massive number of tourists has prompted the construction of hotels, department stores, restaurants, and cafés.

The manufacturing sector, especially geared towards the supply of components to Nordic companies, will also pursue its steady growth. The combination of dramatically lower costs and a highly trained workforce, reinforced by the past successes enjoyed by Finnish and Swedish companies operating in Estonia, will lead to investment in similar manufacturing and assembly plants.

The traditionally strong wood and forest products industry will also continue to grow steadily. More value-added manufacturing of the abundant timber, which is either harvested in Estonia or shipped in from Russia, will likely take place in Estonia itself.

Environmental issues

Estonia suffers from heavy air pollution from sulphur dioxide in the oil-shale emitted by power plants in the northeast. In the former Soviet military bases (Paldiski and Sillamae), soil and groundwater are contaminated with petroleum products, radioactive waste, abandoned equipment, and chemicals. Many of Estonia's smaller lakes in agricultural areas are heavily affected by organic waste. Coastal sea water is polluted at many sites.

Energy

Estonia is self-sufficient in electrical power; its two large oil-shale power plants have a generating capacity of about 3,000 MW, twice Estonia's domestic demand. Because of its large oil-shale reserves, Estonia is self-sufficient and thus need not rely on other fuel sources. In the past, the power plants produced and exported energy to Russia and Latvia, but these markets have largely disappeared. Negotiations are currently underway with a US energy company to form a joint venture to modernize and manage the two oil-shale fired plants, while bringing them into conformity with international environmental standards.

Financial sector

The Estonian financial market fits a characteristically European environment where banks and financing institutions play the dominant role. In 1997, Estonia launched the 'Export Developing Programme' of PHARE, put in place by the Estonian Trade and Investment Board, and set up on the basis of the Estonian Investments Agency. A key objective of the programme is to improve the competitive power of the Estonian economy by developing export activities that prepare Estonia for accession to the EU. Support includes assisting exporters to penetrate new markets, increasing the efficiency of export promotion services, and developing priority sectors.

Furthermore, commercial banks provide financing for exports, with guarantees whenever possible. The banks advise their customers on bank loans as well as on loans granted by other credit institutions. All Estonian commercial banks have extensive correspondent relationships with foreign banks, as well as with most of the larger financial centres.

Telecommunications

Foreign investment in the form of joint business ventures has greatly improved telephone service in Estonia. The Estonian government made a controversial long distance telephone concession agreement with a consortium of Swedish and Finnish firms. This has supplied the country with up-to-date and, in many cases, digital phone lines available throughout the country. In areas where the population density was too low to warrant installation of fixed-line systems, other wireless systems were installed.

In addition to its fixed-line system, Estonia has three mobile phone service providers and a excellent, well developed system. Because of close proximity to Scandinavia and its advanced mobile phone industry, the country has the highest number of mobile phone users per capita in Central and Eastern Europe. Mobile phones and pagers are widely used in Estonia. The Ministry of Transport and Communications is expanding mobile phone services to form rural networks. Fibre-optic cables to Finland, Sweden, Latvia, and Russia provide a worldwide packet switched service; two international switch systems are located in Tallinn.

Information technology has evolved quickly in the country and Estonia now has one of the highest number of Internet users in Central and Eastern Europe. The government has undertaken a major commitment to provide all schools in the country with Internet access. Internet services are available throughout most of the country; already in 1999, six Internet service providers (ISPs) offered their services.

Transportation

Surface transport in Estonia is adequate, but the growing quantity of motor vehicles is increasingly depreciating the road system. The country possesses only a limited number of major highways. One of the most important, the Via Baltica, will improve driving conditions within the Baltic region by linking the Baltic States with major West European cities via Finland and Poland. The new highway is also expected to help expand trade and tourism.

Railways handle a constantly growing amount of transit trade for Russia through Estonia's modern ports. Unlike the situation in Latvia, where the majority of petroleum products are transported from Russia via pipeline, nearly all of the petroleum transiting Estonia is hauled in railcars. The privatization of the railways linking Estonia's ports to Russia's Great October railroad should sharply increase the railways' capacity thanks to new management and significant investment.

The greater part of transit cargo passes through Tallinn's expanding ports. Estonia's main ports are modern, and relatively well managed and enjoy low labour costs. They are deep enough to accommodate the largest Baltic Sea ships, and are generally ice-free.

4.5 Legal environment and regulations

Crime and corruption

Although Estonia has launched a programme to improve the effectiveness of its police force, the country has a relatively high rate of violent crime and has in fact witnessed a proliferation of street crime. Muggings, car vandalism, and car thefts have multiplied considerably. Foreigners alone or in small groups may be at risk in Tallinn at night, especially if they have been drinking alcohol. Adults may own and carry firearms in self-defence. Very few crimes are solved, and it is often quite difficult to obtain police assistance. Local police contingents are understaffed, inadequately equipped, and rarely speak English.

Taxation, accounting and auditing rules

The Estonian taxation system was reformed in 1993 in an attempt to avoid tax evasion. Since then, Estonia has had a flat taxation system, with only one income tax rate for both companies and individuals, set at 26%. In 2001, the government eliminated corporate tax on income that is reinvested in the domestic economy. Enterprises with more than 30% foreign capital may receive two- to three-year tax holidays and a reduced rate for up to five additional years. According to the Income Tax Act, dividends received by a resident native or by a non-resident direct investor are tax exempt. Over one half of government revenue is derived from indirect taxes, notably from VAT (18%).

Laws on establishing and conducting business

The Commercial Code that was adopted on 15 February 1995, and which is in many ways similar to German business legislation, establishes the basic principles of entrepreneurship modelled on European traditions and standards. Commercial operations in Estonia are divided into six types: the general partnership (*täisühing*), the limited partnership (*usaldusühing*), the limited liability company (*osaühing*), the joint-stock company (*aktsiaselts*), the co-operative association (*tulundusühistu*), and the branch (*filiaal*). For foreign investors, the most common way of conducting business is the branch, which has fewer filing requirements. One can find descriptions of the different types, as well as English-language guidelines on how to establish such firms in Estonia on the websites of either the Estonian Investment Agency (www.eia.ee) or the Estonian Chamber of Commerce and Industry (www.koda.ee).

Estonia recognizes and enforces secured interests in property, both chattels personal and real. Mortgages are quite common for both residential and commercial property and leasing, as a means of financing, is widespread and efficient. The legal system protects and facilitates acquisition and disposal of all property rights, such as land, buildings and mortgages. All Estonian governments have pledged to return property to the owners from the pre-Soviet occupation. This has been a long, complicated process that remains incomplete, especially for non-residential real estate.

Business organizations available to foreigners

Regardless of their ownership structure, all companies may, under Estonian law, carry out foreign trade relations. State-owned enterprises have neither exclusive rights nor special privileges in their purchases or sales involving exports or imports. The government encourages joint ventures and licensing arrangements with foreign manufacturers. Many foreign companies have established a presence in the Estonian market with subsidiaries and joint ventures. Several Estonian firms are interested in using their long-established contacts in the former Soviet Union to market foreign goods, and Estonians cite a number of selling points for using the country as a gateway to Russia.

Restrictions on foreign investments

There are relatively few restrictions on foreign investors. Exceptions include transport, energy and certain utilities, where the government requires licenses for investment. However, this requirement is applied in a routine and even-handed manner.

Protection of intellectual property rights

The Estonian legal system protects property rights, including intellectual property. Estonia adheres to the Berne Convention, WIPO and TRIPS. The country has not yet joined the Rome Convention, which protects the rights of producers. However, adherence to that treaty is one of the preconditions for becoming a full EU member. Estonia amended and adopted a copyright law and criminal code in 1998. It complies with EU directives granting protection to authors, performing artists, record producers and broadcasting organizations.

Visa requirements

Passport and visa requirements for Estonia are subject to change and business travellers are well advised to use the following information only as a general guideline. Estonian consulates provide the list of countries whose citizens do not need an entry visa for Estonia. The Estonian embassy or consulate online visa information is the best source for current, detailed requirements. In the event that a visa is required, the three Baltic States (Estonia, Latvia and Lithuania) have established a reciprocal visa policy, where a valid visa for any of the three states will be accepted in the other two.

Temporary residence and work permits are issued together for a period of five years. Applications should be submitted to the nearest Estonian consulate. Citizens of Australia, the UK, and the US may also submit applications to the Citizenship and Migration Board in Tallinn. Along with the application and the appropriate fee, applicants must submit a passport; a certificate of mental health, TB, and HIV; a marriage licence, if appropriate; four photographs; school/college diploma; and an official invitation from an employer in Estonia. Some original documents are required; these are photocopied at the consulate and returned. Processing can take up to one year.

Distribution and marketing

Distribution channels in Estonia are similar to those in developed markets. Goods may be sold through an agent, distributor, established wholesaler, or by selling directly to retail organizations. Privately owned wholesale and trading houses are particularly strong in certain specialized sectors, such as electronics, electrical components and instruments, pharmaceutical and healthcare products, technical products and machinery, raw materials and chemicals.

One exclusive agent/distributor is usually appointed to cover the entire country. Estonian importers often represent several different product lines. In selecting a representative, the exporter should check whether that company handles competing products. There is no clearing house of information for finding a partner in Estonia. When seeking agents, distributors or partners in Estonia should contact local trade associations for a list of importers or contact the Estonian Investment Agency.

As in other emerging markets, direct marketing is showing a steady development in Estonia. Typical direct marketing as advertising includes direct mail and direct response advertising through radio and television. Although more recent, mail order, direct selling, and telemarketing are also generating direct sales.

Estonia's Advertising Law has been operational since January 1998. The law prohibits advertisements that are offensive racially or sexually, and includes provisions on child-related advertisements. Advertising tobacco products is prohibited and advertising alcohol is strictly limited. Nearly half of the advertising in Estonia is conducted through the national and local printed press. About 26% of advertising is conducted by way of television, while radio, magazines and outdoor media have a total share of close to 10%.

The international advertising magazine *Advertising Age*, identifies four Estonian advertising agencies: Inorek & Grey, Brand Sellers DDB Estonia, Bates Adell Saatchi & Saatchi, and Zavod. In 1997 Inorek & Grey showed the biggest turnover of US$ 1.4 million. Among the major Estonian periodicals with the largest circulation, one can cite *Postimees* (circulation 67,000), *Eesti Päevaleht* (36,000), *Sõnumileht* (30,500), *Õhtuleht* (15,000), *Eesti Ekspress* (58,000), and *Äripäev* (12,000).

4.6 Business environment

Currency/foreign exchange

The Estonian currency is a free currency with no restrictions on its transfer or conversion. There are no restrictions, limitations or delays involved in converting or transferring funds associated with an investment (including remittances of investment capital, earnings, loan repayments, or lease payments) into a freely usable currency and at a legal market-clearing rate. There is no limit on dividend distributions, as long as they correspond to a company's official earnings records. If a foreign company ceases operating in Estonia, all of its assets may be repatriated without restriction. These policies have been fixed for many years and there is no indication that they will be altered in any way. Foreign exchange is readily available for any purpose.

Privatization

Since regaining independence in 1991, Estonia has established and achieved some of the most aggressive market reforms in Central and Eastern Europe. The country has largely completed its privatization with only a few infrastructure enterprises still remaining under government control. In 2000, the privatization of the railways, the power generating company, and associated oil-shale mines were completed. A small number of municipal-owned enterprises have yet to be privatized but they constitute a tiny fraction of the overall economy.

Foreign direct investment (FDI)

Estonia's government maintains a highly favourable attitude toward foreign direct investment (FDI). The law on foreign investments, enacted in 1991, affirms the liberal treatment of foreign investments in Estonia and provides potential investors with detailed information on investing in Estonia. In 1994, the Estonian Investment Agency (EIA) was established. This is a publicly funded agency under the administration of the Ministry of Economic Affairs. The EIA aims to boost the Estonian economy through the promotion of foreign direct investment.

In its efforts to harmonize with EU practices, Estonia is adjusting its foreign investment laws and regulations. The government does not screen foreign investments, but it has established requirements for certain sectors to regulate and delineate ownership responsibilities. Estonia requires licenses for foreign investors involved in mining, energy, gas and water supply, railways and transport, waterways, ports, dams and other water-related structures, and telecommunications and communication networks. The Estonian Central Bank issues licenses for foreign interests seeking to invest in or establish a bank. Government reviews and licensing are definitely a matter of routine and non-discriminatory. Estonia's openness to FDI has extended to its nearly complete privatization programme.

The government has sought to establish free trade agreements in order to attract export-driven investments for three primary markets: the EU, the developing markets of Central and Eastern Europe, and the newly independent states of the former Soviet Union. Estonia has mutual investment promotion and protection agreements with the United States, Denmark, Finland, Sweden, France, Norway, the Netherlands, Germany, Switzerland, Poland, China, Israel, the United Kingdom and Austria.

Free economic and trade areas

Free trade zones are operating in Muuga Port (one of the four harbours that forms the Port of Tallinn complex), Valga and Võru (southeast Estonia). A free economic zone is being established in Sillamae (an industrial area in Estonia's northeast). There are also several warehouses located in border areas where goods may be stored for up to one year (extendable), free from import or export duties.

Major booming sectors

Services, especially transportation and tourism, will be the principal growth sectors for the next few years. Manufacturing and the forest products sector are also likely to continue to grow.

Major trade partners

In 1999, the major import trading partners were Finland (23%), Russia (13.2%), Sweden (10%), Germany (9.1%), and the United States (4.7%). The chief export trading partners were Sweden (19.3%), Finland (18.8%), Russia (8.8%), Latvia (8.8%), Germany (7.3%), and the United States (2.5%).

Free-trade agreements

Estonia has free-trade regimes with EU and EFTA countries and also with Latvia, Lithuania, Ukraine, Slovakia, Slovenia and the Czech Republic.

Tariff system

Estonia's liberal foreign trade regime, which contains few tariff or non-tariff barriers, is almost unique in Europe. The government has also restricted its role by avoiding import tariffs (except for agricultural products from certain third countries) and limiting excise taxes to a small range of products. The continued success of the external trade regime depends heavily on restructuring and revitalizing companies in the agricultural and industrial sectors. Because of Estonia's goal to become an EU member and adopting EU internal market procedures, foreign investors may be confident that future Estonian trade practices will resemble those of the EU.

Value added tax (VAT)

Nearly all imports as well as domestic production are subject to a value added tax (VAT). The VAT rate in Estonia is 18%; it is assessed on the CIF plus the amount paid in duties. Exemptions from VAT cover medicines, medical goods and equipment for funeral services, goods imported for non-profit purposes and other specific goods and services, the turnover of which is tax-free in Estonia. An excise tax is also levied on tobacco products, alcohol, gasoline and motor vehicles.

Major customs documentation for importing and exporting

The Estonian government is currently developing new customs regulations. Expensive cameras, large amounts of money, artwork, furs and fine jewellery should be declared on a customs form and stamped by customs officials upon entry; this protection serves as proof of prior ownership upon departure. Items, such as paintings, artwork, sculpture, antiques or other cultural objects may need an export license or special permission to be taken out of the country. Export duty may be charged on these items. Special permits may be required to import firearms, medicines and articles of cultural value.

Some employers place restrictions on the size of household shipments, either by weight or volume, or by excluding certain larger objects. Before deciding whether or not to include your vehicle in your household shipment, it is advisable to check with your employer whether any such restrictions will apply in your circumstances.

Driving

Vehicles imported into Estonia are subject to excise duty based on the age and engine capacity and VAT of 18%. One needs the original vehicle registration to bring it into Estonia. Third-party-liability insurance for vehicles is required in the country and should be purchased in Estonia. Green card insurance is also required. State and private coverage offered in Estonia is limited, and expatriates are advised to obtain an extensive policy that covers damages, personal injury and theft. Road conditions may be poor, and one may encounter unexpected cyclists and horse-drawn vehicles on the roads.

European nationals must possess the current European driving license to operate vehicles in Estonia. Others may drive with valid national licenses. An International Driver's Permit (IDP) must be supported by a valid driver's license from the home country. If stopped for any reason, especially in case of a traffic violation, the IDP can save the foreign driver hours of delay.

4.7 Etiquette and cultural issues

Culture and negotiating style

Estonians are generally well educated and possess a wide range of scientific, technical, and other skills and methodical approaches to work. Baltic people in general gained a reputation in the former Soviet Union for orderliness, hard work, and efficiency. Many professionals and employees in the private sector work long hours. They are eager to become acquainted with Western techniques of production, marketing, administration, and management.

Commercial ties to Scandinavia and Germany date back to the Middle Ages and continue to influence business behaviour, where the atmosphere is usually formal and reserved. Estonians show a great deal of courtesy and respect for others and take such behaviour seriously. They are reserved and cautious in their friendships, which they believe are lifelong endeavours reserved for those with whom one has spent a lifetime.

Although the peoples of Estonia share a strategic location and a history of absorption into other countries, they are unique and proud of their individual histories and cultures. They enjoy discussing their independence and showing their historical sites and are the most Western of the three Baltic States. Having never considered themselves to be a part of the USSR, they have remained strongly patriotic.

Baltic governments are keen to attract foreign capital through privatization laws and other legislation favourable to foreign investment. Foreigners, especially those from Western democracies, are particularly welcome. The Baltic people regard their independence as a window of opportunity. They want free enterprise and democracy and a chance of prosperity that Westerners might help them to achieve. The sizeable Baltic populations in the USA, Canada and the UK, and the recognition of Baltic independence have ensured the West a deep friendship with the people of Estonia, Latvia, and Lithuania, even during the darkest days of Soviet rule. English-speaking foreigners in the Baltic States may find that the mere use of the English language can open doors.

Business entertaining takes place in the home, in restaurants or cafés. A service charge is included in the restaurant bill. If invited to a home, take a small gift for the hostess. It is appropriate to return the hospitality by hosting your associates for a meal or other entertainment.

There are few, if any, restrictions on public smoking – no smoke-free zones in restaurants. Drinking water in Estonia is chlorinated, but is not considered entirely safe because the filtering system does not remove viruses. As an alternative, bottled water is available everywhere, although foreigners might not like its high salt content.

Greetings, gestures, conversation

The greeting protocol in Estonia involves a handshake in all professional situations and for most social contacts. Young people greet their elders first, and men greet women first. One should rise to extend a greeting. Estonians avoid using first names until invited to do so, and use professional titles with the last name. They maintain eye contact during conversation and using their hands as they talk. A visitor should not use hands for gesturing or carry on a conversation with one's hands in pockets. It should be noted that adults do not chew gum in public.

5
Hungary

5.1 Basic facts

A former Soviet satellite, Hungary has developed into a leading Central European economy over the past 10 years and has attracted one of the highest per capita levels of foreign direct investment (FDI) in the world. Among the Central European countries, Hungary has certainly the stable, reliable commercial environment that attracts foreign companies. It is a NATO full member and will soon be a member of the European Union (EU). With about US$ 19.7 billion in FDI since 1989, Hungary has been a leading destination for FDI in Central and Eastern Europe, including the former Soviet Union (FSU).

Hungary has a total area of 93,030 sq km and its neighbours include Austria, Slovakia, Ukraine, Romania, Yugoslavia, Croatia and Slovenia. Its population of just over 10 million is one of the smallest in Eastern Europe. Hungarians are the dominant ethnic group with 96% of the total population, while the remaining minority groups are Gypsies, Romanians, Croatians, Germans and Slovaks. The population is overwhelmingly Christian, with Catholics representing about 68%, and Protestants, mostly Calvinists, at about 25%. The major cities are Budapest (population 1.86 million), Debrecen (209,000), Miskole (181,000), Szeged (171,000) and Pecs (163,000)

Hungarians speak Magyar, the national language, but proficiency in English, Russian, and German is quite common. In fact, in addition to Hungarian, business is conducted in any of these three foreign languages. The rate of literacy for those over 15 is an extraordinary 96%.

The national currency is the forint, made up of 100 fillér.

Although the country is not rich in natural resources, it possesses relatively important quantities of bauxite, coal, and natural gas, in addition to fertile soil, favoured by a temperate climate of cold, cloudy, humid winters and warm summers. Unlike other former Soviet satellites, Hungary enjoyed a much more modern infrastructure in the 1970s and the 1980s. In exchange for the country's pro-Soviet stance in foreign policy, the Soviets allowed Hungarians to experiment with liberal economic policies. Such policies resulted in innovative enterprises and the manufacturing of superior quality products. Today it benefits from modern communication systems, although some private homes still have no telephone. Most Hungarian families have television and radio, and although quite expensive, local broadcasts and cable are available. The country has four daily newspapers, with nationwide circulation, magazines and other publications. The transportation system is relatively good – and inexpensive. All means of transportation, such as subways, taxis, train and bus networks are available.

Despite its longer experience of a liberal economy, Hungary remains a transition economy. Thus, the problems it faces are, in many ways, similar to those in the other former Soviet satellites. Among the major problems is the lack of transparency in creating and applying legislation. Although observers have noted progress in recent years, intellectual property violations, including piracy of audio and video media, software, food products and toys are common. Corruption is still widespread despite serious attempts by the authorities to stamp it out. In fact, Hungary's grey economy is estimated at about one-third of the country's gross domestic product (GDP) and competes with legitimate business dealings.

Among other issues of concern to foreign investors is consumption, which is not growing at the rate many had anticipated in the early 1990s. The slow economic restructuring imposed by international financial institutions in 1995 is partly to blame for the slow growth. Economic restructuring is practically complete, but its results have yet to be evaluated.

5.2 Historical background

The millennium of King Stephen's founding of the Hungarian state was celebrated on 25 December 2000. The 1699 Treaty of Karlowitz awarded all of Hungary to Austria, which stripped the Hungarian nobility of its traditional rights and privileges. The military defeat of the Austro-Hungarian monarchy in 1918 led to a dramatic reduction in both the size and the population of Hungary. The 1920 Trianon Treaty trimmed its territory from about 325,000 to 93,000 sq km, and the population from 20.9 to 7.8 million, leaving sizeable Hungarian minorities in neighbouring Slovakia and Romania.

In the 1930s, Hungary moved increasingly closer to Germany, regaining lands from Slovakia, Romania, and Yugoslavia. It also sided with Germany during World War II. But Germany occupied Hungary from March 1944 until the Soviet Red Army drove out Nazi troops in early 1945. A free election in November 1945 gave a majority to the Smallholders' Party (SP), but a second, rigged, election in 1947 gave a majority to the Communist Party, which nationalized property and abolished other political parties. As in the rest of Eastern Europe, Stalinism dominated Hungary until Stalin's death in 1953. A popular uprising took place in Budapest on 23 October 1956. Prime minister Imre Nagy declared Hungary's neutrality and withdrawal from the Warsaw Pact, a move that prompted a Soviet invasion of Hungary on 4 November.

In 1968 Hungary introduced the 'New Economic Mechanism', a reform package designed to increase enterprise autonomy and the role of markets in economic decision making. This type of experiment with the market was practically non-existent in the other East European satellites and thus provides one of the main reasons why Hungary has been among the fastest growing transition economies and was able to liberalize the economy so quickly and reorient trade towards capitalist global markets. The experiment resulted in a boom in agricultural and consumer goods production. However, income inequality increased and global recession following the 1973 and 1979 oil-price shocks undermined the reform efforts. Worsening terms of trade, combined with excessive imports of Western technology and consumption goods, increased the country's foreign debt to more than US$ 11 billion by the early 1980s.

5.3 Political environment

Hungary's government operates within the framework of a parliamentary democracy, with a freely elected legislative assembly. Parliament elects the president for a five-year term. The current president, Ferenc Madl, elected on 5 June 2000, has few formal powers, even though he is commander-in-chief of the armed forces and guarantor of the democratic political system. Upon election, the president becomes non-partisan. He/she nominates the prime minister but the national assembly appoints the prime minister elected by majority vote. The national assembly (*Országgyüles*) has 386 members; 176 elected by majority vote from single-seat constituencies; 152 elected by party list votes (5% barrier) from 20 multi-seat constituencies. The remaining 58 seats are awarded to achieve proportional representation. Owing to this feature, polling percentages do not provide accurate predictions of the number of parliamentary seats, as absolute votes dwindle when they are non-winners. The term of office in the national assembly is four years.

Two parties, the Hungarian Socialist Party (HSP) and the Federation of Young Democrats-Hungarian Civic Party (Fidesz-HCP, centre right), have alternated in their leadership of the country since the mid-1990s. The pro-Western and pro-business stance of the two parties has created one of the most favourable business environments in the region. In the 2002 elections, after one of the most fiercely fought election campaigns since 1990, Fidesz and its coalition partner, the Hungarian Democratic Forum, won 48.6% of the vote and took 188 seats in the parliament, while the Socialists won 46.1% of the vote and took 178 seats. But with the support of the small centrist grouping known as the Alliance of Free Democrats (SZDSZ), which won 19 seats, the Socialists can form a majority coalition government.

In the judiciary branch, the Hungarian constitutional court is made up of 11 judges. The president of the supreme court is appointed by the president of the republic and elected by a two-thirds vote of the national assembly.

The Hungarian government remains committed to protecting political rights – a condition for accession to the EU. Because of concern over persecution of ethnic Hungarians in neighbouring countries, Hungary signed treaties with Slovakia and Romania in 1995 and 1996 respectively, and these defined and protected the rights of the sizeable Hungarian minorities in each of those countries.

5.4 Economic environment and infrastructure

Hungary's central bank (National Bank of Hungary) has demonstrated its commitment to economic growth by cutting interest rates twice in less than one month and five times in total since September 2001. However, the currency remains strong and consumer-price inflation has slowed significantly. Despite the slowing EU and global economy, Hungary's current account deficit shrank in 2001.

The country's most formidable economic challenges stem from structural reform. While resolute in making the transition to a full-fledged market economy, Hungarians decided in 1996 to establish a welfare system. One of the first steps was to adopt the pension reform legislation in the summer of 1997, thus making Hungary the first country in the region to have addressed this important, but politically sensitive problem. This has left Hungary's public finances vulnerable to economic downturns.

In 1998, the government decided to increase spending on investment, including on infrastructure. The Hungarian economy has staged a remarkable recovery in recent years. In the period 1990–93, it declined by approximately 18%. But the growth of the economy reached 2.9%, 1.5% and about 1%, in 1994, 1995, and 1996 respectively. Although the absolute GDP for 1996 was still well below the 1989 levels, Hungary achieved an estimated 5.5% real GDP growth rate in 2000.

Macroeconomics

Despite the country's formidable real GDP growth in 2000, it fell to about 4.2% in 2001. However, it is forecast to remain at that level in 2002 and 2003 or a little lower despite the ongoing slowdown in the EU, which absorbs three-quarters of Hungarian exports. These GDP forecasts incorporate the realities of the global economic downturn and might vary accordingly. For instance, a prolonged US recession could have a more damaging effect on Hungarian output.

Hungarian sovereign debt was upgraded in 2000 to the second-highest rating among Central European transition economies. Inflation – a top economic concern in 2000 – is still high at almost 10%, pushed by higher world oil and gas and domestic food prices. The Orban government has not yet addressed economic reform measures, such as health-care reform, tax reform, and local government financing.

During the first half of 2001 inflation continued to rise and reached 10.8% in May of that year. Inflation would be substantially higher without continued below-inflation increases in household energy and pharmaceutical prices, owing to government controls, which still affected 18% of the consumer price-index basket in 2000.

Hungary entered transition with the heaviest foreign debt burden in Central Europe. Falling interest rates and a growing domestic investor base has allowed extensive repayment of foreign currency with forint-denominated debt, which comprised more than 60% of public debt by mid-2000. Gains from the stabilization and privatization programmes have been used to reduce the foreign debt. According to data from the National Bank of Hungary, total external debt at the end of March 2001 stood at about US$ 26.1 billion.

Hungary began developing close political and economic ties with Western Europe following the collapse of the USSR in 1991. Thus, in December 1991, Hungary signed with the EU an Association Agreement, which encompasses political, economic, and cultural co-operation. The country joined NATO in 1999 and is a front runner in a future expansion of the EU. It continues to work towards accession to the EU, which it expects to achieve in 2004–2005.

The Europe Agreement, signed on 16 December 1991 and which came into force on 3 February 1994, regulates the present contractual relationship between Hungary and the EU. This agreement aims at preparing Hungary for full membership of the EU following restructuring of the economy and strengthening democracy. The EU has prepared an Accession Partnership that mobilizes all forms of assistance within a single framework. Hungary has also benefited from the EU's PHARE programme, which remains the main financial instrument in helping Hungary prepare for accession to the EU.

Environmental issues

In February 2000, Hungary experienced a massive cyanide spill into a Romanian tributary of Hungary's Tisza River. This caused an environmental catastrophe and had a major impact on the government and public's attitude towards the environment and pollution. A Romanian gold mine was blamed for the spill. Like its neighbours, Hungary faces all kinds of environmental problems that require immediate attention. It has taken only moderate measures and devotes less than 1% of the state budget to environmental protection. Nevertheless, the government has recently introduced regulations, including the Environmental Act, the Water Management Act and the new Decree on Hazardous Wastes, which have become the driving forces for increasing pollution-control expenditures. The authorities planned to introduce an environmental tax in 2001. A Waste Management Act is currently before parliament but lacks support because it is not perceived as aggressive enough. Furthermore, Hungary's eagerness to join the OECD and the EU has compelled the government to pay greater attention to environmental issues.

Energy

Hungary has privatized nearly all of its gas and electric generation and distribution facilities. Foreign energy firms have purchased power generation plants and plan to modernize and expand capacities to meet the expected additional energy utilization. The state-owned Paks nuclear facility generates approximately 43% of Hungary's electricity and hopes to double production by 2005. Gas and electricity prices have risen progressively and are expected to reach world market levels.

Financial sector

Hungary has introduced changes into the banking system in order to meet the conditions of OECD membership. A company with foreign participation is permitted to hold foreign investors' capital contribution in a hard currency account. The corporation can then use the funds to purchase capital equipment, spare parts, and building materials necessary for the manufacture of commodities or for meeting other costs incurred in hard currency. Foreign corporations, even if not registered as an entity in Hungary, may open foreign-denominated accounts in order to conduct business.

Telecommunications

Telecommunications has been one of the fastest growing sectors in Hungary. This is understandable given that in the early 1990s, Hungary had one of Europe's least developed telecommunications systems. Major investment by Ameritech and Deutsche Telekom in the local company, Matáv, has led to dramatic improvements in the number of lines installed and in customer satisfaction. Some parts of the country enjoy 100% digital service, and have a choice between 450,900 or 1800 MHz mobile service. This high level of service is in sharp contrast to the early 1990s when the installed base was limited to 1.5 million lines and a penetration rate of 15 lines per 100 persons, resulting in a call completion rate of only 40%. The telecommunications sector was opened to competition in December 2001 when Matáv's monopoly expired.

Transportation

Hungary enjoys a transportation infrastructure that is more developed than its neighbours. However, four-lane highways only cover part of the country and the government has announced expansion plans that include linking all major cities by four-lane highways over the next seven years. Indeed, the government has undertaken considerable efforts in building road infrastructure, as illustrated by the completion of the highway that links Budapest to Vienna. The distance between the two cities can now be covered in less than three hours. In addition, Hungary is preparing to build a European Corridor from Venice to Kyiv through Hungary.

The country's air transportation is lacking in domestic air service and airport capacity. The major airport in Budapest, Ferihegy, doubled its capacity with the expansion of Terminal 2 in late 1998. It plans to transform former Soviet air bases into domestic passenger and cargo airfields to fill the gap in domestic air service.

In contrast to air transportation, Hungary has an extensive railway system. Railroads serve approximately 158 million passengers and carry 43 million tons of goods annually across 7,600 km of track, of which 2,184 km are electrified. The tracks need upgrading to allow for high-speed trains. The country plans to modernize the ticketing and information management systems.

5.5 Legal environment and regulations/judicial system

Hungarians have allowed foreign ownership up to 100%, with the exception of designated 'strategic' holdings, some defence-related industries and the national airline MALÉV. Since July 1996, government approval is not needed for foreigners to invest in financial institutions and insurance; all that is required is official notification. From 1 January 1998, foreign financial institutions have been permitted to operate branches and conduct cross-border financial services, in keeping with Hungary's commitments at the time of its OECD accession in May 1996.

Foreign-owned companies that are Hungarian legal entities may acquire real estate, with the exception of agricultural land. Under the Investment Act, a company incorporated in Hungary may only acquire real estate 'required for its economic activities'. However, this has not prevented US and other foreign entrepreneurs from engaging in property development. The Land Law (Act 4 of 1994) restricts the purchase of land by foreigners to 6,000 square metres, but allows for leases up to 10 years for up to 300 hectares.

Only Hungarian nationals can purchase arable land at present. The liberalization of restrictions on arable land ownership was derailed in 1997 by a vociferous opposition campaign. The proposed legislation would have allowed any company registered in Hungary (regardless of ownership) to buy land for agricultural use within the same county where its headquarters are located, provided it had been engaged in agriculture for at least five years. Nonetheless, Hungary will have to lift restrictions on foreign land ownership as part of its accession to the EU.

The country does not impose restrictions on the ownership of real estate by Hungarian companies with foreign participation. This includes companies that are 100% foreign-owned, assuming that such ownership is necessary to conduct business. In all other cases, the municipal authority is authorized to grant permission to foreign legal or natural persons to acquire real estate.

Laws on establishing and conducting business

The use of local agents and distributors is recommended in those instances when establishing a sales subsidiary is not feasible. Commercial sections of embassies can provide a head start to firms seeking an agent or distributor in Hungary. Registration of a new business entity must be applied for at the Court of Registration. A new Companies Act (Act CXLV of 1997), which came into force on 16 June 1998, is intended to substantially reduce the tim e required to register a new company. If the Court fails to act on the registration within 30 days for limited liability companies (Kft.) and joint-stock companies (Rt.) and within 60 days for unincorporated business entities, the registration becomes effective automatically.

Foreign entities planning to set up businesses in Hungary are advised to consult an experienced solicitor and accounting firm. Furthermore, foreign businesses should be aware that obtaining and renewing work and residence permits has become increasingly onerous as the government attempts to crack down on illegal residents. Thus, it is advisable to hire a law or accounting firm or a company that specializes in this type of work to assist with the process of obtaining such permits.

Business organizations available to foreigners

Foreign individuals and corporations can choose among several investment alternatives. Forms of business enterprises include general and limited partnerships, co-operatives, and joint ventures. Act CXXXII, currently in effect, allows the formation of branch offices of foreign companies beginning from January 1998. This act is applicable to companies established after 16 June 1998.

In addition to the forms of business described above, foreign companies may establish a representative office, service office or information office, which are allowed to conduct marketing and technical support but not to engage in trade. One may, for example, choose to participate in the privatization programme or to acquire shares in a company directly from the owners or via the stock exchange. Investors may also decide to form a joint venture with one or more Hungarian or foreign partners. Alternatively, an investor may choose to set up a new company or an accredited representative office.

The other forms of enterprises are a union, a joint enterprise ('KV'), a limited partnership ('BT'), and an unlimited partnership ('KKT'). Alternatively, investors may prefer to operate through a representative or service office. As of 1998, branches of foreign companies were still not permitted in Hungary, even though a draft amendment to the Companies Act has been under consideration; this draft amendment should allow foreign companies to open branches in Hungary. Today, if a foreign investor wishes to set up an operation in Hungary, but does not wish to set up a corporate entity, the only options open are a representative office or a service office. Both of these constitute local operations of a foreign entity and have only a limited scope of permitted activities. While the representative office would normally act as an 'agent' between local customers or clients and the founding entity, the scope of activity of a service office is more limited and would normally be understood as being a permanent service establishment to service local customers.

The establishment and operation of joint ventures in Hungary has been permitted since 1972. The foundation of companies operating with foreign participation is subject essentially to the same treatment as that of exclusively Hungarian-owned companies. In 1989, the earlier licensing procedure was abolished. Today, it is sufficient to have the company simply incorporated in the Trade Register. Foreign investors are allowed to purchase shares in Hungarian firms up to 100% majority holdings. Joint ventures and 100% foreign-owned ventures – as with all businesses in Hungary – are entitled to pursue foreign trade activities. It is also possible to establish joint ventures in duty-free zones. In contrast to certain other countries, there are no specific duty-free zones delineated for establishing joint ventures. The land area of any enterprise or that of plants already existing or under construction can be declared as a duty-free zone by customs authorities.

Since 1 January 1994, Hungary has permitted the establishment of offshore companies. Under the law on corporate taxation, offshore companies enjoy an 85% tax preference. Such a company must be a limited liability company or shareholders' company registered in Hungary, and must be wholly foreign owned.

Franchising

Franchising is a relatively new concept in Hungary and most market segments are still underdeveloped. Current inefficiencies and a growing middle class indicate sizeable franchising opportunities in Hungary. There are currently around 300 franchise businesses operating throughout the country and they represent between 4% and 5% of total retail sales. Estimates reveal that 40% of the franchises are foreign and 60% are Hungarian-owned. As in many emerging markets, the majority of franchises are in the fast-food sector, followed by other retail sectors, such as clothing, photo service, copying/printing, petrol stations, business services and hotels. Franchisers such as McDonald's, Burger King, and Pizza Hut are well established in Hungary. Porst (a German film developing chain), Eastman Kodak, Adidas, and car rental companies such as Hertz are also well established in the country. These corporations have successfully adjusted their structures, marketing, and services to fit Hungary's transition economy by selling sub-franchises, providing financing, setting lower master franchise fees or using foreign master franchisees. However, despite its growth, franchising, as a proportion of the retail sector, still lags considerably behind the United States, Japan, and Western Europe.

Establishing an office

A business is established by drafting Articles of Association (Deed of Foundation in the case of single-person entities), which must be filed with the local Court of Registration within 30 days and must contain the following information: name, address, initial capitalization and names of members or shareholders. The business must pay a number of fees. Businesses are also required to register with the State Taxation Office (APEH), the Central Statistical Office, the local Chamber of Commerce and the Social Security office. In addition, foreign companies may have to establish a representative office, service office or information office, which are allowed to conduct marketing and technical support. However, as noted above, these cannot engage in trade.

Taxation, accounting, and auditing rules

In 1997 the government introduced a new act on corporate tax and dividend tax that limited the corporate tax to 18%. A 20% withholding tax replaced the 23% 'supplementary tax' that existed hitherto.

The EU's fourth and seventh directives on company law and the international accounting standards (IAS) have strongly influenced Hungary's accounting codes and practices. Nearly all business entities must prepare annual financial reports on a calendar-year basis. A simplified yearly report consists of a less detailed balance sheet and profit and loss statement. A company must prepare a consolidated yearly report if it has a majority stake in, or exerts management control over, another entity. The law designates the format of the annual report, which must furnish a realistic representation of the financial position of the business. The law also stipulates a number of obligatory bookkeeping and reporting principles, such as comprehensibility, completeness, consistency and precaution, and requires that there be a physical stock-taking of all tangible assets. Hungarian law applies depreciation and amortization rates so that the costs of replacing assets over their useful life can be written off. Goodwill can be amortized over at least five years, but in no case, over more than 15 years.

An external auditor must audit all legal entities, apart from small enterprises (this requirement is being phased in over a five-year period). Publication of a yearly report, including the auditor's opinion but excluding the business report, is compulsory for all joint-stock companies and limited liability companies whose foundation capital exceeds Ft 50 million and in a number of other specific instances.

Incentives for foreign investment

The current environment in Hungary encourages foreign investment and participation in virtually all aspects of the private economy; accordingly 30,000 foreign companies have established operations.

Act 24 of 1988 (as amended) on Investments of Foreigners in Hungary (the 'Investment Act') governs the establishment and operations of companies with foreign participation, and grants significant rights and benefits to foreign investors. It guarantees national treatment for foreign investments and abolishes the general requirement of government approval. It also provides protection against losses resulting from nationalization, expropriation, or similar measures, and guarantees free repatriation of invested capital and dividends.

Investment protection

The Hungarian authorities are committed to protecting foreign investors, both individuals and corporations, against illegal expropriation. They will compensate in full any losses incurred in the unlikely event of nationalization, expropriation, or similar measures; this would be done without delay in the currency of the initial investment. Hungary has signed a number of bilateral investment protection treaties with several countries, including Austria, France, Germany, the Netherlands, Sweden, and the United Kingdom. The same protection is offered through the World Bank's Multilateral Investment Guarantee Agency (MIGA).

Hungarians are concerned about the prevalence of bribery and corruption, which accounts for about 30% of GDP. However, officials are hopeful that the acceleration of reforms will eventually reduce that figure.

Protection of intellectual property rights

The Hungarian patent legislation provides protection for a 20-year period, provided that the patent is used within four years of the date of application or three years from the date of issue. There have been a few cases of litigation due to infringements of intellectual property rights. Pharmaceutical companies and toy manufacturers have been especially affected. Although copyright protection extends to literary, scientific and artistic creations, including software, the main issue concerning intellectual property rights (IPR) protection in Hungary is the lack of enforcement, notably in the area of software, sound recordings, videotapes, movies, and cable television. Moreover, in cases of transgression, court proceedings can be very time-consuming. Businesses can register their trademarks in Hungary but it is a rather lengthy process, which might take from six months to one year. The law requires that foreigners appoint a local attorney to represent them. Registrations are valid for ten years and can be renewed. The US Department of Commerce has reported that US enterprises have protested against trademark violations, especially in retail clothing and food products.

Distribution and marketing

Hungarian retail and wholesale distribution is developing towards Western standards. In the past, large, state-owned monopolies controlled distribution, which was largely supply-driven. During the transition period since 1989, the monopolistic state-controlled trading companies have been privatized and/or broken up, but a smooth-working demand-driven system has not fully developed and some inconsistencies remain. Choice of size and styles still needs to improve, particularly in clothing and apparel. However, the use of newer technologies, such as electronic data interchange (EDI), is beginning to significantly improve delivery of goods.

Large-scale wholesaling is still embryonic and this is why it is not unusual for retailing and wholesaling to be combined, sometimes even together with manufacturing. Although Hungary's retail sector now includes some larger department stores and supermarkets, small family-run stores are still quite common. Examples of foreign chains with operations in Hungary include Auchan (France), Metro (Germany), Michelfeit (Austria), Ikea (Sweden), Baumax (Germany), Humanic (Austria), Julius Meinl (Austria), Penny Market (UK), Cora (France), Marks & Spencer (UK), and Tesco (UK). A Hungarian corporation, Fotex Holding Co., has made a significant impact on the retail sector. Fotex is involved in such diversified market segments as optics, film developing, audio media, household appliances/consumer electronics, cosmetics and furniture. Recently, indoor shopping malls have arrived in Hungary and are now rapidly expanding not just in the Budapest area, but also in other cities, such as Gyor, Székesfehérvár, Debrecen, Miskolc, Pécs, Szeged, Kecskemét, Szombathely, Nyíregyháza, and Szolnok.

Hungarians have eliminated state subsidies and price controls for many products, thus allowing market forces to determine prices. The state still supports some basic services, such as utilities, mass transit and petrol. However, recent price increases are gradually bringing rates in line with costs. The one sector that the government still continues to heavily subsidize is that of pharmaceuticals.

Hungarian consumers, like most Eastern Europeans, are price-sensitive. The recent weakening of their purchasing power, due in part to high inflation, devaluation, and the special import tariffs – all part of the 1995 restructuring programme – have exacerbated that tendency.

Hungarian purchasing decisions are increasingly subject to sophisticated print and electronic media techniques. Billboards and kiosks are layered with the latest advertisements, geared towards young people and the rising middle class, with promotions of trendy Western lifestyles. It should be noted, however, that shoppers of all ages and lifestyles are often loyal to Hungarian products perceived to be of high quality. For mainstream Hungarian consumers, price and traditional habits (e.g. frequenting the local shop) still govern purchasing behaviour. Consumer campaigns, special offers and discounts have become common marketing practices in Hungary today.

The most important Hungarian firms use one form of advertising or another. In order of preference, television, radio, press, and outside billboards/signs remain the most popular media. Hungary's Competition Law prohibits any advertisement that deceives consumers or jeopardizes the reputation of competitors. In June 1997, the country introduced a new Advertising Law, which, according to most observers, is the most liberal in Europe.

Direct marketing is still in its infancy in Hungary. Only recently have telephone and direct mail soliciting been exploited. The lag is due partly to the poor quality of telephone access in the past, including the frequent change in phone numbers. But, the lack of familiarity with such marketing techniques also helps to explain the scarcity of direct marketing. Firms such as Avon, Amway, Oriflame and Tupperware have successfully used alternative forms of marketing that consist of personal presentation marketing.

5.6 Business environment

Hungary conducts over 70% of its trade with OECD countries, including over 60% with the EU. Before 1990, 65% of Hungary's trade was with the Soviet-dominated communist common market (COMECON or

CMEA) countries. Trade with the United States has increased considerably and the US is now Hungary's sixth largest trading partner, while Hungary is America's 64th largest trading partner. According to Hungarian trade officials, bilateral trade between the US and Hungary has increased 66% in the past six years and is expected to continue growing.

Currency/foreign exchange

Hungary's currency, the forint, is fully convertible for current account purposes. In 1995, the National Bank implemented a pre-announced crawling peg foreign exchange system. Since 2000, the forint has been valued exclusively against the Euro. Previously, the forint was valued against a currency basket consisting of 30% US dollar and 70% Euro. The forint is currently devalued at a rate of 1.1% per month. It is exchangeable for all current transactions and for some capital transactions, including repatriation of capital and profits by foreign investors, provided that the original investment is registered with the Foreign Exchange Office. Certain capital transactions are still subject to controls. However, liberalization measures currently underway will probably lift those controls. It is no longer necessary to obtain permission from the National Bank of Hungary to receive loans of more than 12 months from outside of the country, although the Bank must be notified that such loans have been received.

The Investment Act guarantees foreigners the right to repatriate 'in the currency of the investment' any dividends, after-tax profits, royalties, fees, or other income deriving from the operation or sale of the investment. The Act also grants foreign employees of a foreign investment the right to transfer all of their after-tax salaries. There are no onerous foreign exchange requirements, and there are no reported instances of delay in repatriations.

The government has gradually eliminated nearly all restrictions on long-term capital account transactions. As of 1 January 1998, restrictions were eliminated on (a) non-resident purchase of collective investment securities to open-ended investment funds; (b) resident firm acceptance of foreign credits or loans in excess of US$ 50 million; (c) resident firm loan payments abroad; (d) resident persons borrowing abroad; and (e) resident investments in instruments of OECD-based issuers of less than investment grade. Restrictions remain on non-resident investments in instruments with less than one-year maturity.

Foreign investors may keep export receipts and other cash contributions in convertible currencies in a foreign exchange account. The company may use these funds to import, duty-free in some circumstances, goods considered as part of the investment. Alternatively, it may import goods using foreign exchange bought in HUF.

Privatization

Hungary stands as a model of telecommunications, banking, and energy sector cash privatization. The government has opened major sectors to private investors. More than one-third of all FDI has come from Hungary's privatization programme. The programme has emphasized strategic investment rather than mass privatization, an approach that has successfully revitalized many failing state-owned enterprises. The State Privatization and Holding Company (APV) manages and sells state-owned properties, with Ministry of Finance approval on issues concerning the banking sector. The APV's mandate was to expire at the end of 2001 and be replaced by two organizations: a holding company that will administer the state's residual interests in companies, and a second body which will handle APV's claims and liabilities.

Most sectors have been privatized, including telecommunications, energy, and banking, as well as the national airline. By the end of 2001, roughly 85% of the economy was in private hands. Majority share sales of state-owned assets are, to all intents and purposes, complete; minority, blocking, and golden shares in major firms are next to go, and will proceed through the stock exchange. New infrastructure projects, such as the recently completed tender for the next generation, DCS 1800 MHz mobile phone system (won by a UK–US consortium) are also underway. Radio and television are currently undergoing privatization. Hungary embarked on transforming the retail sector to private ownership in the early 1980s.

Major privatizations scheduled for 2000 and 2001 include Malev Hungarian Airlines (although the government still owns shares), Antenna Hungaria, the national broadcasting company, the steelworks company Dunaferr, electrical company MVM (49%), and a sale of 25% stake in Hungary's largest corporation, MOL Hungarian Oil and Gas Company.

Hungary's success in transforming itself into a market economy is evident from the fact that the private sector now produces about 80% of GDP. Foreign owners control 70% of financial institutions, 66% of industry, 90% of telecommunications, 60% of energy production, and 50% of the trading sector.

Foreign direct investment (FDI)

Due to the transformation of its economy in the past decade or so, Hungary is now recognized as a worthy business partner. Foreign ownership of and investment in Hungarian firms is widespread, with cumulative foreign direct investment (FDI) totalling US$ 23 billion in 2000. The Economist Intelligence Unit expects Hungary to attract some US$ 2 billion of FDI a year until 2005. Hungary leads the region in FDI and accounts for over one third of all FDI in Central and Eastern Europe, including the former Soviet Union. Its successful economic restructuring programme has resulted in a substantial betterment of the country's macroeconomic conditions. The private sector now produces most of the goods and services, thus reversing decades of inefficient central planning. Products at least partially produced by foreign-owned companies account for almost 75% of its exports. The industrial sector has received some 55% of FDI.

Foreign direct investment has so far been concentrated in western Hungary and in Budapest, due to more developed infrastructure and proximity to the EU. However, eastern Hungary offers a well trained workforce and a long tradition in industry, agriculture, and research. There are also special incentives for doing business in eastern Hungary.

The United States is the foremost investor, with over US$ 5 billion. Most of America's main multinationals are present in Hungary. Among these are General Electric, General Motors, Ford, Ameritech, US West, Pepsi Cola, Coca-Cola, McDonald's, Lockheed, AES, Tenneco, Alcoa, Guardian Glass, Marriott, Procter & Gamble, and IBM. Not only have these companies invested considerable amounts of money, but they also have reinvested repeatedly, indicating their positive experience with Hungary's well-educated, productive, and relatively low-cost labour market.

Foreign investment in Hungary typically takes one of four forms: establishing a new (greenfield) business; entering into a joint venture; obtaining equity in a state enterprise through privatization; and, making a portfolio investment or participating in a capital increase. Local subsidiaries are typically incorporated as a limited liability company (known by its Hungarian abbreviation Kft.). Other commonly used forms are joint-stock companies (Rt.), joint ventures, business associations, general and limited partnerships, and sole proprietorships. Many foreign companies operate through representative offices, and establishing branches has become easier under the revised Branching Act which became effective in January 1998.

Major booming sectors

Tourism is Hungary's second-largest industry behind agriculture. Since 1997, following years of stagnation, tourism has shown signs of increasing vitality, as illustrated by high numbers of visitors and hotel occupancy rates. In order to accommodate the anticipated longer-term tourism industry growth needs, the authorities decided to launch several infrastructure programmes, which include the expansion of Budapest's International Airport, the construction of new highways, and the modernization of existing ones. The Government has offered a five-year tax exemption programme to hotel construction investments in underdeveloped regions.

The energy sector provides another set of interesting opportunities for foreign investors. Most Hungarian power generation plants are obsolete and ineffective. Some thermal units function with an efficiency level of less than 25%. Given the low quality and high cost of mining Hungarian coal, coal-fired plants are condemned to be either decommissioned or replaced by modern fluidized-bed technologies in the next 10 to 15 years.

There is unlimited demand for environmental technologies in Hungary. Hungarians are eager for financing in that sector. With the privatization of many power plants, chemical, and pharmaceutical companies, the authorities hope that Western investors might instil a higher level of environmental awareness. More importantly, they hope that those investors would also attract the new technologies that are required to address the country's environmental concerns.

Agriculture is another potentially hot sector for foreign investment. The country has a long tradition of being an agricultural exporter. It imports high quality planting seed for propagation and production. The United States' exports of vegetable, grass, forage and, in particular, field corn seeds have been well received. However, some limitations exist for new exporters because the market is well established and trade ties are entrenched. In addition, Hungary imposes a tariff rate quota system on certain exports.

In the industrial sector, the computer market represented part of a growing IT market of about US$ 600 million in 1996. Imports accounted for about 80% of the total market in 1996. The US was the largest exporter, with a 24% market share. The number of PCs sold in Hungary is an impressive 110,000–120,000 per year. In 2000, there were 16 Internet service providers and 650,000 Internet users.

Mobile telecommunications have also been a fast-growing sector. The number of subscribers is expected to approach the 2.5 million mark in 2000. Westel Radiotelephone Co Ltd (450 MHz), Westel 900 (900 MHz), and Pannon GSM (900 MHz) are the three main service providers. The American US West and the Hungarian Matàv have been the major investors in Westel Radiotelephone and Westel 900. Pannon is a joint venture that ties together a group made up of Scandinavians, Dutch and Hungarians. This sector has experienced substantial investments in the last few years.

Yet another market that has expanded rapidly in the past few years is cosmetics and toiletries. This expansion was due mostly to the liberalization of trade and to the increasingly sophisticated consumer demand. The competition on quality and price between multinational and local companies has been fierce. Various French, German, Italian and American companies have opened subsidiaries in the country. Renowned, large corporations, such as Colgate-Palmolive, Procter & Gamble, Johnson & Johnson, and Clinique have all acquired a share in the Hungarian market.

Importing and exporting

Imports to Hungary fall into one of two categories: (1) 'liberalized' imports, or items for which no permission is required, and (2) 'non-liberalized' imports, commodities which require permission from the Ministry of Industry and Trade. Hungary requires an import licence for goods and services that do not figure on the 'liberalized' list. Furthermore, international trade in certain 'strategic products', such as energy sources, fuels, precious metals, and weapons requires a special licence from the Ministry of Industry and Trade. It takes two or three weeks to obtain a licence if the application is submitted through the Joint Venture Club at the Chamber of Commerce in Budapest. 'Non-liberalized' imports are also subject to an annual quota, and a list of these quotas is published every six months. The quotas are issued on a 'first-come, first-served' basis. Nevertheless, if the full quota is not used within 120 days of being granted, the ministry may re-allocate it to another applicant.

Tariff system

The Hungarian customs tariff is based on the harmonized system. It follows the Brussels tariff nomenclature. The dutiable value of imported products is calculated according to the rules defined by GATT/WTO and, generally, includes the commercial value of the goods plus the costs associated with getting them to the Hungarian border, such as transport, insurance and storage. The type of product and the country of origin largely determine the customs duty rates.

Labour and education

Foreign investors in Hungary will find it increasingly difficult to locate enough highly skilled local labour. Measures to remedy this potential problem include bringing back expatriates to work as financial controllers or top account managers, increasing training, or lobbying the government to help improve labour mobility.

Educational levels in Hungary are comparable to those of Western Europe. A high standard of general and vocational education has been important in attracting foreign employers to Hungary, especially in new technology sectors. In 1999 the car maker Opel reported that the workforce at its Szentgotthard component plant was significantly better educated than its counterpart in Germany, with more than half holding a degree or equivalent qualification. Among Central European countries, Hungary consistently ranks highest in education spending.

5.7 Etiquette and cultural issues

Business in Hungary is conducted in a Western style and formalities are important in business dealings. Hungarians use titles, discuss business courteously and treat their business counterparts with respect. They are formal in their business customs and use titles, such as doctor, professor, director, Mr, Mrs, or Miss, always employing the last name. Greetings on a first name basis are reserved for close friends and family. Adults commonly greet each other with a firm handshake when meeting and parting. A man invariably waits for a woman to extend her hand first. Thus, status is very important, as is hierarchy. Hungarian management is conducted in a top-down manner.

Regardless of progress made during business meetings, Hungarians would customarily invite business associates to dinner. When a businessperson visits a Hungarian's home, which is rare since most business entertainment is done in restaurants, he/she should remember to take his/her shoes off upon entering the house. Hungarians usually offer their guests slippers. It is usually appropriate for the business guest to bring flowers, a box of chocolates or liquor. Hungarians usually regard dinner as a time to relax and build rapport rather than an occasion to discuss business. In fact, business is seldom discussed over dinner.

Western European dress customs have conspicuously influenced Hungarians. Businessmen habitually wear conservative suits. Organizations are male-dominated at every decision-making level.

Culture/negotiating style

Although many business people will find Hungarian business culture and behaviour no different from that in Western and Central Europe, they should be aware of some of its unique features. Indeed, while

Hungarian culture displays many aspects of Southern European cultures (a preference for relationships, indirect communication style, formality and so on), the Hungarian sense of punctuality and observance of schedules and deadlines is very similar to the chronometric behaviour of Northern Europeans (Germans, Scandinavians, Swiss). Thus, when planning a business trip to Hungary, it is important to make appointments beforehand and to be punctual.

Because of their penchant for building relationships, Hungarians prefer face-to-face negotiations. But negotiations are likely to be slow and time-consuming precisely because, as in Mediterranean societies, they like to build rapport before getting down to business. Furthermore, they will use roundabout language in their negotiations as in cultures that cross-cultural communications specialists call 'high context'. The impact of the heavy bureaucratic past is still evident. Unlike Americans, they do not appreciate a presentation that begins with a joke. Like the French, they believe that starting with a joke undermines the seriousness of a business negotiation. Just like the Germans, Hungarians appreciate presentations that provide lots of information, hard facts and technical data.

Business people should bear in mind that Hungary is today one of the most, if not the most, affluent of the democratic countries in Central and Eastern Europe, where business opportunities are plentiful. Hungarians welcome the foreign investments that are needed to make their country prosperous. They are particularly well disposed to companies that can bring in new skills and technology transfer

At their business dinners and lunches they generally avoid discussing politics and religion, which is perhaps another hangover from the Soviet-dominated past. But it is wise to remember that Hungarians are proud of their heritage, especially of their artists, musicians, composers and philosophers. They are equally proud of their very rich food and wines. Although the most popular dish, goulash is only one of many delicious Hungarian recipes, which include halaszle (fish soup), stuffed peppers, stuffed chicken, crepes, strudel and pancakes. A healthy lifestyle is not popular in Hungary. They drink and smoke heavily too.

Hungary has often been referred to as the 'nation of horsemen' because of its equestrian history. Indeed, horses today continue to play a noticeable role in recreational and tourist activities.

5.8 Conclusion

Hungary is today one of the most favourable markets for business in Central Europe. Within a decade of the collapse of the Berlin Wall,

Hungary had made important strides in creating the foundations of a market economy. Hungarians have created the required legal framework to attract foreign companies. For their part, foreign firms brought the necessary know-how and capital, but also the sense of profit orientation that many Central and Eastern Europeans lacked. Undoubtedly, Hungary is today a developed country rather than a developing one, even though there still exist many problems at various levels. In January 2002, some managers reported that although English and German are widely spoken, communication in Hungary is still a major problem. While many companies brought highly skilled managers from their home country, these managers have had difficulty adapting to the local culture. They also have difficulty understanding the bureaucracy, the accounting system, and other such issues. Retaining staff has proven more arduous due to switching salary scales. Given that salaries in Hungary are very low, employees would switch jobs when they find another that offers higher pay. Foreign managers have stated that the change of mentality in the manufacturing sector from a planned to a liberal economy has been more complicated than anticipated. Furthermore, the 'work ethic' is still missing.

Although Hungarians generally like Westerners, are open to the West and would like to be like the West, they still display xenophobic signs. Foreign visitors will also notice Hungarians' tendency to complain continuously and to always focus on the negative aspects of things. As put by a Western-educated Hungarian manager, 'our people have a half-empty glass attitude'. Yet, the young are eager to experience change and look forward to coaching that will alter the predominant negative attitude. This is probably one of the reasons why most foreign businesses still prefer Hungary to Poland or even the Czech Republic.

6
Latvia

6.1 Basic facts

Located on the Baltic Sea and the Gulf of Riga, Latvia is bordered in the south by Lithuania (453 km), in the north by Estonia (339 km) and in the east by Belarus (141 km) and Russia (217 km). Latvia covers an area of 64,589 sq km that consists, for the most part, of a low-lying plain with some moderate elevations in the east, the tallest of which is 311 m. Arable land accounts for 27% of the total land mass, and although it has no specific crop pattern, 13% of the permanent land use is given over to pasture. Forests and woodlands account for another 46%. The climate is continental with moderate winters largely due to the country's maritime position.

As a result of massive post-war immigration, Latvia has a distinctly multi-ethnic population of nearly 2.4 million. It is made up of 56.5% Latvians, 30.4% Russians, 4.3% Belarusians, 2.8% Ukrainians, and 2.6% Poles. The dominant religions in Latvia are Lutheran, followed by Roman Catholic and Russian Orthodox. Taking into account the very large number of mixed marriages, many people in Latvia belong to more than one ethnic group. The treatment of some minorities, especially Russians, many of whom are denied citizenship because of an insufficient knowledge of the official language (Latvian, also known as Lettish), long remained a hot issue in domestic politics and a bone of contention in Latvia's relations with Russia, as well as one of the impediments to European Union (EU) membership. The government amended the corresponding laws in late 1998 to allow everyone born in Latvia after 1991 to become citizens on request, but Latvia's pursuit of those accused of Soviet-era crimes and rising rhetoric on both sides have caused relations to remain strained.

Latvia has both a negative population growth rate (–0.84%) and net migration rate (–1.32 migrants per 1,000). Just over one third of Latvia's population is concentrated in Riga (805,000), the capital, which is also the largest city in the Baltic region. Other large cities are Daugavpils (117,000 inhabitants) and Liepaja (96,000). Outside the capital, however, many of the goods and services taken for granted in developed countries are absent.

Latvia's national currency, the lat (the official symbol is LVL, and 100 santims are 1 lat), is freely convertible. In order to maintain stability, the lat has been loosely pegged to Special Drawing Rights (SDR), the IMF's basket of currencies.

Means of communication

Latvia has eight AM and 56 FM stations, with one short-wave radio station, 74 television stations, and 11 Internet service providers. The leading newspaper, *Diena* (The Day) is published in both Latvian and Russian. Leading business newspapers include *Dienas Bizness* (The Day's Business), published in Latvian, and *Biznes i Baltiya* (Business and the Baltics), published in Russian. *Vakara Zinas* is a popular tabloid. *SM-Sevodnia* is widely read by the Russian-speaking population.

6.2 Historical background

Because of its strategic geographic location, Latvia has frequently been invaded by other bigger nations, which has determined the fate of the country and its people. Latvia means 'the land of the Lett-speakers' and has a history dating back to 9000 BC. Its territory was originally settled by ancient Baltic tribes and first conquered by the Vikings. Later, in the twelfth and thirteenth centuries, the Germans converted Latvia to Christianity, founded the city of Riga and dominated the largely peasant and serf population. Under their control, a confederation of feudal nations called Livonia grew up. It included today's Latvia and Estonia.

German control of the area continued for three centuries and came to an end in the mid-1600s, when Latvia was partitioned between Sweden and Poland–Lithuania. At the end of the eighteenth century, Peter the Great absorbed Latvia into the Russian empire. Consequently, Latvia became Russia's most developed province, its industry developed quickly and the number of inhabitants grew significantly. Nevertheless, the awakening of strong national feelings amongst the Latvian nation marked most of the nineteenth century, with the first newspapers in the Latvian language, as well as the emergence of several cultural features.

Profiting from the confusion in the aftermath of World War I, Latvia proclaimed its independence in November 1918. Soviet Russia immediately recognized Latvia's independence and relinquished its authority and claims to Latvian territory for all time. Latvia became a member of the League of Nations and played a full part in the activities of democratic nations. Thanks to the rapid economic growth that took place in the second half of the 1930s, the country achieved one of the highest standards of living in Europe. However, the benefits of its sovereignty were short-lived. In 1939, as a result of the Hitler–Stalin non-aggression pact, known as the Molotov–Ribbentrop agreement, Latvia was occupied by Soviet troops and annexed to the Soviet Union. In June 1941, several thousand Latvians were deported by force to Siberia. Subsequently, Latvia was captured by German occupation forces, which deported about 90% of the Jewish population. Finally, in 1944, Latvia once more came under Soviet occupation. An extensive Russification campaign began; rural areas were bludgeoned into collectivization, and the country was forced to adopt Soviet farming methods. Post-war genocide, forced deportations to Siberia and mass imprisonment reduced the population by more than one third.

During its brief period of independence, Latvia had built a relatively well developed market economy. However, large-scale nationalization imposed by Stalinist Russia transformed the country in the early 1950s. Its economy began to mirror that of other Soviet republics – a heavily industrialized system dominated by large-scale, highly specialized enterprises governed by the central planning apparatus. Trade was limited to the republics of the USSR. Russian workers were poured into the country, their numbers noticeably diluting the proportion of Latvian nationals. Although living standards were above the Soviet average, they were far behind those of Western Europe.

The era of *glasnost* and *perestroika* in the late 1980s led to increasing popular demands for independence. Nationalist and independence movements swamped the Baltic. On the 50th anniversary of the signing of the secret Soviet–Nazi pact, one million Latvians, Lithuanians an Estonians joined hands to symbolize their united wish for the independence of the Baltic States. They created a 600 km human chain connecting Vilnius to Riga and on to Tallinn. This unprecedented protest was one of the mechanisms that set in motion the collapse of the Soviet Union. On 4 May 1990, Latvia declared its independence. Clinging to power, the Soviet Union responded with military force, but eventually retreated in the face of pressure from the international community. In September 1991, Latvian independence was finally recognized by the USSR.

The first president, Guntis Ulmanis, was elected in 1993 and remained in office until 1999. He oversaw the period of transition from a satellite of Russia to an independent state with a successful and growing economy. Latvia is now a member of the United Nations, the Council of Europe, the World Trade Organization (WTO), and is also a candidate for admission to the European Union (EU) and NATO.

6.3 Political environment

Since independence, Latvia has been a parliamentary republic. The constitution (*Satversme*) of 1922 was revalidated on 21 August 1991, and a few of its provisions have since been amended (e.g. the voting age is now 18 years of age, and the parliamentary term is four years). The most important state institution is the unicameral parliament (*Saeima*). It is made up of 100 representatives elected for a four-year term by direct popular vote. It elects the president for a four-year term, appoints public officials, discusses and votes the laws. The president appoints the prime minister, initiates legislation, and fulfils all necessary representative duties. He has the right to dissolve parliament. However, confirmation by means of a referendum is required, and a negative result leads to the automatic dismissal of the president. The government consists of a cabinet of ministers headed by a prime minister. The prime minister nominates the members of the cabinet, who are then subject to approval by parliament. Finally, the judicial branch is composed of the Supreme Court, to which parliament affirms the appointment of all judges.

Since the restoration of independence in 1991, the Latvian political scene has been turbulent. Coalition party disputes have resulted in the collapse of most Latvian governments before the end of their term. After the general election in October 1998 and after separations from and changes of parties, the distribution of the 100 seats of parliament is as follows: People's Party (24 seats), Latvia's Way (21 seats, a centrist, pro-European party), TB/LNNK (15 seats), Party for Human Rights (16 seats), Social Democratic Workers' Party (12 seats), Social Democratic Alliance (5 seats) and Independents (8 seats). Latvia's ninth government since the restoration of independence was formed in May 2000 and is led by prime minister Andris Bērzi4š, a popular and highly regarded leader of Latvia's Way. Government policies reflect a broad public consensus in support of economic reform, democracy and the rule of law. The integration of Latvia into the EU and NATO remains one of the most important goals of this government. This ambition serves as a stimulus as Latvia modifies its legislation to comply with EU require-ments and strives to strengthen its regulatory and judicial institutions. The current president is a former-psychology professor, Mrs Vaira Vīse-Freiberga, the first woman president in Eastern Europe. Elected in June 1999 as a compromise candidate, she is a Canadian-Latvian who has spent most of her life in Canada. Nevertheless, she has succeeded in becoming a pragmatic popular leader.

Foreign relations

Latvia is a member of several international organizations, including the United Nations and many of its specialized and regional agencies. Some of these institutions include the International Bank for Reconstruction and Development (World Bank) and the International Monetary Fund (IMF). It is also an associate partner of the Western European Union (WEU). Negotiations for accession to the EU began in early 2000. The govern-ment has set its goal to fulfil the conditions for EU membership by 2002. Latvia has concluded bilateral investment agreements with the majority of European and CEE countries and the United States. It is a member of the Council of Baltic Sea States (CBSS), the European Bank for Reconstruction and Development (EBRD), the Organization for Secur-ity and Co-operation in Europe (OSCE), and the Council of Europe. In contrast, Latvia's relations with Russia remain strained. Tensions with the Russian government arise over border agreements as well as restrict-ive transport, customs, and banking regulations that target trade and financial transactions with Latvia.

6.4 Economic environment and infrastructure

Macroeconomic tendencies

Latvia is still a transition economy undergoing changes for eventual integration into various Western European political and economic institutions. As a result, the government has adopted a comprehensive reform package involving price and trade liberalization, privatization, and macroeconomic stabilization. As the first Baltic state to join the WTO, the government's (unrealistic) goal was to join the EU by 2002.

Like most Eastern European states, Latvia was negatively impacted by the Russian financial crisis and went into recession in 1999, with GDP growth plummeting to 0.1%. The crisis also had a negative effect on unemployment, which rose to 9.1% (up from 6.7% in 1997), and resulted in budget revenues stagnating and investment and industrial output falling (the latter by 8.8%). A stand-by agreement for US$ 45 million was signed with the IMF at the end of 1999. Fortunately, the economy has since recovered. Growth was a robust 6.6% in 2000, and unemployment fell to 7.7%. Inflation remains low at around 2%, anchored by the peg to the SDR. The country has almost completed its privatization programme, and the private sector now accounts for two-thirds of GDP. The gross debt represents 13.9% of GDP. As Latvia proceeds with its EU convergence efforts, the outlook could improve further, despite some minor concern about the fiscal deficit (2.7% of GDP against 2% for the IMF target) as well as the current account deficit (6.8% of GDP). The latter is essentially due to heavy imports of capital and intermediate goods, which are needed for restructuring.

However, the improvement in macroeconomic conditions has had a social cost. Since 1991, poverty has been rising; real wages have been decreasing, and there is growing inequality of access to healthcare and education, resulting in a lower life expectancy. The hidden unemployment is such that the overall unemployment rate is estimated to be 14.5%, with large divergences throughout the country. More worrying is the fact that a high proportion of job seekers consist of the long-term unemployed and the young. Pensions are on average equal to 40 LVL a month, that is half the estimated subsistence level.

Industry

During the Soviet era, Latvia's industry essentially serviced the military-industrial complex and specialized in producing electronics, radio and communication resources, chemical and pharmaceutical products, heavy machinery and foodstuffs. Independence resulted in the immediate closure of the Russian markets, so that many companies that used to be the flagships of Latvian industry simply disappeared overnight, while several others needed to be converted rapidly. Today, industry accounts for 20.2% of GDP and has successfully managed its reconversion. There are now four distinct industrial centres in Latvia: Riga, Daugavpils, Liepaja, and Jelgava. Riga produces 50% of the total value of industrial production in the country and is quite diversified, Daugavpils specializes in synthetic resins and plastic materials, Liepaja in iron and steel, and Jelgava in motor vehicles and machinery.

Energy

Latvia is poorly endowed with fossil fuels and is, therefore, a net energy importer. Its supply of energy resources are made up of 34% of natural and liquefied gas, 32% of oil products, 24% of hard fuel (coal, wood, and peat) and 10% of electricity from hydro plants. The recently privatized Latvijas Gas controls the extensive network of natural gas pipelines and depot facilities. The oil and oil products market is fully liberalized and has many local and foreign competitors, while the electricity sector is primarily under the control of the state-owned monopoly, Latvenergo (Electrical Power Energy).

Latvia imports all of its oil, mostly from Russia, Belarus and Lithuania, with only a small amount coming from the EU. The potential existence of unexplored oil offshore reserves in the Baltic Sea is currently being investigated. However, oil exploration has not yet started, as financial feasibility has not been proven. Natural and liquefied gas are imported from Russia in the summer and injected into the Incukalns underground reservoir, the third largest in Europe. Gas is then available during the winter. About three-quarters of the electricity generating capacity of the country is hydroelectric and is located on the Daugava River. The shortages are covered by imports from Russia, Estonia and Lithuania, as well as by coal imported from CIS and Poland, and local fuel (peat and firewood). The government also supports private initiatives for small-scale hydro power, wind generators and co-generation equipment by purchasing their production at double tariff.

Agriculture

The agricultural sector has declined dramatically in recent years. Currently it has a share in GDP of only 3% (against 21% in 1990) but employs about 15% of the total workforce and utilizes almost 40% of Latvia's total land area. The major agricultural products are cereals and grains (spring barley, winter wheat, winter rye and oats), sugar beets, potatoes, vegetables, as well as stockbreeding. A small domestic market and growing external competition, combined with low productivity, quality problems and an extensive under-capitalization in farming are the main obstacles to the development of the sector. The main goal of agricultural policy is, therefore, to restructure agriculture (where possible accompanied by compensatory measures) so that it can be integrated in the European single market.

It is worth noting that there are also 3.2 million hectares of forest in Latvia, of which 87% is productive or partly productive and 13% is protected. This opens up broad opportunities for future commercial development in this sector.

Financial sector

The Bank of Latvia is the independent central bank of the republic. Its principal objective is to regulate money in circulation by implementing monetary policy to maintain price stability in Latvia. It is in charge of issuing the national currency, organizing and maintaining settlement and payment systems in the country, and monitoring the development of the banking system. It acts as a lender of last resort and sets the reserve requirements for commercial banks. However, since 1 July 2001, the Bank of Latvia is no longer in charge of the regulation and supervision of the banking system. The latter has been taken over by the Financial and Capital Market Commission (FCMC), thus, allowing the Bank of Latvia to concentrate more on macro-prudential analysis. The FCMC will be completely independent, setting its own budget and raising its own revenue from fees paid by market participants.

Following a rapid expansion in the 1990s, the commercial banking sector ran into a deep crisis in 1995, which resulted in the development of supervisory and regulatory systems, as well as in the closure of several less competitive institutions. In 1998, the financial sector was severely hit once again, this time by the Russian crisis. Rigas Komercbanka, the country's third largest bank, was declared insolvent and closed in March 1999. A major restructuring followed, marked by increased statutory capital and further increased regulations from the Bank of Latvia, combined with mergers, acquisitions, and the entry of strategic foreign investors in core banks.

By the end of 2000, the banking sector in Latvia was again solid, adequately capitalized and well regulated in conformity with the EU standards. It finally consolidated in 27 commercial banks, still a large number given the country's size, with approximately 60% of the banks' capital in foreign hands. Latvia's five largest commercial banks are Parekss Banka, Latvijas Unibanka, Hansabanka, Rietumu Banka, and Latvijas Krajbanka with total combined assets of LVL 1.12 billion (about US$ 1.87 billion). Foreign banks have the right to open subsidiaries and branch offices in Latvia and licences are granted using the same procedure applied to domestic banks. At present, there are three foreign banks operating in the country, two German banks and one Estonian.

The Riga Stock Exchange is the only stock exchange in Latvia. It is owned by commercial banks in Latvia and broker unions. At the end of 2001, the Latvian equity market had a market capitalization of US$ 0.7 billion, with a monthly volume of US$ 17.5 million and a total annual turnover of 30%.

The Latvian insurance market is new and has attracted several foreign investors. The sector consolidated in 12 insurance companies at the end of 2000, with 50% of the capital coming from foreign investors. The most important foreign insurers in Latvia are Codan (Denmark) and Alte Leipziger, Schreiber Maron Anstalt, Kolnische Ruck (Germany), and consolidation is expected to continue in the near future.

Telecommunications

With the restoration of independence, an immediate priority of the Government was to update the outdated telecommunications network. Consequently, large investments have been made both on telecommunications and high-speed data transmission networks. The fixed lines telecommunications network is controlled by the local operator, Lattelekom, which belongs to the state (51%) and to Tilts Communications (TC) from Denmark (49%), which in turn belongs to Finnish Sonera (90% of shares). In return for monopoly status until 2013, all Lattelekom lines were to be upgraded to digital lines before 2003. This is an unlikely target, since on 1 January 2001, only seven cities and 52.2% of all Lattelekom lines were connected to digital networks. Consequently, discussions started to shorten the monopoly of Lattelekom. In particular, in February 2001, the Ministry of Transport granted Baltkom GSM a licence to provide international telecommunications services in Latvia.

The market for mobile telecommunications is extremely dynamic due to the competition between the two operators, Latvijas Mobilais Telefons (LMT, 70%) and Baltkom GSM (30%). There were more than 400,000 mobile phones in Latvia at the end of 2000, which represented 15.76% of the population. It is anticipated that three Latvian UMTS licences will be awarded during 2002, one to each of the two existing operators and one that will be auctioned. There are also several Internet service providers in Latvia. The most important are Delfi (40% market share), Lattelekom's Apollo, Telia, and Latnet.

Transportation

One of Latvia's strongest business attractions is its location as a commercial, financial, and transportation hub for the Russia/Baltic region. Therefore, revenues from transit carriage constitute approximately 66% of its export of services or 10% of GDP. Latvia enjoys a well developed road network (59,178 km of highways, 22,843 km paved roads and 36,335 km unpaved) carrying traffic from the main Latvian ports eastward and from north to south along the Via Baltica.

Ports are an important part of the transit system as more than 90% of handled cargo is transit freight. Major ports and harbours are in Daugavpils, Liepaja, Riga, and Ventspils, and there are 300 km of permanently navigable waterways inside the country. The Latvian merchant marine consists of a total of 14 ships of 1,000 GRT or greater, four cargo ships, four petroleum tankers, and six refrigerated cargo ships. The country possesses a total of 50 airports, 36 with paved runways and 14 with unpaved runways. Its national airline, airBaltic, operates direct flights to Copenhagen, Stockholm, Helsinki, Frankfurt, Kyiv, Vilnius, Tallinn and Budapest. Finally, Latvia is internally connected through a total of 2,412 km of railways, of which 2,379 km are broad gauge, 33 km narrow gauge and 271 km are electrified.

Environment

Current environmental concerns include air and water pollution owing to the lack of waste conversion equipment, as well as soil and groundwater contamination owing to chemical and petroleum dumping at military bases. In particular, the Gulf of Riga and the Daugava River remain heavily polluted.

6.5 Legal environment and regulations

Crime and corruption

Latvia has been strongly criticized for its corruption by both the World Bank and the EU in recent years. Several corruption scandals involving cabinet members have even led to the demise of numerous ministers and even prime ministers. Bribe-taking infects all levels of authority – from low-level bureaucrats in a position to delay administrative procedures to high-ranking officials awarding government contracts. The customs service, the traffic police, the judicial and dispute-settlement mechanisms are especially vulnerable. Although the legal framework to fight these problems is already in place (the Corruption Prevention Programme, adopted in February 1998, and the new Criminal Law, adopted in April 1999), law enforcement institutions still lack effectiveness. The lack of transparency in business regulations increases the problem. However, as a result of close co-operation with experts from the World Bank, a co-ordinating institution, the Corruption Prevention Council, has been created to implement a national strategy to combat corruption. The crime rate is another source of concern for those considering business in Latvia; it climbed almost 20% in 1999. Organized crime, car theft, burglaries, prostitution, smuggling and pickpockets frequently target foreigners.

Judicial system, dispute settlement and bankruptcy procedures

The Latvian legal system is based on civil law and the new constitution, dating from 1991, provides for the basic rights and freedoms of all citizens. The judiciary is independent, but insufficiently trained and highly subject to corruption and bribery. Weakness in the judiciary and inadequate enforcement of the rule of law are the most important reasons for corruption. To make matters worse, according to several surveys, the cost of the bribe is often unpredictable; the outcome of the case once the bribe is paid is not certain, and the time between filing a claim and the final decision is often disproportionate. As a consequence, most conflicts are rather settled out of court.

There are three arbitration institutions in Latvia: Riga international arbitration, arbitration under the auspices of the Privatization Agency, and arbitration conducted by the Latvian Chamber of Commerce. These institutions are currently more often utilized than the Latvian courts to settle commercial disputes. The Civil Procedure Law contains a section on arbitration courts, providing full compliance with international standards, and also governs the enforcement of rulings of foreign non-arbitral courts and foreign arbitration. The country is also a member of the 1958 New York Convention on the recognition and enforcement of foreign arbitral awards, ensuring that the judgments of foreign arbitral courts made in accordance with the convention can be enforced in Latvia. In addition, the Civil Procedure Law stipulates that judgments of foreign non-arbitral courts are enforceable in Latvia.

It should be noted that there are two laws governing bankruptcy procedures in Latvia: the 1996 Law on Insolvency of Enterprises and Companies, and the Credit Institutions Law. The latter regulates bankruptcy procedures for banks and other financial sector companies. Parliament has also adopted a new Collateral Law to strengthen the security of registering pledges on moveable assets.

Taxation, accounting, and auditing rules

In January 2002, enterprises and individuals operating in Latvia were subject to a flat 22% corporate income tax on their worldwide income (for residents) or on their Latvian-source income (non-residents). Capital gains must be included in taxable income for most companies. A 10% withholding tax is also imposed on dividends paid to foreigners and management and consultancy fees. A 25% withholding tax is applied to payments to persons registered in low-tax countries. The withholding tax may be reduced or waived because of a double tax treaty. At present Latvia has signed tax treaties with some 20 countries.

The Law on Accounting and the Law on Annual Reports of Enterprises regulate bookkeeping and financial reporting in Latvia. They are based on the fourth and seventh European Directives and are, therefore, in line with international standards. Accounts must be kept using the monetary unit of the Republic of Latvia, and Latvian must be used as the language of accounting. Companies with a significant foreign ownership may use a second language, with the prior approval of the auditors. All annual reports are subject to a mandatory audit. It should be noted that the majority of Latvian banks have joined the international accounting system, SWIFT, that provides standardization, effectiveness and security.

Laws on establishing and conducting business

Latvia's foreign investment law provides for unrestricted repatriation of profits associated with an investment. Investors can freely convert local currency into foreign exchange at market rates and can freely obtain foreign exchange from Latvian commercial banks. Expropriation of foreign investment is possible in a very limited number of cases specified in the Law on Real Property Expropriation, and compensation is mandatory. Nevertheless, there have been no cases of arbitrary expropriation of private property by the Government.

Various forms of business organizations available to foreigners

According to Latvian law, foreign companies may conduct business activity under one of the following three forms of business representation: limited liability company (*Sabiedriba ar Ierobezotu Atbildibu*, or SIA); joint-stock company (*Akciju Sabiedriba*, or AS); or a representative (branch) office of a foreign company. Limited liability and joint-stock companies must be listed with the Latvian Enterprise Register. A limited liability company has the rights of a legal entity and may be established by an individual or another company with a minimum statutory capital of LVL 2,000. Limited liability companies may have up to 50 shareholders.

The structure and legal requirements for establishing joint-stock companies are more complicated and are, hence, less popular with foreign investors. Companies with more than 50 shareholders, providing securities in public offerings, or former state enterprises using privatization certificates, must be established as joint-stock companies. A joint-stock company also has the rights of a legal entity. The minimum statutory capital is LVL 5,000. The establishment of banks, insurance companies, currency exchanges, and pawnshops requires a larger statutory capital. The establishment of a foreign bank branch is also subject to the approval of the Bank of Latvia. Minimum legal capital for joint-stock companies is to be increased to LVL 25,000 in the near future. Representative offices of foreign companies may be established for an initial period of five years. However, as representative offices do not have separate legal entity status, they are not allowed to carry out commercial activities in Latvia. Other full liability forms of business representation are closed to foreigners. These include: sole proprietorships, partnerships, and enterprises of social and religious organizations, companies with supplemental liability, non-profit companies, and co-operative societies. Private enterprises have competitive equality with public enterprises with respect to access to markets and business operations.

Restrictions on foreign investments

Under the 1991 Foreign Investment Law, the laws of Latvia apply equally to domestic and foreign investors. There are, however, some exceptions. In particular, foreign investors are prohibited from controlling timber-harvesting companies, organizing lotteries and gambling casinos, and operating radio or television stations. There are also certain restrictions on the purchase of land (but foreign investors may lease land for a period of up to 99 years), as well as necessary authorizations to establish foreign-owned insurance companies or banks.

Investment incentives

Since January 2001, foreigners investing more than LVL 10 million in less than three years benefit from a corporate income tax rebate of 40% of the investment and a carry-over of 10 years, upon acceptance by the government. High technology companies with ISO 9001 or ISO 14001 quality certificates also benefit from a 30% corporate income tax rebate. Finally, the government has prepared a series of incentive schemes for investment, both foreign and domestic, in several free ports, special economic zones (SEZ), and in special support regions (see below).

Protection of property rights

The government has adopted modern laws establishing the protection of copyrights, patents, trademarks and intellectual property rights. However, due to insufficient resources of the agencies concerned, the enforcement of intellectual property rights laws remains weak. At the same time, Latvian authorities are taking more proactive steps to confiscate pirated films, videos and software. Applications for the grant of a patent or registration of a trademark, in Latvian, English, Russian or German, can be made through the Latvian patent office. Nevertheless, consultation with a Latvian attorney is recommended before establishing a business or an intellectual property right in Latvia.

Entry requirements

Several countries have negotiated visa-free entry for periods of 90 days per calendar year. Nationals of other countries need to apply for a tourist visa prior to entry. Foreigners willing to work in Latvia must first obtain: (a) a residence permit or a special visa if he or she is a shareholder of a company registered in Latvia or an accredited representative; and (b) an official work permit.

6.6 Business environment

Privatization

After several unsuccessful attempts, privatization in Latvia effectively started in 1995 under the control of the Privatization Agency. The process followed the Estonian model and was based on the principles set in the 1991 Decree 'On the State Property and the Fundamental Principles of Conversion' and the mechanisms of the 'Law On Privatization of State-owned and Municipal Property'. Privatization included international tenders for large companies, direct sales of minority stakes, public auctions, public offerings on the stock exchange, and privatization certificate distributions to every resident in Latvia (based on the length of their period of residence). Foreign investors were given fair access to most enterprises that were eligible for privatization. The only performance requirements concerned the maintenance of a certain employment level and reinvestment in the company. However, these privatization requirements were always subject to negotiation.

Overall, it must be said that Latvia's privatization programme has been somewhat muddled and half-hearted. Although privatization of small and medium-size companies is almost complete, privatization of housing has been very slow, and the privatization of utilities, energy companies and transport only started in 1997. The privatizations of several entities (e.g. the electrical monopoly, Latvenergo, the Latvian Shipping Company, and the telephone company, Lattelekom) were postponed because of major political disagreement. Nevertheless, one has to recognize that the main factor behind the foreign direct investment (FDI) inflows into Latvia has been the privatization process.

Foreign direct investment (FDI)

The government actively encourages foreign direct investment (FDI) and has taken significant steps to improve the country's business climate. Thanks to intensive privatization, FDI grew considerably in 1996 and 1997. However, as a result of the Russian financial crisis, growth fell sharply in 1998 by about 50% to 4% of GDP. However, FDI started again in 2000 and represented 19.2% of GDP. The major investors come from Scandinavia (33.7%), the remainder of the EU (25.1%), the CIS (7.8%) and America and the Pacific (11.9%). The preferred targets are finance (23%), manufacturing (22%), trade (20%), communications (11%), services (10%), and transport (8%).

Free economic and trade areas

The Latvian government established free ports in the Riga and Ventspils portareas. In general, the free ports provide for exemptions from indirect taxes, including exemptions from customs duties, value added tax, and excise tax. Special economic zones (SEZ) have been created in Liepaja, a port city in western Latvia, and Rezekne, the centre of an east Latvian region that borders on Russia. The SEZs offer additional incentives, such as 80–100% reduction of corporate income taxes and real estate taxes. However, since the IMF objects to free trade zones, due to anti-competition and tax collection difficulties, Latvia has agreed to forego creating any new free trade zones. It is worth noting that requirements for companies applying for a license to operate under a free port or SEZ vary from one zone to the other.

Major trading partners

In 2001, 61% of Latvia's trade volume was with Europe. The chief exporting partners include Germany (16.9% of exports, 17% of imports), followed by the United Kingdom (14% of exports), Sweden (10% of exports, 7% of imports), and Russia (12% of exports, 12% of imports). Main exports are timber products, textiles, metal ware, chemicals and machines. Main imports are commodities, machinery and equipment, chemicals, fuel, textiles and foodstuffs.

Foreign trade agreements

On 10 February 1999 Latvia was the first of the Baltic States to join the World Trade Organization (WTO) as a full-fledged member. This provides an opportunity to enjoy most-favoured-nation (MFN) status in exports of goods to 140 countries. Latvia has free-trade agreements with 26 countries, including those of the EU, EFTA, several CEFTA countries and Ukraine, although the existing free-trade agreement with Ukraine does not extend to food commodities. Latvia also has MFN trade agreements with 21 other nations, including the United States, Canada, China, India, Australia, the CIS countries, and Hungary.

Value added tax (VAT)

Value added tax (VAT) is charged on any supply of goods or services or import of goods, as well as self-consumption. VAT rates are 18% or 0%. A new 9% rate will come into force on 1 January 2003 for a specific set of products (medicine, literature, etc.). Foreign investors are entitled to exemptions from VAT and customs duties on fixed assets that are imported as long-term investments. There is also an exemption from VAT and import duties if goods are imported for processing on a temporary basis.

Documentation

Importers or agents must complete a customs declaration and a customs freight delivery note at the border. The following documents are indispensable: contract (or copy) of the transaction, invoice, and consignment note, bill of lading indicating the amount, weight, and value of goods, an original copy of the certificate of origin (form EUR.1 or form A), a notarized registration certificate of the entrepreneur or company, specific licences if transportation of particular goods is restricted, a warranty entitling the holder to act on behalf of the entrepreneur or business company, certificates verifying that the goods in transit are not hazardous to health or the environment, and a Latvian language label with information on the contents/ingredients, producer, country, importer's name, and consumption end-date is mandatory for food products. Such a label should be attached to each retail package, unless the original product package contains the required information. The Ministries of Agriculture and Economy issue licences in compliance with a quota system.

Import licences

Imported products have to be approved for sale in Latvia. Licences currently must be acquired for the import of alcohol, fuel, and arms. Some products, for example, grains and sugar, have no licensing requirement. However, a formal procedure for registering imports remains for statistical purposes. For food imports, a producer's declaration or a food conformity certificate, issued by an accredited laboratory, is required.

The National Food Centre (NFC) tests and certifies all commodities prior to issuing retail sale permits. The Latvian veterinary department applies unified import certification of meat and meat products, dairy products, and fish. Veterinary legislation is currently being adjusted to EU accession requirements.

Standards and quality control

Meat imports are subject to border inspection controls for bovine spongiform encephalopathy (BSE), classical swine fever, and salmonella by the State Veterinary Department.

Labour

There is a legally established minimum wage in Latvia, currently LVL 50 per month, and all companies must abide by this minimum. The influence of the unions on the wage-setting process is modest. Employers are required to pay a social security tax to cover the cost of a retirement pension and access to the State healthcare system (currently 28% of salary and an additional 9% is paid by the employee). In the year 2002, this tax should decrease to 33%, payable in equal parts by the employer and the employee.

Infrastructure of doing business

The marketing of consumer products in Latvia, previously inhibited by the lack of large distributors or wholesalers, is changing as distribution and sales channels develop. Currently, private food wholesale companies such as Interpegro, Prodimpex, and Hanzas Uznemums, process the importation of food and grocery items for wholesale and retail operations. Seasonal agriculture and food products continue to be sold at farmer's markets located in the larger cities. There is also a growing network of small grocery and produce stores. Traditionally, Latvians shop for groceries in small, specialty stores. However, several large supermarkets have appeared in recent years. This change is largely due to the establishment of a Norwegian–Latvian joint venture, Varner Baltija, which has established the Norwegian retail chain, Rimi, in Latvia.

Nowadays, there are no laws regulating the relationship between a foreign company and its distributors or agents in Latvia. Due to the small size of the Latvian market, one distributor/agent is often used to cover the entire country and may also carry products from several industry sectors. Franchising arrangements are regulated under the 'Law on Competition' but franchising is currently not a common or well understood business arrangement. Joint ventures with local partners are common practice today and a recommended arrangement for companies with little or no experience of East European business practices. Some Latvian companies have registered with the Latvian Chamber of Commerce and Industry and may be good choices for partnerships. However, it is always necessary to check the background of all potential partners. Basic information and credit ratings of local companies may be obtained from Latvian business information companies. Advertising and trade promotion is growing in Latvia and can be carried out in both print and electronic media.

Major booming sectors

Although Latvia is a small country, it is a potentially attractive market for such products as IT equipment and services, capital machinery and equipment, and consumer products. Its favourable position at the centre of the three Baltic States provides a perfect location as a commercial, financial, and transportation hub for the Russian/Baltic region. The best prospects for foreign exports include IT equipment, telecommunications equipment, electronic components, electrical machinery, light industry equipment, transportation vehicles, and pharmaceutical products.

6.7 Etiquette and cultural issues

The Baltic States have historical and commercial ties to both Scandinavia and Germany that date back to the Middle Ages. These ties have left a considerable mark on business behaviour in this region. As a result, the business atmosphere is rather formal and reserved. Men wear tasteful, conservative suits, while women generally prefer skirts and dresses to slacks. Both men and women generally avoid ostentatious displays of wealth and luxury items. It is customary to shake hands with both men and women. Latvian men may also kiss the woman's hand, and some will exchange kisses on the cheek, depending on the degree of acquaintance. Courtesy and respect for others are also very important. It is customary to rise while greeting others, and to greet women and elders first. It is considered rude to use excessive hand gestures, to speak with hands in pockets or to chew gum in public. It is worth noting, however, that Latvians are heavy smokers and that there are no restrictions on smoking in public.

Punctuality is a virtue, and Latvians expect foreign visitors to be punctual for all appointments. Meetings begin on time and are not interrupted, a characteristic of Germanic societies. Meetings usually start with an exchange of business cards. Latvians use professional titles, thus, using first names should be avoided unless invited to do so. Business entertaining in restaurants or cafés is common, but home entertaining is also quite frequent. When invited to a private home, it is recommended that you bring the host or hostess a small gift (e.g. chocolates, cognac, flowers, etc.). Guests are always offered refreshments and should try to finish everything on their plate. Business is usually not discussed at social meetings. If you are invited, remember that Latvians appreciate reciprocity, which is customary in the country.

They are rather deal-oriented as opposed to relationship-oriented in their business behaviour. Like Germans, Latvians get down to business fairly rapidly. But in contrast to North Americans or North Europeans, making direct contact with Latvian business partners is not as effective as when done through referral or presentation. Similar to what happens with the Japanese, the best prospects for business contacts take place at trade shows.

Negotiating with Latvians

Although Latvians are very Westernized, negotiating a contract usually takes longer than in the United States or Western Europe. Perhaps because of the history of the country, it takes longer to establish trust. Furthermore, as in many other former Soviet-dominated nations, bureaucratic slowness influences the pace of negotiation. Foreign business people should be aware of the 'hardball' tactics (e.g. use of bogus deadlines to pressurize counterparts) that Latvians use in negotiation. Like Americans, they prefer comprehensive contracts. Foreign business people should be aware that the new generation of Latvians are quite efficient and conduct business negotiations in a direct, effective fashion. Though less devious than their Soviet-influenced elders, young Latvians can use negotiation tactics with surprising ease.

6.8 Conclusion

Since independence from the former Soviet Union, Latvia has experienced continued stability and the strengthening of democratic institutions. Its friendly and open environment for inward investors was the key to its transition to a market economy. Given its past successes and its enviable current status, Latvia hopes to be among the first candidate countries to join the EU. It is making consistent progress but lagging behind the other two Baltic States, essentially because of corruption. Solving this problem would open up a new bright and clear future for it.

7
Lithuania

7.1 Basic facts

Located on the Baltic Sea, at the gateway between the European Union (EU) and the CIS, Lithuania is the largest of the three Baltic State (65,300 sq km). It has common borders with Latvia (453 km) in the northwest, Russia–Kaliningrad (227 km) in the south, Belarus (502 km) in the east and southeast, Poland (91 km) in the south, and the Baltic Sea (99 km) in the west. Most of the countryside consists of lowland plains, with numerous small lakes in the eastern part of the country, and hilly uplands. The highest point is Juozapines Hill, near Vilnius, at 294 metres. Woodlands cover about a quarter of Lithuania, and more than half of the coast is sheltered by a sandbar that is about 100 km long and less than 4 km wide, known as the Curonian Spit National Park. Lithuania also has over 700 rivers, the longest of which are the Nemunas, Neris and the Venta. Five areas of wetlands (Cepkeliai, Kamanos, Nemunas Delta, Viesvile and Zuvintas) are designated protected areas. The climate is transitional between maritime and continental, with wet and moderate winters and summers. The average daytime temperature is –5 °C (23 °F) in January and 23 °C (80 °F) in July.

The total population is 3.7, of whom 81.3% are Lithuanian, 8.1% are Russian, 6.9% Polish, and 3.2% from other ethnic groups (Belarusians, Ukrainians, Latvians, etc.). Soon after its independence, Lithuania granted full citizenship rights to all ethnic groups in the country, thus ensuring a politically stable environment and the ethnic homogeneity of its population.

Lithuania is divided into 44 regions and 11 municipalities. Vilnius (0.57 million inhabitants) is the state capital. Located at the confluence of the Vilnele and Neris rivers, it is the economic, cultural and political centre, the capital of finance and the main link between Lithuania and the rest of the world. Other important cities are Kaunas (0.4 million inhabitants), Klaipeda (0.2 million), Siauliai (0.15 million) and Panevezys (0.13 million). The official language is Lithuanian, which belongs to the Baltic family of Indo-European languages. Polish and Russian are widely spoken. The primary religion is Roman Catholicism, followed by Lutheran, Russian Orthodox, Protestant, Evangelical Christian Baptist, Muslim and Jewish. All five major cities in Lithuania have their own universities, so that the literacy rate and the percentage of university graduates are among the highest in the region.

Since 1993, the Lithuanian currency has been the litas (LTL); 100 cents make 1 litas. It is freely exchanged with foreign currency, but only by credit institutions licensed by the Bank of Lithuania to perform foreign exchange transactions. The litas was originally pegged to the US dollar under a currency board system at a rate of 4 litas to 1 US dollar. On 2 February 2002, Lithuania terminated the litas – US$ peg in favour of the Euro at a rate of LTL 3.4528 to the Euro. It plans to replace the lita by the Euro in 2007 or 2008.

Means of communication

The independent Lithuanian printed media has flourished since independence and includes a wide range of economic newspapers and speciality magazines. The media are free and independent of the state. Nevertheless, several investigative journalists covering organized crime have been harassed and received death threats. The public television channel is less popular than several commercial channels, but politicians still influence its editorial policy, mostly through managerial appointments.

7.2 Historical background

Although Baltic tribes established themselves on what is presently known as Lithuanian territory during the seventh century BC, it was only in 1236 that Duke Mindaugas united the Lithuanian ethnic lands and established the state of Lithuania. In 1253, Mindaugas embraced Christianity – essentially for political reasons – and accepted the crown from the Pope of Rome, thus becoming the first and only king in Lithuanian history. In 1385, Grand Duke Jogaila of Lithuania married Queen Jadvyga of Poland and united the two countries. Several decades of military and political prosperity followed, when Lithuania annexed many Belorussian, Russian and Ukrainian territories and extended the state border all the way from the Baltic Sea to the shores of the Black Sea.

In 1569, Lithuania signed the Union of Lublin with Poland, by which the two countries agreed to share one king (also bearing the title of Grand Duke of Lithuania) and a joint legislature, the Seimas (Parliament). Nevertheless, Lithuania's state sovereignty was preserved, since the treasury, the currency, the laws and the army remained independent. In 1655, the Grand Duchy of Lithuania became enmeshed in wars with Russia and triggered several conflicts with Poland. Despite an alliance with Sweden, the country lost virtually all its sovereign rights and was finally partitioned in 1772, 1793 and 1795 between Russia (most of the country), Austria and Prussia. A policy of Russification immediately started, and printing books in Lithuanian using the Latin alphabet was outlawed. The name of Lithuania therefore disappeared from the political map of Europe for 123 years.

During World War I, its territory was occupied by Germany. In February 1918, even though the German Army and authorities were still in control of the entire country, Lithuanian representatives assembled in Vilnius to proclaim the restitution of the independent state of Lithuania. The new state was recognized by Sweden in December 1918. It survived a Soviet attempt to create a Lithuanian–Belorussian Soviet Republic and a late Polish campaign aimed at reincorporating Lithuania into Poland. Although all other major countries recognized Lithuania from 1920 to 1922, its war of independence against the Bolsheviks, Poles and the remnants of the German and Tsarist armies continued until 1923. At that time, a constitution establishing a parliamentary democracy was adopted, but a military coup in 1926 by the nationalist Tartinkai Party resulted in a dictatorship. Lithuania began to reconstruct its economy, recovered the Baltic Sea port Klaipeda, thus gaining a gateway to the world, restored a system of national education and developed extensively its agriculture.

During World War II, the country was almost physically annihilated. The Nazis initially seized part of Lithuania but in June 1940, the Soviet Union occupied the country and initiated mass deportation of the Lithuanian people to Russia and Siberia. In June 1941, Germany attacked the Soviet Union and reoccupied Lithuania. Hundreds of thousands of Lithuanian Jews were executed or sent to Auschwitz to be killed. In the summer of 1944, the Red Army crossed the Lithuanian border and once again, the entire country fell under Soviet domination. However, the Lithuanians were almost glad to see the Russians, as they were horrified by the way the Nazis had treated human beings. Unfortunately, the enjoyment did not last long. In accordance with the Yalta and Potsdam agreements, Lithuania was once again treated as a part of the Soviet Union. Agriculture was collectivized, churches closed, Lithuanian political parties were disbanded and rapid industrialization was set in motion. In addition, the Soviets undertook even more repressive measures and deportation campaigns than those before the war. Overall, it is estimated that Lithuania lost approximately 30% of its population during the period 1940–53.

It was only in 1988, after three years of the *perestroika* movement initiated by Mikhail Gorbachev, that representatives of the intelligentsia in Vilnius founded Sajudis, a democratic reform movement to liberate Lithuanians from Soviet occupation. Representatives of Sajudis won several elections and began to call officially for separation from Moscow. On 23 August, a human chain 600 km long joined two million Lithuanians, Latvians and Estonians together hand in hand along the Vilnius–Tallinn road.

In February 1990, Sajudis representatives won the elections to the Supreme Council (the legislature), declared the restoration of Lithuanian independence on 11 March and elected Vytautas Landsbergis as its chairman (*de facto* president). Moscow responded with economic sanctions, embargoes on fuel and medical supplies, and sent troops to seize Lithuanian television, radio and other vital central state institutions in Vilnius. Under pressure from Western nations, the Soviets and Lithuanians negotiated. The declaration of independence was suspended, and Moscow agreed to restore shipments. But the national sentiment among the people was kept alive and a national referendum on 9 February 1991 produced an absolute majority for the restoration of an independent state. After the unsuccessful Russian coup against Mikhail Gorbachev, Lithuania renewed its pressure for recognition of its independence. Moscow finally recognized the independence of Lithuania in September, immediately followed by other major states. In September 1991, Lithuania became a full member of the United Nations and in August 1992, the last Russian soldiers left Lithuanian territory.

7.3 Political environment

As stated in its 1992 constitution, Lithuania is an independent democratic republic, where power is exercised by a unicameral parliament (*Seimas*), the president of the republic, the government and a series of courts.

Parliament votes and adopts legislation drafted by the government or the president. It controls the activities of the government, ratifies international treaties to which the country is a party and approves the budget. It also appoints judges to the supreme and constitutional courts and can propose referenda. Parliament consists of 141 members elected for a maximum four-year term; 70 of them are elected on the basis of a nationwide party-list vote (the proportional representation formula) and 71 are determined on the basis of the results of elections in single-mandate districts (majority winner).

The country's president is the head of state and the commander-in-chief of the armed forces. He is directly elected for a five-year term, with a maximum of two consecutive terms. He nominates the prime minister (who must then be approved by parliament), and has author-ity to dissolve parliament, initiate laws or send draft legislation back to parliament for reconsideration. He also participates in the proposal of judges for the Supreme Court and nominates three judges to the consti-tutional court. The government – composed of the prime minister and other cabinet ministers – is responsible collectively and individually with the president to parliament for developing and implementing the domestic and foreign policies of Lithuania. He has the authority to initiate legislation, but may be removed collectively or individually by no-confidence votes in parliament.

The country's judiciary consists of common courts dealing with civil and criminal matters (the supreme court, the court of appeal, district courts and local courts), as well as specialised administrative courts inves-tigating administrative litigation (the highest administrative court and district administrative courts). Parliament appoints the judges to the Supreme Court. The president appoints the judges to the court of appeal (with the approval of the Seimas) as well as judges to the district and local courts. In addition, the constitutional court is an independent judicial body with the authority to determine whether the laws and other legal acts of parliament or the president are in conformity with the constitution.

Lithuanian politics has been anything but stable since independence. The latest parliamentary elections took place in September 2000. A social democratic coalition regrouping the socialist Democratic Labour Party of Lithuania (LDDP), the Lithuanian Social-Democratic Party (LSDP), the New Democratic Party (NDP) and the Lithuanian Russian Union (LRS) came first with 31.1% of the votes. Other major parties included the liberal New Union (NS), with 19.6%), the Lithuanian Liberal Union (LLS), with 17.3%) and the conservative Homeland Union-Conservatives of Lithuania (TS-LK), with 8.6%). All remaining parties scored less than 4.2% of the votes. Rolandas Paksas was nominated prime minister and formed the twelfth government since 1990, but he had to resign in July 2001. The current prime minister is Algirdas Brazauskas, the former president of the republic from 1993 to 1998 and the popular chairman of the Social Democratic Party. He intends to maintain the continuity of the country's foreign policy and has pledged to pursue EU and NATO membership while sharpening the focus on domestic social issues. The next elections are to be held in October 2002.

The current president is the Lithuanian-American citizen Valdas Adamkus, who was elected in 1998 by a margin of less than half of one per cent. He is a former high-level official of the US Environmental Protection Agency but had to renounce his US citizenship before his inauguration. He remains a powerful and popular figure and a strong guiding force for the country.

7.4 Economic environment and infrastructure

Macroeconomic tendencies

After a sizeable reduction in GDP during the first years of its transition, Lithuania enjoyed a period of robust economic expansion during 1994–98. In 1999, the country was hard hit by the consequences of the Russian financial crisis the previous year, and GDP declined by 4.2%. Since then, GDP growth (5.9%, 2001) has exceeded both the government and the IMF expectations. The recovery was driven by strong export growth and complemented by a gradual increase in domestic demand. The share of GDP produced by the private sector (70%) has steadily increased with the creation of new businesses and the consistent privatization process.

Inflation has declined steadily from 45.1% in 1994 to 2.0% in 2001, thanks to a strict monetary policy. In 2001, flat wages in real terms and the lagged effects of the earlier appreciation of the litas against the Euro were even enough to compensate for a 6.2% increase in food prices and non-alcoholic beverages, and a 21.1% rise in communication tariffs. The strict monetary policy should continue, as indicated in the Lithuanian government's memorandum to the IMF. All litas in circulation are backed at 149% by foreign currency and gold reserves under a currency board system, which is likely to stay in place until the country joins the Euro zone. Interest rates in Lithuania are currently among the lowest in Central and Eastern Europe, due to active crediting policies of banks and increasing competition.

In 2001, the state budget deficit was LTL 0.65 billion compared to the LTL 0.91 billion positive planned figure. The current account deficit narrowed to LTL 2.29 billion (4.8% of GDP, 15% lower than in 2000) and is projected to remain around 5.8% of GDP in 2002. Total public debt stood at LTL 12.90 billion and total foreign debt stood at LTL 9.86 billion (20.6% of GDP); most of it is long-term debt. In September 1996, Lithuania was the first country of the former Soviet Union to obtain a credit rating. Current ratings are: Standard & Poor's (BBB), Moody's (Ba1), Fitch IBCA (BBB+).

The state of the labour market is still unsatisfactory and the high unemployment rate (12.5% in 2001) must be considered one of the most urgent problems of the country. Unemployment is essentially structural: it affects primarily the unqualified workforce in the regions, while there is a shortage of qualified workers in urban areas. Unofficial unemployment is important, as employees in insolvent enterprises are often on unpaid forced leave, but are reluctant to terminate their employment contracts for fear of loosing severance pay. Finally, about 20% of the active population work in the shadow economy without labour contracts to avoid taxes and high social security contributions. The wages are among the lowest in Central and Eastern Europe (average of 1056 LTL/month per capita, with a minimum monthly salary of 430 litas). However, these figures vary greatly between town and country.

Industry

Understanding the industrial situation in Lithuania today requires going back to the middle of the twentieth century. When Lithuania was annexed by the Soviet Union in 1944, the USSR put great emphasis on the development of heavy industry. The overall process was designed to make Lithuania economically dependent on Russia in the present as well as in the future: Lithuania depended heavily upon the Soviet republics for imported raw materials and fuels, and since the country did not have much use for all the newly produced heavy industry products, the bulk of these goods were sent to Russia. In a few years, intensive industrialization gave birth to enterprises specializing in petroleum refining, shipbuilding (Baltija Shipyard), agricultural machinery, machine tools, electrical and electronic products, metallurgy, construction materials and food processing.

However, when Lithuania declared its independence, its heavy industry was soon massively impaired as a result of the immediate shrinkage of orders from republics of the former Soviet Union. Lithuania had to quickly diversify its industrial production and reorient its exports to Western Europe. This led to the development of an important light industry (in particular textiles, knitting, sewing and leather goods), chemicals and pharmaceuticals, information technology, timber and wood industries.

Energy

In 2000, Lithuania's sources of energy were oil products (34%), natural gas (27%), nuclear power (29%), as well as hydro energy, coal, peat, and wood (10% in total). Most of its energy resources were used to produce electricity (42%) and heating (19%). With the exception of forests and peat, Lithuania has very limited energy resources and must therefore import the majority of its fossil fuel supplies, essentially from Russia and Ukraine. The privatized gas pipeline company, Lietuvos Dujos (Lithuanian Gas), imports most of its gas from Russia, while the oil sector is controlled by the Mazeikiu Nafta (Mazeikiai Oil) public company (33% stake held by the US company Williams International). The oil sector comprises the Mazeikiai oil refinery (one of the largest in Eastern Europe and the only one in the Batltics), the Birzu Naftotiekis pipeline, and a new oil terminal at Butinge. The latter enables Lithuania to import North Sea oil in the case of a disruption of oil supplies from Russia.

As the cost of imported fossil fuels rose, Lithuania relied increasingly on nuclear energy. In 1995, the Chernobyl-style Ignalina Nuclear Power Plant (INPP) alone provided 87.5% of the country's electricity. It is located in northeastern Lithuania, close to the borders with Latvia and Belarus. Lithuania also operates 13 thermal electricity plants, the Kruonis Hydro-Accumulative Power Plant, the Kaunas Hydroelectric Plant and several smaller plants. As local demand is considerably less than the built-in capacity, a large amount of electric power is exported to Belarus, Latvia, Estonia and Russia. However, one of the necessary conditions for Lithuania to become a full and equal member of the EU is the closing of both reactors of the INPP by 2007. In the meantime, the Swedish government, the European Bank of Reconstruction and Development, the United States, Norway and Japan have provided a total of over US$ 220 million in assistance to upgrade the safety standards and to assist with the shutdown and transition to other energy sources.

The Lithuanian electricity sector is still 90% state-owned, and the government is under intense pressure from both the EU and IMF to restructure and privatize the sector. It has begun to move towards the privatization of energy with the formation of joint-stock companies for the electricity grid and various oil and gas companies. A Canadian investment bank, CIBC Wood Gundy leads the restructuring of Lietuvos Energija – one of the country's biggest companies. The process should result in the break-up of electricity generation, transmission and distribution, and non-core activities into several independent companies.

Agriculture

The temperate climate and fertile soil of Lithuania has sustained a centuries-old agricultural tradition. Shortly before the outbreak of World War II, agriculture was the dominant economic sector, with nearly three quarters of Lithuania's labour force employed on private farms. Then, the forced collectivization by the Soviets rapidly wiped out all the traditions of family farming. Until 1989, collectives (*kolkhozes*) and state farms (*sovkhozes*) ran 93% of all arable land, and residents used the remaining 7% as summer plots (which were far more productive than their state-owned counterparts). Since independence, much of the country's farmland has been privatized into numerous small household plots (2–3 hectares on average) and medium-size private farms (8.5 hectares on average), while a few larger farms (380 hectares on average) have picked up where the former *kolkhozes* and *sovkhozes* left off. However, most of the newly created farms are inefficient. They lack buildings and appropriate machinery to work the land, and their poor access to capital prevents their aging owners from acquiring seeds and animals. Thus, agricultural production has declined, and there are large plots of land in some areas that are not being farmed at all. Nevertheless, agriculture, hunting and forestry sectors still play a significant role in the economy, contributing 6.3% of the 2001 GDP and employing an estimated 17% of the workforce. The major products are grains, sugar beets, livestock, dairy products (mainly cheese, butter, milk powder) as well as some fruit and vegetables.

Reorganizing the agricultural sector is an important aspect of the government reform programme, with the aims of (a) achieving self-sufficiency in agricultural produce; (b) making agricultural products competitive on foreign markets; and (c) reducing the environmental problems (e.g. water and soil pollution by nitrates, soil erosion, loss of grasslands due to abandonment and overgrown bushes or ploughing). Among recent successes in the Lithuanian agriculture is the development and marketing of organic farm products, which have become increasingly popular in the country.

Financial sector

The Lithuanian financial sector is relatively small, with total assets equivalent to about 30% of GDP. It is dominated by banks (87% of the assets), but also comprises securities firms, insurance companies, and leasing companies. The country has a standard two-tier banking system consisting of a central bank (the Bank of Lithuania) and commercial banks. The Bank of Lithuania – owned by the state and therefore suffering somewhat from a potential lack of independence – has exclusive rights to issue bank notes, implement monetary policy, ensure the stability of the national currency and supervises commercial banks' activities.

The commercial banking system has undergone substantial consolidation and restructuring since the banking crisis of 1995. Several banks were liquidated, others merged or were sold to foreign investors. As a result of the restructuring process, there are now nine commercial banks and four foreign bank representative offices operating in Lithuania. They offer a large range of services, including leasing, insurance, asset management, investment banking and term deposits in foreign currencies – although the Foreign Exchange Law limits the use of foreign currencies for commercial transactions in the country. In addition, 42 credit unions service 12,400 members and essentially provide small credits. The three largest banks control about 85% of total banking system assets. Following the privatization of Lithuanian Agricultural Bank in the first quarter 2002, foreign investors now own more than one half of the share capital of seven commercial banks and control 89% of the banks' capital in Lithuania.

Government debt and securities of private companies in Lithuania are traded on the National Stock Exchange of Lithuania (NSEL). The latter was created in May 1993 in co-operation with the SBF-Bourse de Paris and is regulated by the Securities Commission. Shares are dematerialized and accounted through entries in the Central Securities Depository, which also provides custody services for foreign institutions. Several brokerage firms and brokerage departments of commercial banks trade sporadically some 40 companies, but most of the trading volume concentrates on the six largest capitalizations. The lack of pension funds (the law for a voluntary scheme was passed in 2001), the low interest of insurance companies and the over-restrictive requirements for establishing open-ended investment funds have so far hampered the development of the securities market.

Nevertheless, there are still plans for expanding co-operation with the Tallinn and Riga Stock Exchanges and even joining the Scandinavian Stock Exchange alliance, Norex, which would provide a one-stop exchange for all Nordic and Baltic financial instruments.

With six life insurance and 27 non-life insurance companies, the country's insurance sector is small and highly concentrated – the three largest companies write 63% of non-life insurance policies and 94% of life insurance policies. Nevertheless, it is likely to develop significantly in the years ahead.

Telecommunications and IT

The telecommunication sector in Lithuania is characterized by solid growth (28% in 2001) in both the fixed-line and the mobile phone markets. Lietuvos Telekomas (Lithuanian Telecom), with 1.5 million subscribers, holds a monopoly in the fixed-line market until 2003. The company was privatized in 1998 through the acquisition of 60% of its shares by Amber Teleholdings, a Swedish/Finnish consortium. On the mobile phone side, there is intense competition between the various operators: Mobilios Telekomunikacijos and Omnitel (joint Lithuanian, Danish and Luxembourg ventures), and Tele2. The forecasts are that the penetration of mobile communications should exceed 40% by the end of 2002.

The computer and peripherals market in Lithuania is well developed, both in the business customer segment and the fast developing household consumption market. In recent years, the government has focussed on creating the necessary infrastructure to meet the demands of a Western information society. Consequently, the Internet market is now booming. This explains the high growth rate of fixed-line telephones, but also raises numerous competition issues. In particular, all Internet service providers are forced to buy communication channels from Lithuanian Telecom at wholesale prices, while at the same time they have to compete with the monopolist.

Transportation

Strategically located at the gateway between the EU and CIS, Lithuania serves as a main artery between east and west, north and south. In 2001, the added value in transportation, storage and communications sectors accounted for LTL 5.31 billion or 11.1% of GDP. The country has one of the best transportation infrastructures in Central and Eastern Europe. The 21,000 km of well-kept, high-quality, state-owned road system provides favourable conditions for international traffic and is constantly extended. A network of four-lane highways links the major industrial centres. The 2,000 km of railways (Russian gauge track) are being modernized, and there is a 22-km European-gauge line from the Polish border to Sestokai station. The Klaipeda State Seaport is one of the few ice-free ports on the eastern coast of the Baltic Sea. It offers regular ferry and cargo services to other European seaports, handles more than 21 million tons of cargo every year, and is the only port in the region to receive funding from the EBRD and the European Investment Bank to finance major expansion projects. Finally, three state-owned international airports (Vilnius, Kaunas and Palanga) and two state-owned national companies (the soon to be privatized Lithuanian Airlines and Air Lithuania) offer efficient freight and passenger services. Lithuania is constantly upgrading its transport infrastructures, with the aim of integrating them into the Trans-European Networks (TEN). It co-operates with IFI programmes (EIB, EBRD, WB) and the EU's PHARE programme. Among the major projects are the EU's International Corridor No. 1 on a north–south axis (the Via Baltica motorway and the Tallinn–Riga–Kaunas–Warsaw railway) and Corridor No. 9 in an east–west axis consisting of 9B (Kyiv–Minsk–Vilnius–Kaunas–Klaipeda) and 9D (Kaunas–Kaliningrad).

International relations

Lithuania is a member of numerous international organizations, including the United Nations, the World Bank, the International Monetary Fund (IMF), the World Trade Organization (WTO), the Council of Baltic Sea States (CBSS), the European Bank for Reconstruction and Development (EBRD), the Organization for Security and Co-operation in Europe (OSCE), and the Council of Europe. Lithuania is also an associate partner of the Western European Union (WEU).

The country is actively engaged in negotiations with the EU regarding its future accession. President Adamkus has repeatedly stated his desire and the necessity for Lithuania to join the EU. Already 17 of the 30 chapters for EU accession are completed, and the government is working on the necessary harmonization of legislation. Lithuania is expected to become a member by 2004.

Compared to its neighbours Estonia and Latvia, the country enjoys relatively good relations with Russia, due in part to its friendly policies toward the residents of Kaliningrad (the Russian enclave on its Western border along the Baltic Sea) and a liberal citizenship law. However, there are still certain sources of tension, for example Lithuania's willingness to enter the North Atlantic Treaty Organization (NATO) or the sale of state-owned enterprises to non-Russian interests.

7.5 Legal environment and regulations

Crime and corruption

Street crime (e.g. mugging and purse snatching or car theft) is a problem, especially at night near tourist restaurants and hotels. Getting help may be difficult, since police forces suffer from a shortage of manpower, resources and equipment and often do not speak English. Corruption is also a serious problem and has hampered Lithuania's progress in recent years. It undoubtedly represents a significant obstacle to doing business in the country. The most widespread kind of corruption (in terms of the number of incidents) is bureaucratic corruption, but business and preventive corruption are now common tools for doing business. On 18 February 1997, the government adopted a resolution creating an independent, specialized unit within the Ministry of Interior, called the Special Investigations Service (SIS). Its purpose is to combat corruption (including organized crime) and crimes committed against the civil service. The SIS also collects, analyses and collates different kinds of information from various sources and has developed a framework of information analysis to combat corruption. Since 1998, it has exposed several hundred cases of corruption. Unfortunately, in practice, Lithuanian judges are usually more lenient in passing sentences for corruption, that is, imprisonment is often suspended. Nevertheless, in 2001, Lithuania adopted a new law on corruption, a code of ethics for SIS staff and a national anti-corruption strategy. It has also become a signatory to the Council of Europe Criminal Law Convention on Corruption.

Judicial system, dispute settlement, and bankruptcy procedures

The Lithuanian legal and regulatory system has been extensively reformed to harmonize it with EU requirements. All laws must be in compliance with the constitution, and all international treaties and conventions ratified by Parliament (*Seimas*) prevail in cases of inconsistency with Lithuanian national legal acts.

Dispute resolution by arbitration is a relatively new idea in Lithuania, but is gaining popularity since it offers a relatively inexpensive and prompt solution. Lithuania is a party to the 1958 New York Convention on the Recognition and Enforcement of Foreign Arbitral Awards, and the 1996 Commercial Arbitration Law applies to the resolution of commercial disputes, irrespective of the place of arbitration (national or international). Arbitral awards (including those granted in any state that is a party to the 1958 New York Convention) are enforced in accordance with the procedure prescribed by the Code of Civil Procedure of the Republic of Lithuania.

The Enterprise Bankruptcy Law was enacted by parliament on 17 June 1997 and revised in March 2000. It provides for the definition of insolvency and conditions for the institution of bankruptcy proceedings, and seeks to facilitate the bankruptcy procedures for creditors. The 2001 Enterprise Restructuring Law also provides for a new insolvency procedure – restructuring – as an alternative to bankruptcy for enterprises with temporary financial difficulties.

Taxation, accounting, and auditing rules

Since 2001, Lithuania has reduced its corporate income tax flat rate from 24% to 15%. A 13% tax rate applies to smaller enterprises. Income earned from a primary job in a Lithuanian company is taxed at a flat rate of 33%, after deducting non-taxable minimum income as established by the government. Income earned from a secondary job in a Lithuanian company is taxed progressively at rates varying from 10% to 35%. Finally, income derived from employment with a foreign company is taxed at rate of 20%.

The 1992 Principles of Accounting Law specifies the accounting and bookkeeping requirements for enterprises. Accounting records must be prepared in litas and in the Lithuanian language and, if necessary, in a foreign language.

Laws on establishing and conducting business

The Investment Law permits the incorporation of an enterprise wholly or partially owned by foreigners as well as the acquisition of shares in an existing company. A foreign investor can sell, donate, mortgage or otherwise dispose of his shares as he/she wishes. There are no specific prohibitions or limitations, provided the investor does business in accordance with Lithuanian law. The latter provides equal protection to foreign and domestic investors. After tax payments, foreign investors have the right to repatriate the profit, income or dividends in cash or otherwise, or reinvest the income without limitation.

Various forms of business organizations available to foreigners

In accordance with the Enterprises Law, the following types of enterprise may be established: the individual (personal) enterprise, the general or limited partnerships, the public or private limited company, the co-operative society and the agricultural company. The individual company belongs to a single owner, who is fully liable on his wealth for all obligations resulting from the company's operations. The company must be identified by the name of the owner. Partnerships are unlimited liability structures that group several individuals or legal entities called partners. In a general partnership, all partners remain jointly liable for all the partnership's obligations, while the limited partnership allows limited liability partners (but at least one general partner). Companies are legal entities liable for their obligations only to the extent of their assets, and their owners (shareholders) are liable only to the extent of the amounts due to be paid for their own shares. Private companies have a minimum authorized capital of LTL 10,000 and at most 100 shareholders. Public companies are required to have a minimum authorized capital of LTL 150,000. Finally, co-operatives are legal entities with changeable composition and capital, while agricultural companies are limited liability entities deriving at least 50% of their income through the sale of agricultural products or services. All enterprises must register the name of the firm with the State Patent Bureau prior to its registration. All enterprises with foreign capital must (a) obtain consent from the local municipal authorities for the stated activity of the enterprise and (b) register with the Ministry of Economy.

In addition to the above-mentioned structures, Lithuanian law provides for the establishment of three types of group enterprises: concerns, consortia and associations. Concerns are economic structures unifying enterprises related by common interests and shares cross-holdings. Consortia are temporary by nature; they are typically formed to work on large-scale projects. Associations are legal entities representing the interest of their members.

Restriction on foreign investments

In accordance with Law on Investment Article 8, foreign capital investment is prohibited in the sectors of national security and defence (except for investment made by foreign entities meeting the criteria of European and Transatlantic Integration, for which Lithuania has opted, provided that this is approved by the State Defence Council) and in the organization of lotteries.

Investment incentives

There are currently no laws establishing special incentives for foreign investments, although significant tax incentives still apply to foreign investments that were made in 1993–97. On a case-by-case basis, the government may grant some specific incentives to strategic investors.

Protection of property rights

Foreign investments in Lithuania are protected by the constitution against nationalization or requisition. Lithuanian authorities have no legal rights to create any obstacles to an investor in using or disposing of his property unless he has violated the laws of the country. In the event of justified expropriation, the investor is entitled to compensation equivalent to the market value of the property expropriated in a convertible currency. However, since independence, there has been no case of expropriation of private property by the government. In addition, Lithuania has signed several international agreements and bilateral contracts to encourage investments and to ensure mutual investment protection.

It has transformed its intellectual property regime from a Soviet-style system into a modern system. Parliament has passed several laws governing the enforcement of copyright, patents, trademarks and firms' names, including amendments to the criminal and civil codes. In 1992, Lithuania joined the World Intellectual Property Organization (WIPO) and signed the Paris Convention for the Protection of Industrial Property in 1994. It also entered into an agreement with the European Patent Office on Co-operation in the Area of Patents and became an extension state for the validation of European patents. The fight against software piracy commenced in 1999, on the initiative of the Infobalt Association and the BSA local committee. Although pirated recordings and software are still obtainable, they are frequently confiscated and destroyed by the police.

Entry requirements

A valid passport is required to enter Lithuania, but most foreign citizens do not need a visa for a stay of less than three months per half-year. An expatriate wishing to work in Lithuania must obtain a work permit and a residence permit. Usually, it takes five to ten weeks to obtain a work permit. A separate application must be submitted for all family members.

7.6 Business environment

Privatization

Lithuania's privatization programme started in 1991 and was considered a crucial part of the transition to a free-market economy. The privatization process has been at the core of many of the country's economic reforms. It can be divided into three major stages. From September 1991 to July 1995, there was a phase of mass privatization using vouchers with some elements of cash sales. Nearly 1.5 million Lithuanian residents, approximately 40% of the population, became shareholders. From July 1995 to November 1997, there was a large cash privatization at market prices of several state and municipal properties (generally recognized as state monopolies), in which Lithuanian and foreign investors participated on an equal footing. The third phase started in November 1997, with the adoption of the Law on privatization of State-Owned and Municipal Property. The law provides for several methods of privatization, including public sales (through the stock exchange), public auctions (highest bidder), public tender (best written price and investment proposal), direct negotiations (often includes social aspects), as well as leasing with an option to purchase. The Lithuanian State Privatization Agency was reorganized into a subdivision of a new state institution, the State Property Fund. Its major roles include the preparation of lists of companies slated for privatization (to be approved by the government), the determination of methods and conditions of privatization, the administration of the sales transactions, as well as the assessment of privatized property and that in the course of privatization.

In July 1998, Lithuania signed the largest-ever privatization contract in the Baltic States, with the sale for US$ 510 million of 60% of AB Lietuvos Telekomas (Lithuanian Telecom) to Amber Teleholdings, a consortium of the Swedish Telia and the Finnish Sonera firms. Other key companies earmarked for privatization are Lithuanian Airlines, Lithuanian Gas, Lithuanian Energy and Lithuanian Railways.

Foreign direct investment (FDI)

With every passing year of independence, the Lithuanian market is attracting more and more foreign investors. Thus, it is now a leading destination for foreign direct investment (FDI). The latter shot up by 14.2% in 2001 to reach the total of LTL 10.66 billion. The major investors were Denmark (18.6% of the total), Sweden (16.1%), Estonia (10.0%), Germany (9.2%) and the USA (8.3%). The majority of FDI was in the manufacturing industry (25.6%), trade (20.4%), financial intermediation enterprises (19.9%) and communication services (14.7%). As a high-skilled low-cost alternative to production in the West, several multinationals have chosen to locate production facilities in Lithuania, for example Siemens, Philips, Motorola, Mars/Masterfoods, Kraft Food International, Lancaster Stell, Philip Morris, Carlsberg and Cargill among others.

Free economic and trade areas

Since 1995, Lithuania has been developing free economic zones (FEZ) in Klaipeda, Kaunas and Siauliai, three key transport and industrial centres. In addition to streamlined and simplified customs and administrative procedures, companies in FEZs are exempt from customs duties, VAT and excise taxes, road taxes and real estate taxes. There are no foreign exchange restrictions and complete withholding tax exemptions for repatriated profits and dividends. Last but not least, there is an 80% corporate tax reduction for the first five years and 50% for the next five (better tax conditions are even granted for investments of over US$ 1 million). The same legal guarantees are provided for companies located inside a FEZ as for those outside.

Major trading partners

In 2001 compared to 2000, Lithuanian exports increased by 20.3% and peaked at LTL 18.33 billion, and imports increased by 15.1% up to LTL 25.13 billion. Imports still exceed exports, so that the foreign trade balance remained negative. The majority of Lithuanian trade was with EU countries (47.9% of exports, 44.4% of imports) followed by exports to CIS countries (19.5% of exports, 29.7% of imports). Compared to the year 2000, trade with EU countries is of growing importance. Exports to EU countries increased by 20.4% and exports to CIS countries by 44.7%, while imports from EU increased by 18.0% and imports from CIS by 8.0%. The country's main export partners are United Kingdom (14.0%), Latvia (12.6%), Germany (12.5%) and Russia (10.9%), while the major import partners are Russia (25.6%), Germany (17.4%), Poland (4.9%) and Italy (4.3%). Exports consist essentially of textiles, machinery and equipment, chemical products, wood, miscellaneous manufactured articles, transport equipment, and mineral products as well as base metals and articles thereof. Major imports are energy resources (oil and gas), as well as raw materials, timber, and ferrous and non-ferrous metals.

Major booming sectors

The best prospects for foreign investors are in light industry (in particular textiles and clothing manufacturing), computer-related services (software development, maintenance, database services, systems management consulting, e-commerce applications), and building renovation and construction materials. There should be plenty of opportunities in the field of energy and power generation as soon as the state-owned power generation companies are privatized, as well as in pollution control and waste management. Finally, if loans to agribusiness finally become available, the market for food processing equipment will boom.

Free-trade agreements

Lithuania has established commercial relations with more than 160 countries and signed free-trade agreements with more than 20, including the EU and several of its neighbours. Lithuania has also granted the most-favoured-nation (MFN) trade status to 22 countries.

Value added tax (VAT)

Value added tax (VAT) is levied on imports at a standard rate of 18%, and on the added value created and sold within the process of manufacturing goods, performing works or providing services. The tax period for VAT is a calendar month. Reduced rates apply to heating services (9%) and services of public transport (5%). Exported goods and services (including goods that have been temporarily imported for processing) as well as medical, educational, scientific and cultural goods and services are exempt from VAT.

Tariff system

The February 1998 Customs Tariffs Law states that all goods imported into Lithuania are subject to taxation, except in special cases stipulated by this law. Since the tariff system is rather complicated, it is recommended that the services of a customs clearance agent be used. Goods are taxed according to their classification and their country of origin. The classification derives from the EU Combined Customs Tariffs and Foreign Trade Statistics Nomenclature. Depending on the type of classification, customs tariffs may be calculated *ad valorem* (from the customs value of the goods), specific (as a rate per unit), or compound (both *ad valorem* and specific). The country of origin may be classified as autonomous (countries without MFN status), conventional (countries with the MFN status granted through international agreements with Lithuania) or preferential (countries with a free trade agreement). In addition, seasonal import duties are applied to certain goods.

Besides import duties, importers must pay excise taxes varying from 10% to 75% on alcoholic beverages, tobacco products, luxury goods and cars, publications of an erotic and/or violent nature and fuels. Imported goods exempt from customs duties are also exempt from excise tax. It should be noted that export duties are currently levied on only one type of goods leaving Lithuania, that is, leather articles, which are subject to a tariff rate of 15%.

Major customs documents for importing and exporting

Both import and export procedures may be executed at customs offices located at border posts or within the customs territory of Lithuania, as determined by the customs office. All imported/exported goods must be declared and cleared with the necessary documents, that is, a certificate of origin, purchase and sale documents (contracts, invoices), transport documents, a customs invoice (if duties and taxes are assessed) as well as sanitary, veterinary, hygiene and quality certificates if necessary. Import licences are required for oil products, alcohol, tobacco and tobacco products, foodstuffs for specific purposes, as well as arms and ammunition. Export licences are required for oil products, raw wood, narcotics and alcohol. The Ministry of Environment, the Ministry of Economy or the Ministry of Agriculture grants import/export licences, depending upon the nature of the goods.

7.7 Etiquette and cultural issues

Culture

With 53 museums, 13 professional theatres, several state orchestras, chamber groups and a few large art collections, Lithuanians enjoy a rich and diverse cultural life. In particular, Vilnius benefits from the cultural activities of numerous theatres, opera and ballet performances, as well as classical and popular concerts and recitals. Several cinemas in Vilnius show English-language films with subtitles.

Lithuanian culture – particularly stained-glass art, painting and sculpture – was abundant during the independence period between the two world wars. Jonas Maciulis, known as Maironis, is often regarded as the founder of modern Lithuanian literature, which is dominated by poetry that depicts the nation's soul and its memory imbued with the tragedy of history. Songs have also helped to preserve the identity of the nation now that the population has moved to the cities.

Greetings, gesture and conversation

Commercial ties with Scandinavia and Germany dating back to the Middle Ages have left a considerable mark on business behaviour in Lithuania. Although Lithuanians have a reputation for being more spontaneous and emotional than Estonians and Latvians, the business atmosphere is still rather formal and reserved. Men wear tasteful, conservative suits, while women generally prefer skirts and dresses to slacks. Both men and women generally avoid ostentatious displays of wealth and luxury items.

They expect foreigners to be punctual for all appointments and meetings should, therefore, be arranged well in advance and confirmed in writing (spontaneous visits are not common in Lithuania). It is customary to shake hands and exchange business cards at the beginning of a meeting. Foreigners should pay attention to professional titles and make use of them, but avoid using first names unless invited to do so. Men greet women first, and may either shake or kiss the lady's hand. Good friends will kiss on the cheek. Gifts (such as small items inscribed with a company logo) may be presented when meeting a new associate. Lithuanian business people have a reputation for solid scientific and technical skills, as well as a methodical approach to business discussions. Always keep eye to eye contact during conversations, do not gesture with your hands or keep your hands in your pockets or chew gum in public.

Social entertaining is usually organized in restaurants and should not be used as an occasion to discuss business, unless your host initiates it. It is appropriate to return the hospitality. Remember that Lithuanians tend to be heavy smokers and that there are no restrictions on smoking in public and no smoke-free zones in restaurants or offices. If you are invited to a home, take a small present for the hostess, such as a bouquet of flowers (always take an odd number of flowers, since even numbers are reserved for funerals). Finish everything on your plate – leftover food is a sign you did not like the dish.

8
Poland

8.1 Basic facts

Poland is the second largest country in Central Europe, after Russia. The country occupies an area roughly the size of Great Britain and Ireland combined. It is also the most densely populated country in Eastern Europe and constitutes more or less the geographic centre of Europe. Warsaw, the capital is also the largest city with approximately 1,643,000 inhabitants. Other large cities include Lodz (784,000 inhabitants), Krakow (734,000), Wroclaw (633,000), Poznan (581,000), Gdansk (457,000), Szczecin (417,000), Lublin (354,000), and Katowice (336,000), and Bydgoszcz (385,000). The total population of Poland is 38.6 million.

Sharing borders with Belarus, the Czech Republic, Germany, Lithuania, Russia (Kaliningrad Oblast), Slovakia and Ukraine, as well as 491 km along the Baltic Sea, Poland's total land mass (312,685 sq km) covers a vast area of mostly flat plains, which have traditionally offered little protection from invasion. Up to the end of World War II, Poland had been invaded or crossed by the armies of Austria, Russia, Germany, France, Italy, Sweden, the Huns, Mongols and Turkey. This explains why the Soviet Union imposed control over Poland, and other Eastern European countries, to create a buffer between a perceived aggressive West and the USSR. Furthermore, the fact that Poland is crossed by a system of navigable rivers, mainly the Oder, the Vistula, and the Bug, and canals which drain into the Baltic Sea where nine major ports occupy the 524 miles of sea shore, makes the country an important trade link.

Poland is one of the most homogenous societies in Eastern Europe. The great majority of its 38.6 million inhabitants are Poles (97.6%). Small minorities of Germans (1.3%), Ukrainians (0.6%), and Belarusians (0.5%) make up the rest of the population, which has a negative (−0.04%) growth rate and a negative immigration rate (−0.49 migrant per 1,000). On average the birth rate is 1.38 children per woman and life expectancy of the total population is a little over 73 years.

The Polish language and the Catholic Church are the two main strings that have helped to hold the Polish nation together during years of partition and war, especially in the twentieth century. Polish is the main language spoken today and although it belongs to the Slavic language group, it is based on the Roman alphabet and, as such, is easier for Westerners to read than other Eastern European languages. Roman Catholicism is the dominant religion; 95% of Poles are Catholic and approximately 75% practise their religion. The Catholic Church is an integral part of Polish society with no division between church and state. The Church has taken on institutional roles in the past in the form of representation of and support for the people's resistance to outside rule, as was the case against the ruling Communist Party and Soviet domination in the 1980s, for instance. Other religions in the country include the Eastern Orthodox Church and Protestantism. Poland has a high literacy rate at 99% of the total population over the age of 15 (99% male, 98% female) and education is a valued institution.

Polish society is divided into three groups: peasants, workers and the intelligentsia. Some 62% of Poles live in urban areas. Those living in rural areas are considered peasants and have a much lower quality of life and education. The working class is the largest group and is comprised of everyone working for wages. The intelligentsia is the elite in Poland today tracing its roots back to the old class of landed gentry.

Poland has a mostly temperate climate, but winters are cold with frequent precipitation, and can be severe as there are no natural barriers against the cold Siberian wind blowing in from the East. Polish summers are mild with frequent rain and thundershowers.

Natural resources available in the vast plains include coal, sulphur, copper, natural gas, silver, lead, and salt. One of Poland's most valuable natural resources is arable land, which accounts for 47% of the country's total land mass, of which 1,000 sq km irrigation supports 1% permanent cropland and 13% permanent pastureland. Major agricultural products include potatoes, fruits, vegetables, wheat, poultry, eggs, pork, beef, milk, and cheese. Another 39% of the land is covered with forests and woodland. Among the major industries are machine building, iron and steel, coal mining, chemicals, shipbuilding, food processing, glass, beverages, and textiles.

Means of communication

Major newspapers circulate throughout Poland and special interest magazines, business journals, niche publications, and specialized newspapers have proliferated. Classified advertising is highly developed and effective. The leading daily newspapers include *Rzeczpospolita*, *Gazeta Wyborcza*, *Zycie* and *Trybuna*, whereas *Prawo i Gospodarka* and *Puls Biznesu* are the most important daily business journals. Major weekly magazines include *Wprost* and *Polytica*. *Business News Poland*, a business journal printed by Boss Economic Information, also appears on a weekly basis. The *Warsaw Business Journal* and the *Warsaw Voice* are two English-language weeklies that cater mainly to foreigners in the country.

8.2 Historical background

World War II began when Germany attacked Poland on 1 September 1939. At the end of the war in 1945, Poland had lost nearly half of its pre-war territory but was compensated with German lands in the west. Eventually, the country regained from the Germans its Western provinces, rich industrial and fertile agricultural areas. It also regained its historic borders of the eleventh to thirteenth centuries when the country was originally took shape. Undoubtedly, the repossession of this territory constituted a considerable economic advantage. Unfortunately for Poland it was governed after the war by a puppet regime. The ruling Communist Party, Polish United Workers' Party (PZPR), seized power in the newly founded People's Republic of Poland (PRL) and instituted a centrally planned economy. Poland was aligned on the Soviet Union diplomatically, militarily and politically. Its trade was also closely tied to its powerful eastern neighbour. With the exception of agriculture and handicrafts, virtually all the economic sectors were nationalized.

In the 1980s the 'Solidarity' movement, originally set up as an illegal labour union of Gdansk workers, with the strong backing of the Catholic Church and Western government institutions, grew into a 10 million-strong social movement against the communist authorities. With the demise of the USSR in the late 1980s the movement culminated in the election of Lech Walesa as president of the new Republic of Poland and the dissolution of the PZRP. Once the new Polish government was formed, the Solidarity movement fell apart as a united front. The Republic of Poland has been a democratic state since 1989 and has enjoyed democratically elected governments. The country is divided into 16 provinces (*wojewodztwa*). Although in 1997 Walesa lost the presidential election,

Solidarity is still credited with laying the foundation for what is referred to today as the 'Polish miracle'.

8.3 Political environment

On 16 October 1997, the National Assembly adopted a new constitution that limited the role of the president *vis-à-vis* the government, established an independent central bank, and entrusted monetary policy to an independent committee. In September 2001, the Democratic Left Alliance (SLD) and its electoral allies won the parliamentary election. However, their failure to win an absolute majority forced them to invite the centre-left Polish Peasants' Party (PSL) into a coalition. From late 1997 until September 2001, Poland was governed by a coalition of Solidarity Electoral Action (AWS) and the Freedom Union (UW). AWS is itself a coalition of more than 30 centre-right and right-wing groups.

Executive power in Poland is shared between the president and a government composed of a prime minister and cabinet ministers. The president is elected for a term of five years and is limited to two terms. There are two rounds of voting, the second held only in the event that no presidential candidate attains an absolute majority in the first round. The president is head of state and commander-in-chief of the armed forces. He has the right to initiate legislation and veto bills from the lower chamber of parliament (*Sejm*). However, a two-thirds majority in the *Sejm* overturns a presidential veto. The prime minister is the head of government, but the president appoints the prime minister and all other members of the government, including cabinet members, upon the recommendation of the prime minister. These appointments are then subject to absolute majority approval by the *Sejm*.

Legislative power rests in the hands of a bicameral parliament, the *Sejm* and the upper chamber (*Senat*). The 460 members of the *Sejm* are elected by proportional representation for a four-year maximum term. With the exception of guaranteed seats for small German and Ukrainian ethnic parties, only parties with at least 7% of the total vote can claim seats in the *Sejm*. The 100-member *Senat* is elected by a plurality method in which candidates receiving the most votes in a district win the seats. There are 47 two-seat constituencies and two three-seat constituencies and all members serve a four-year term. The *Senat* may amend or veto bills sent by the *Sejm*, although final approval rests in the hands of the *Sejm*, which has the power to overturn such amendments or rejections.

Despite Poland's impressive economic growth in recent years, the current government's popularity has been damaged by societal instability.

The splintering of political alliances between the free market Freedom Union and the pro-reform wing of Solidarity has resulted in alliances between the anti-reform wing of Solidarity and the ex-communist Democratic Left Alliance. These shifting alliances have made it difficult for the government to steer its reform policies through the Sejm.

8.4 Economic environment and infrastructure

Poland, with a private sector that is now responsible for 70% of economic activity, has witnessed one of the most successful transitions from a state-controlled to a market economy. However, in contrast to development in the private and industrial sectors, the large agricultural sector remains handicapped by structural problems such as surplus labour, inefficient small farms, lack of investment, and a sluggish effort at privatization. Poland's determination to gain membership in the European Union (EU) has driven many of the country's economic policies. The objective of the main economic and monetary policies has been to reduce the country's account deficit and reduce inflation. The restructuring and privatization of sensitive sectors, such as coal and steel, has begun in earnest but much remains to be done and as in many economies in transition, unrelenting reform measures have generated considerable social upheaval.

Macroeconomic tendencies

Poland's annual gross domestic product (GDP) growth has been about 5–7%, although it dipped to just over 4% in 1999 following the Russian financial crisis and remained at 4% in 2000. The projected GDP for 2001 was estimated at 1.8%. The service sector in Poland contributes an estimated 60% of GDP and employs 48% of the labour force. Today, Poland ranks above all but six of the 15 EU member countries in total GDP. Globally, it ranks 25th out of 191 countries in terms of GDP, 30th in terms of population, and 62nd in terms of GDP per capita. Inflation experienced a gradual decline from 1994 to 2000. The rate of inflation increased from 8.4% in 1999 to 11.6% in 2000 (from July 1999 to July 2000). Due to unavoidable industrial and agricultural restructuring, the labour market continues to deteriorate and unemployment, which had fallen to 10% in 1994, climbed again to 14.4% in 2000.

The zloty (symbol Zl) is Poland's currency; 100 groszy are 1 zloty. The zloty has consistently depreciated against the US dollar since 1995, but is showing signs of stabilizing. In March 2000, the zloty was freely floated against other currencies. Polish currency may not be imported or exported by residents or non-residents. Unused zlotys must be exchanged for other major currencies upon departure. The government plans to adopt the Euro upon accession to the EU.

Industry

The industrial sector, which includes manufacturing, construction, energy, and mining contributes to 35% of GDP and is estimated to employ 33.9% of the labour force. The key industries in Poland are coal mining, iron and steel, machine building, chemicals, shipbuilding, food processing, glass, beverages, and textiles. Poland is a major Central European producer of steel. In 1996, it was the second largest producer of copper in Europe and Central Eurasia, and ranked among the top 10 world producers. Similarly, the country was the third largest mine producer of zinc and the second of lead, sixth of silver, and seventh of sulphur. During the same year, Poland was also a leading European and Central Eurasian producer of lime, nitrogen, and salt. Additionally, strong and growing demand for construction materials is expected to continue through the next decade for both housing and major commercial projects.

Energy

Although coal production is declining due to environmental concerns and preparation for accession to the EU, it is still currently the dominant fuel in Poland's economy. Weglokoks, the successor to the state-owned coal monopoly since 1993, is still owned by the State Treasury and is Poland's largest coal exporter. Coal, which accounted for 94% of Poland's primary energy production and over 65% of total consumption in 1998, is likely to remain a key energy source in the future. Coal exports to customers in Europe and the former Soviet Union have also historically served as a major source of foreign exchange. A comprehensive restructuring programme, aimed at maximizing efficiency and paying off some of the industry's US$ 4.5 billion debt, is in the pipeline with the objective of closing down as many as 30 of the current 53 inefficient mines. These changes have positive economic and environmental implications, both of which are important for accession to the EU. The state-owned Polish Oil and Gas Company is earmarked for privatization, and this should bring the country in line with EU regulations.

Owing to Poland's limited natural gas reserves, increased consumption will undoubtedly lead to a significant increase in natural gas imports. Poland is a net energy importer with over half of all its imported gas coming from Russia, and smaller quantities from Germany. Reliance on

Russia for natural gas has been alleviated recently with the signing of a natural gas contract with Norway. In 1999, some 99% of Poland's oil consumption derived from imports. Until 1995, all its oil was received from Russia. Today, however, oil is received through a new pipeline from Germany. Demand for oil is expected to increase up to 50% by 2020. With the prediction that Polish oil fields will be depleted in the next 30 to 40 years, exploration projects are underway to discover new oil and natural gas reserves in the hope of offsetting this depletion. Additionally, a 1999 agreement between Poland and Ukraine cleared the way for a joint commitment on the building of a pipeline connecting Caspian Sea oil through Ukraine to Poland, thus enabling Poland and its neighbours to import the crude oil necessary to meet EU motor fuel specifications.

The Polish electrical power sector at present consists of three subsectors: generation, transmission and distribution. As a system, it is the largest in Central and Eastern Europe. The Polish electrical grid, as part of the CENTREL system linking the Czech Republic, Slovakia and Hungary, was connected to Western Europe's system in 1995 and both north–south and east–west connections are currently being expanded under the EU Trans-European Energy Network project. Along with the CENTREL system, Poland also has connections with Ukraine and Belarus and plans for linkage to Lithuania are under discussion. The major problems with Poland's electricity generation facilities derive mostly from pollution and outdated technology, similar to the experience other East European countries.

In order to meet environmental standards set for accession to the EU, Poland has had to improve its environmental standards in energy production. Increased consumption of natural gas as an alternative to coal is considered the key objective to meeting stricter regulations. Clearly, the environmental situation has improved since 1989 due to the decline in heavy industry and increased environmental awareness of postcommunist governments. But the biggest concern remains air pollution due to sulphur dioxide emissions from the many coal-fired power plants as well as the resulting acid rain that has caused forest damage. Water pollution and the disposal of hazardous wastes are also major concerns for Poland.

Agriculture

The agricultural sector, producing primary food crops of barley, maize, potatoes, rice, sugar beets and wheat, as well as meat products of beef and veal, chicken, duck, game, goose, horse, lamb, pork, rabbit and turkey, employs an estimated 18.2% of the entire labour market. Prior to World War II, Poland was an agrarian state but agriculture now represents only about 5% of the country's GDP, and production does not currently meet domestic demand in this sector.

Financial sector

The Polish banking system is efficient and is probably one of the best regulated and best supervised in Central and Eastern Europe. The system is supervised by the central bank, the National Bank of Poland (NBP), which is responsible for issuing money, controlling the monetary and credit policy, and granting banking licenses and foreign exchange permits. The post-1989 reforms of the banking and financial sectors led to the division of the Polish National Bank NBP into nine medium size regional banks, the majority of which have already been privatized. There are roughly 83 privately owned banks or commercial companies in Poland, an additional 1,295 independent co-operative banks, and 26 foreign banks. A growing number of foreign banks are also establishing banking operations in the country. In fact, foreign banks now own more than 70% of the Polish banking sector. According to international financial experts, the Polish banking market is likely to be the fastest growing in Europe over the next five years.

The consolidation of the banking sector has also involved insurance companies and is likely to lead to the creation of major financial institutions. Competition from foreign investors and the move towards a fully open and free market have started a trend, wherein large banks are becoming integrally involved in the insurance industry. Poland has the largest insurance market in all of Central and Eastern Europe. In fact, business experts view the Polish insurance market as a good investment opportunity.

Telecommunications

The telephone system in Poland is for the most part underdeveloped and outmoded. However, the government has launched a programme of partial privatization and modernization of the system, with an additional 10 million telephones placed in service in 2000. As of 1998 there were more than eight million main lines and 1.58 million mobile phones in use. The domestic system is comprised of cable and open wires, microwave radio relays, three mobile networks. About 56% of the local exchange is digital. Overall, the Polish telephone network is growing at an annual rate of 20% and privatization is currently underway. Planned investments are estimated at US$ 14 billion over the next ten years.

Information technology

The total information technology market has reached a value of US$ 2.5 billion, with computer hardware estimated at US$ 1.2 billion. The Polish computer market grew approximately 20% in 1999. The personal computer segment has grown by 16% annually. The main purchasers of computer equipment are financial, transportation, telecommunications, manufacturing, trade, administration, science, and educational organizations. Individual users, small and medium size companies, and the education sector significantly increased their purchase of computer equipment in 1999.

The computer services segment is estimated at US$ 570 million with expected annual growth of 30%. Computer education and training, consulting, hardware maintenance and services, and data processing are the most dynamic and promising segment of the Polish information technology market. Internet service, with an expected growth of 30% per year, is also a very promising field.

Due in part to the growth of computer networking in many organizations and the upsizing of database management systems as a result of the ongoing privatization process, the Polish software market grew 25% in 1999, reaching a total of approximately US$ 560 million. The total computer market is expected to maintain a 20% annual growth. At present the financial and industrial segments are the main purchasers, but software sales prospects also include large, small, and medium size companies.

Transportation

Poland has 23,420 km of railways, 381,046 km of highways (249,966 km paved including 268 km expressways and 131,080 km unpaved), and 3,812 km of navigable rivers and canals. A network of pipelines transports crude oil and petroleum products (2,280 km) and natural gas (17,000 km). Major ports and harbours are located in Gdańsk, Gdynia, Gliwice, Kolobrzeg, Szczecin, Swinoujscie, Ustka, Warsaw, and Wroclaw. Poland has 123 airports and international air service is provided through Warsaw.

Poland's transportation network is in dire need of upgrading and refurbishment. To help meet this need, the Polish authorities have planned a new system of toll roads. The programme calls for about 2,500 km of highways to be built in four segments over the next 15 years at a total cost estimated at US$ 8 billion. Prime contractors will build each portion of the highway individually. Poland's geographical location is forcing integration of a portion of the Polish railway network with the European transportation system and thus imposes a higher standard of service in both passenger and freight transportation. Mixed transport has the best prospect for growth. The railway modernization project, from Warsaw to Kunowice, will include the purchase of track rehabilitation machinery, signalling cables, power supply cables, signalling equipment, steel parts for standard turnouts, as well as hot and flat-wheel detection equipment. The project's estimated value is close to US$ 600 million. The EBRD and other international financial institutions will provide the bulk of the funding for this project.

Other economic sectors

Together with Hungary, the Czech Republic, and Slovakia, Poland has been an EU 'associate' member since 1991. In November 1998, it began negotiations for the country's accession to the EU. Unrealistically, the authorities expressed the hope of joining the EU by January 2003. Further economic restructuring, tightening of the public budget, agricultural sector reform, and environmental regulations are some of the chief items on the government's policy agenda as it prepares for accession to the EU.

In March 1999, Poland made a colossal symbolic step in its relations with the West by joining NATO. Its 1996 admission to the OECD stands as a tribute to the country's determination to abide by EU-compatible investment, trade, and legislative rules. Meeting the terms of accession to the EU has been costly to Polish society and the movement towards integration is gradually losing support within the farming sector and the AWS. Indeed, attempts to integrate the Polish agricultural sector into the EU's Common Agricultural Policy (CAP) have created tensions in the farming sector and the AWS, which is made up of centre and right-wing forces. These forces mistrust integration into the commercialized and secular West.

8.5 Legal environment and regulations

Although based on the Napoleonic civil code, Poland's legal system is still influenced by communist legal theory. A new tripartite legal structure is in the making. This structure, called the 'New Economic Constitution', is made up of a new commercial code, new law on economic activity, and new law on public aid to companies. This legal structure will bring Poland into line with EU standards, with the ultimate goal of limiting the role of the state in economic and commercial life through a reduction of burdensome government controls and state subsidies.

Civil code regulations are based on the principles of equality for all persons. Poland's 1997 Constitution protects the rights of private ownership and succession for both domestic and foreign private entities. However, ownership of land presents a special problem. Current law dating from 1996 allows foreign individuals and firms to own an apartment, 0.4 hectares (4000 sq metres) of urban land, or up to one hectare of agricultural land without a permit. The acquisition of real estate exceeding these limits, or the purchase of shares in a foreign-controlled Polish company owning real estate, still require approval from the Ministry of Internal Affairs, with the consent of the Defence and Agriculture Ministries. However, this process was substantially liberalized from 2001 onwards with the New Economic Activity Act, when the sectors requiring concessions were reduced for broadcasting, aviation, energy, weapons, rail transport, highway construction, and private security services. Expropriation has not been a problem in Poland. Polish law on land management and expropriation of real estate stipulates that property will only be expropriated in the case of public works construction, national security considerations, or other cases of public interest, and only on the basis of full market-value compensation.

Crime and corruption

Bribery is a criminal offence and bribes are not tax-deductible. But, although Polish law provides a legal basis for combating corruption and bribery, corruption remains a substantial problem in Poland. It is still commonly and widely practised by customs and border guard officials, tax authorities, and local government officials. Although Poland signed the OECD convention on combating bribery in 1997, there has not been any significant improvement in enforcement of anti-bribery criminal laws. Nevertheless, in its attempt to deregulate and reduce the state's role in the economy, the government has sought to reduce opportunities for corruption.

Judicial system, dispute settlement and bankruptcy procedures

The Polish judiciary consists of the Constitutional Tribunal, the Tribunal of State, the Supreme Court, the Supreme Administrative Court, and other military, administrative, and common courts. The Constitutional Tribunal rules on the constitutionality of existing laws or proposed laws that the president refers to the Constitutional Tribunal. The president appoints Supreme Court judges for an indefinite period, whereas the *Sejm* selects each justice to the Constitutional Tribunal for a nine-year term.

Investment disputes between foreign investors and the Polish government have occurred in the past; however, the government made a commitment to uphold the rights of foreign investors. Deregulation of the economy, including the sale of state-owned enterprises, the government's steady march towards full adoption of EU regulations, and the recent passage of legislation more clearly defining the role of the state in economic activity, should all lead to a reduction in the type of disputes that have prevailed hitherto. Foreign firms and investors generally are wary of the overburdened Polish legal system and prefer to rely on other means to defend their rights. Thus, in the event of investment disputes, they usually choose international arbitration rather than the Polish court system. Contracts involving foreign parties normally include a dispute settlement clause that provides for arbitration in a third country court (usually in Britain or Switzerland). However, decisions by an arbitration body are not automatically enforceable in Poland. Poland is party to four international agreements on dispute resolution, with the Ministry of Finance acting as the government's representative. These agreements are the 1923 Geneva Protocol, the 1958 New York Convention, the 1961 Geneva European Convention and the 1972 Moscow Convention.

Taxation, accounting and auditing rules

A Polish company, including a subsidiary of a foreign company, must account for withholding tax to the Polish tax authorities on any distributable dividends unless a double taxation treaty is in effect (as is the case with the United States).

Laws on establishing and conducting business

Since the legal environment in Poland is in constant flux, it is imperative that business people contact a Polish law office that is fully informed about the latest changes, especially when bidding on a major project, forming a joint venture, or solving trade disputes. Most Polish and international law firms offer business counselling in addition to legal advice and can provide contacts for Polish business partners, investments, or projects to pursue. Several international accounting and consulting firms are also present in Poland and can offer legal advice and business counselling regarding business formation, tax matters, and employee benefits.

Various forms of business organizations available to foreigners

Many businesses with foreign participation in Poland are structured as joint ventures in which the foreign partner contributes capital and technology while the Polish partner contributes land, distribution channels, trained workers, access to the Polish market, and the network within the local government and local business environment. The Polish Foreign Investment Agency (PAIZ), the Polish Chamber of Commerce and other foreign or local organizations are instrumental in making business contacts. Due diligence is recommended and indispensable before entering into any business agreements with domestic partners. Agencies such as Kroll International and Parvus are experienced in obtaining background information on persons and companies in Eastern and Central Europe.

Protection of property rights

As in many emerging markets, piracy of intellectual property in Poland remains a significant problem. However, in 2000 the authorities passed new intellectual property legislation, which brought Poland into compliance with the WTO TRIPS Agreement and the EU. Because of concerns about intellectual property protection in the past, licensing of products, technology, technical data and services has not been widespread in Poland.

8.6 Business environment

Foreign business can make investments in Poland by means of merger and acquisition or 'greenfield' investment. Polish investment law allows foreign participation up to 100%. Companies with foreign investors must be established as joint-stock companies or limited liability companies. This will change under the new draft commercial code, which will also include partnership companies and limited and stock partnerships. Limited liability companies require at least one founder, whereas joint stock companies require a minimum of three entities as founders. In both cases, a minimum initial fee must be paid prior to registration.

In general, Poland does not have screening and licensing requirements for the entry and establishment of businesses by foreign firms, except in cases where ceilings to foreign investment are established. Sectors subject to such ceilings include air transport (foreign investment is limited to 49%), certain fisheries activities (49%), and radio and television broadcasting (33%). Foreign investments in international telecommunications through 2003 and in gambling are not permitted. Approval requirements are also in place for foreign investments above certain thresholds in the insurance sector, certain major capital transactions or the lease of assets with state-owned enterprises. Current investment law restricts investment in areas of public security. However, concessions will be granted in the future for defence production and the management of seaports and airports for investors from OECD countries.

The 1997 Customs Law established eight customs duty-free areas (WOCs) in Poland where business practices are based on the same principles as those applied in the EU. Foreign-owned firms are afforded the same investment opportunities as domestic firms to take advantage of free customs areas, free ports, and special economic zones. The eight free customs areas are located at Gliwice (southern border), Malaszewicze/Terespol (eastern border), Przemysl-Medyka (eastern border), Warsaw-Okecie International Airport (duty-free retail trade within the airport), Sokolka (northeastern region), Szczecin (Baltic port), Swinoujscie (Baltic port), and Gdańsk (Baltic port). Existing free-trade zones are currently involved in storage and packaging goods.

Privatization

Privatization in Poland is progressing rather slowly, especially in areas the Polish government considers strategic sectors: banking, insurance, telecommunications, mining, steel, defence, transportation, energy and broadcasting. A 1995 Parliamentary bill emphasizes commercialization of Polish state-owned industry, or creating treasury-owned joint-stock companies before actually privatizing them. Nevertheless, Poland has privatized almost all of its small state-owned enterprises, most medium-size enterprises, and many large enterprises. The government sought to privatize 70% of the remaining state-owned enterprises by 2001, including the telephone company (TPSA), the national airline (LOT), the dominant insurance company (PZU), banks, steel mills, oil refineries, and the electrical energy sector. The government has invited foreign investors to compete for a strategic interest in all privatization efforts. Of the 8,500 enterprises earmarked for privatization in 1999, 30% have been completed and an additional 25% are in progress. This progress was mainly achieved in the banking, insurance, pharmaceuticals, energy and air transportation sectors. The sale of TPSA, the national telecommunications service provider, to France Telecom is estimated to have generated nearly US$ 2.5 billion in privatization proceeds. Future privatization efforts include six defence enterprises and the restructuring and subsequently privatization of the steel and coal sectors.

Privatization is seen as the key to the modernization and efficiency of the electric power-generating sector. However, estimates predict that it will take a few years before the energy market becomes truly competitive. Before free market pricing can take effect, current long-term supply contracts between power generators and the national grid company, PSE, which account for up to 70% of the electricity produced in Poland, will have to run out. Laws calling for the reduction of the number of generating companies and third-party access to the power grid vesting authority have been put in place. According to government plans, all Polish power plants and distribution companies will be privatized by the end of 2002. The World Bank is involved in financing the Polish power sector including modernization projects within power generation, transmission, and distribution. Although in their efforts to conform to OECD codes of liberalization Polish authorities have promised to lift restrictions on the free movement of capital, certain controls still remain, notably the special restrictions on capital operations other than direct investments.

Foreign direct investment (FDI)

In recent years, Poland has attracted high levels of foreign direct investment (FDI), primarily because of its size, skilled labour force, and low labour cost. This investment has allowed the country to comfortably fund its current account deficits. Indeed, Poland has received over US$ 30 billion of FDI since 1990. In 1999 alone the nation drew US$ 8 billion in FDI, even though ownership of agricultural land remains a sensitive issue and is subject to strict controls.

The Polish government supports and encourages foreign investment; it has openly acknowledged the need for capital as a critical element for the development and modernization of the country's economy. This is precisely why it is recommended that foreign investors emphasize their contributions to the Polish economy and society in order to penetrate the Polish market and preserve good relations. A good public relations plan helps to dispel the image of foreigners coming to Poland to exploit the emerging economy. Undoubtedly, the legal regime the authorities have put in place protects property rights and investment. The legal system also allows private business activity in almost every sector of the economy, provides for equal treatment for domestic and foreign companies, and permits the repatriation abroad of profits and capital.

Performance requirements for establishing or maintaining investments are generally not imposed except in the case of access to investment tax relief and incentives for investments in areas of high structural unemployment. In October 1994 for example, Poland enacted the Law on Special Economic Zones (SEZ), which, as a means of encouraging investment, offered exemptions from income tax, local taxes and fees, as well as the accelerated amortization of fixed assets. The creation of SEZs, in dire need of funds and modern infrastructure, was intended to boost the economies in areas with significant unemployment. However, the impending accession to the EU will ultimately put an end to all special economic zones and as such cannot be considered a permanent advantage to investors. Six SEZ are currently operating in southern Poland, five in the Baltic coast region, and four near the German border. The largest investment offers are in the automobile, building materials, food processing, and plastics industries, as well as in furniture manufacturing. The Polish government also supports exporters through export credit guarantees offered through the state-owned insurance entity, Kuke. This agency provides credit guarantees for both domestic and foreign firms registered in Poland.

Generally, foreign investors receive comparable treatment to domestic investors, both at the time of initial investment as well as after investments are made. However, foreign firms do face potential discrimination in public procurement contracts since public procurement law allows a 20% domestic price advantage and 50% domestic material and labour content requirements.

Major booming sectors

Drugs and pharmaceuticals

In 1999, US$ 2.5 billion's worth of pharmaceuticals were sold in Poland, and experts estimate that the value will increase by 8–9% annually over the next decade. The primary distribution channels are wholesalers, of whom 350 are operative, and pharmacies, of which there are 8,000.

Automotive industry/parts and components

Automobile sales in Poland continue to grow and several international automobile manufacturers, such as Fiat, Daewoo, GM-Opel, Ford, Volkswagen, Peugeot, Scania, and Volvo, are currently present in the market. With 8.5 million passenger cars registered in Poland the market for automobile parts and components has grown significantly over the past few years. Experts estimate that the number of cars will reach 15 million by 2010.

Rehabilitation equipment

There is growing demand for rehabilitation equipment in Poland and this market presents excellent opportunities for suppliers. The best prospects for investors are in high quality wheelchairs, electric wheelchairs, wheelchairs for children, active rehabilitation wheelchairs, sports wheelchairs, pneumatic mattresses, hydrotherapy and physical therapy equipment, and wheelchair lifts.

Electrical power machinery and equipment

The Polish market offers significant sales opportunities for electrical power equipment and services. A new energy law will ultimately force Polish power companies to operate under competitive conditions, requiring a major upgrading of power facilities. The best opportunities for investors involve coal-fired fluidized-bed combustors, pollution control equipment, pumps and compressors, electrical systems, heat recovery systems, turbine generators, and gas and steam turbines.

Airport/avionics and ground support equipment

Poland has 157 airports, including eight major facilities. The authorities plan to enlarge Warsaw Okecie Airport to accommodate long-term traffic growth. Experts estimate future expenditures will reach US$ 2.5 billion. Modernization plans are also underway to expand Poland's other three international airports located in Krakow, Katowice, and Gdańsk. As in most other Central and Eastern European countries, the best prospects for foreign companies concern air traffic control equipment, airport design, and construction services.

Pollution control equipment

The market for pollution control equipment has grown steadily over the past few years and is expected to increase rapidly. The most promising areas are air pollution control, waste-water treatment, waste disposal, and recycling technology.

Food processing equipment

Most analysts expect growth in the Polish market for food processing equipment to remain strong in the coming years. The largest segments of the market involve meat and poultry processing (19%), spirits and yeast (18%), dairy products (12%), sugar and sweets (12%), tobacco products (10%), and breweries (7%). Undoubtedly, the food industry will sustain a steady growth rate of at least 5% over the next few years with investments between US$ 1.2 and US$ 1.5 billion per year. The procurement of food processing technology, including equipment, is slightly below US$ 0.8 billion annually. Equipment for processing fruit, vegetables, tea and coffee offer the best opportunities for foreign companies.

School and office supplies

The market for school and office supplies will continue to grow at a rate of 2–5% within the next three years. Consumer demand for higher quality and more fashionable products has resulted in considerable, constantly growing imports, which amounted to US$ 277.3 million in 1999.

Insurance services

With a population of 40 million, a relatively low insurance subscription rate and a high rate of economic growth, the Polish insurance market offers tremendous opportunities for potential investors. The Polish insurance market has experienced rapid development during the last decade. The overall growth rate of the industry's premium collections in 1998 attained 26.6%. Growth in premium collections for life insurance products was 32.5%.

Defence equipment

The Polish government has identified full and active participation in NATO as one of its top foreign policy goals. As in Hungary, NATO integration goal requirements are driving equipment-related decisions and defence firms are seeking Western partners. Opportunities exist mainly in investment, technology transfer, and co-production work.

Healthcare services

Poland is the largest healthcare market in Eastern Europe and has a slowly growing private sector. As Poland's economy continues to improve and once healthcare reform is fully implemented, there is no doubt that consumers will increasingly turn to private healthcare companies.

Tourism development

Poland ranks among the top 10 for the number of visitors annually and 13th for tourism-generated revenue, and widely recognized as an important destination in the global tourist market. There is a strong demand for new hotels, development of moderate tourist accommodation, and investment in leisure activities such as ski lifts, tennis courts, open and indoor swimming pools, golf courses and bowling halls. In 1999, foreign capital engaged in the Polish tourism sector amounted to US$ 1.5 billion.

Chemical industry

The chemical industry in Poland continues to grow, with production figures increasing in all branches of the industry and in all groups of chemical enterprises. Figures from 1999 show that sales of chemicals, chemical products, and chemical fibres rose by 9%, while sales of rubber and plastics products rose by 20%. A new programme for modernization and privatization of the Polish chemical industry calls for investment through the year 2005 for a total value US$ 3 billion. There is hope that 30% of financing will come from Polish chemical companies, 20% from a Polish investment consortium and 50% from foreign investors.

Major trade partners (imports and exports)

Poland's major trading partners are Germany (36%), Italy (5.8%), Russia (5.6%), the Netherlands (4.7%), France (4.6%), Ukraine (3.8%), and the UK (3.8%). Russia, previously Poland's major trading partner, has fallen substantially behind in commercial exchanges with Poland because Poland now favours trade relations with the West. The nation exports manufactured goods and chemicals (57%), machinery and equipment (21%), food and live animals (12%), mineral fuels (7%) and imports manufactured goods and chemicals (43%), machinery and equipment (36%), mineral fuels (9%), and food and live animals (8%).

Germany has consistently contributed the greatest amount of foreign capital to the Polish economy, while the United States occupies the second place. Germany also ranks first in terms of the number of firms operating in Poland. The manufacturing sector remains the most popular among foreign investors in Poland. They invested US$ 17.3 billion during the period 1989–99. Of this total, US$ 4.6 billion was invested in the food industry, while US$ 4.4 billion was invested in the automotive industry. The second most attractive sector for foreign investors was the financial services sector followed by trade, repairs, and construction.

Free trade agreements

Because of its acceptance of and openness towards the West, Poland has strained its relations with Russia. However, the Russian enclave, Kaliningrad, which is essentially cut off from its motherland, is likely to become increasingly integrated with Poland's economy. Although relations are improving with Ukraine, they remain tense with Belarus. The close proximity to Belarus and Russia serve as reminders of possible tensions to the east and reinforce the desire to create firm links to Western economic and security structures. Poland has also endeavoured to establish mutual trade with its neighbours. Poland, the Czech Republic, Hungary, Bulgaria, Romania, and Slovenia formed an informal alliance, known as Visegrad, which established the Central European Free Trade Area (CEFTA) to increase regional trade. The original objective of this alliance was to inaugurate regional co-operation that was not dominated by the Soviet Union, as was the case with CMEA during the communist era.

Tariff system

Customs duties apply to virtually all products imported into Poland. The tariff schedule, ranging from 0 to 400%, has different rates depending on the type of commodity and the country of origin. Perhaps due to the legacy of the communist era, Polish customs officials are notoriously meticulous with regard to proper documentation. Foreign investors are regularly confronted with higher customs duties than those in EU countries. They are also confronted with problems arising from inconsistent and non-transparent regulations and an overall lack of consistency in all areas of business policy and public administration.

Value added tax (VAT)

The authorities revised the corporate tax code in 1999. The code allowed for greater transparency and lower rates in order to attract new investment. The corporate income tax rate, set at 34% in 1999, will plummet to 22% in 2004. However, companies with foreign participation, either as limited liability or joint stock, are subject to a 38% flat tax rate. There are no separate capital gains taxes. Value added tax (VAT) in Poland is not tax deductible unless it cannot be offset by a company's outgoing taxes.

8.7 Etiquette and cultural issues

Polish society is quite formal, a characteristic that is reflected in the use of polite titles and forms of address. The forms of address Pan, Pani, and Panna, or Sir, Madame, and Mademoiselle, respectively, are often coupled with other titles, such as Doctor or Professor. It is recommended that foreign visitors use the formal 'you' when speaking to locals in the Polish language. Most relationships never progress to a first-name basis. The

French word 'Madame' is also widely used and acceptable for married women.

Formal behaviour also pertains to business meetings. The most senior or high status person will be allowed to enter a room first, followed by the rest of staff in ranking order. Before taking the minutes or tape recording the session, it is polite to request permission.

In general, Poles have great respect for education, which they value more than financial wealth. Thus, given that advancement through education is the preferred means of social climbing, Poles look down upon 'the nouveau riche', or 'zloty millionaires', who have emerged in the new market. Foreign business travellers are advised to make the most of their own personal education credentials, which can be printed on business cards after the name as a subtle means of communication and a way to elicit respect. Business cards are the norm in Poland and are generally given to each person present at a meeting. As Poles tend to bring more than one person to their meetings, visitors should bring plenty of cards and make sure to hand one to each person. It is advisable to have cards printed in both the visitor's mother tongue and in Polish.

Poles are rather reserved and will keep at arm's length during conversation. Although they will often embrace friends while shaking hands, there is usually no touching in a business setting. The Polish language is spoken very softly but Poles also speak with their hands, using many gestures, such as stroking the chin, beard, hair or nose while talking, or waving a cigarette in the air.

Vodka is a genuine part of the Polish tradition and culture. Keeping up with the Polish toast is often difficult for foreigners, as the glass is drained in one gulp, and the bottle is never left half finished. The Polish smoke a lot and almost always provide ashtrays in business meetings. It would thus be offensive to ask people at a meeting to stop smoking.

The Polish family is an extended unit of three generations that often live under one roof. This makes family relations quite important. Doing business in Poland is built upon personal relationships and trust. Polish people do not go straight to the point, but rather have a roundabout way of getting down to business. This conversation helps to build the relationship and is a perfect occasion to show the local party a genuine interest in their country or in their person.

Poles are very sensitive about being referred to as an emerging market. Showing appreciation for the development and progress that Poland has made in the last decade is a good way to create warm and trusting relationships. As is evident in Latin, Asian, and Middle Eastern cultures, Poles also take time before or after a meeting to establish and preserve the personal relationship, which explains why they have a very relaxed approach to time. They normally do not structure their tasks to fit into a designated time slot, but rather will extend the time to fit the task. As a result, they are often running late from previous meetings or tasks. But that does not mean that foreign visitors can arrive late for meetings. On the contrary, they should be punctual.

One holdover from the days of communism is the Polish way of 'getting around' the bureaucratic system through a network of relationships based on personal favours. In this sense, the relationship is always more important than the deal in Poland. In doing favours for others, a relationship is built up, in which others are then obliged to return it in kind and this can be very useful. This is not a system of bribery but rather a concept of honouring obligations and saving face. There is a certain etiquette to this practice. For instance, direct requests for favours must only be made by acquaintances with equal status and within one's own social circle. One would not ask a favour of a superior, unless first doing him or her a favour and creating an obligation for them.

Other characteristics from the past include the tendency to maximize output rather than quality, a lack of service orientation, and the fact that business meetings, like those in the Middle East – albeit for different reasons – will often be interrupted by telephone calls and other incidents. The latter is for the most part due to an unwillingness of senior management to delegate less important tasks to their subordinates.

Women in Poland occupy important positions, such as architects, office managers, and professors and are represented in nearly all professions. Women have been represented at the highest levels of government and business and include Hanna Suhocka, prime minister in the early 1990s, and Hanna Gronkiewicz-Waltz, president of the National Bank of Poland. This is not the norm, however, as Poland in general remains a male-dominated society in the workforce. Long-standing male/female traditions still prevail in Poland and it is not unusual for a man to kiss a woman on the hand, to rise when women enter the room, to hold open doors, or to offer up a seat on the bus. Nearly all women work outside the home and discharge their household tasks after hours. The extended families in Poland usually have an elderly grandmother who helps with the care of the children. Male/female relationships in the workplace are formal. For instance, female secretaries or female nurses would rarely, if ever, be on a first name basis with their male superior. Females are also not invited to after hours socializing events. Especially in the blue-collar environment, men are not accustomed to women managers.

Culture

Titles on Polish business cards can be very useful for the foreign visitor in negotiations because they help identify the status, area of expertize, or ways to approach and prepare for the negotiation. When negotiating in Poland, it is important to remember that it may take a couple of meetings, or longer when dealing with government agencies, to reach a deal. Polish people are interested in establishing a personal relationship before getting down to business with others. Thus, first meetings may be used exclusively to establish the relationship and mutual trust. When dealing in Poland, it is also important to err on the side of formality. This includes following up meetings with a formal letter restating the proposal and thanking the Polish party for their time. Be aware of negotiating tactics which include intimidation where aggressive bargaining techniques are often used, delay tactics which can be frustrating for foreign negotiators who have flight schedules or deadlines to meet, and deferment to higher authorities.

Much business and relationship building is concluded in after hours socializing and drinking. However, foreign visitors are not expected to get drunk and it is not insulting if they decide to opt out of the drinking exercise. Even for those who do not drink, it is best to attend these very important sessions when first making inroads with Polish business acquaintances. Dinner parties often end in lively, late-night discussions. When invited to dinner, it is considered rude to leave early. Foreign negotiators should be aware that this might be used as a tactic when invited to dinner the night before a big negotiation, as tired negotiators are not necessarily good negotiators.

Greetings, gestures and conversation

Shaking hands is the customary form of greeting in Poland. A firm handshake is appreciated, but shaking hands over the threshold of a doorway is a sign of bad luck and must be avoided. Polish men will sometimes follow a handshake with a clap on the back or a quick embrace. Likewise, women and men will kiss each other on each cheek. When two groups of people meet, each individual in the group will greet and shake hands. This will take several minutes, but is an essential ritual. A businesswoman should not be surprised if a Polish man kisses her hand upon introduction, at subsequent meetings, or when saying goodbye. Foreign men are not expected to kiss a Polish woman's hand but may simply shake hands. Men should wait until the woman extends her hand. Often women will just offer a polite nod instead of a handshake when introduced to a man. Women visitors should also be prepared for a series of lavish compliments upon introduction from both men and women. This polite banter is an art that Poles have cultivated for social occasions.

9
Slovakia

9.1 Basic facts

The Slovak Republic (Slovenska Republika, or Slovakia) is a tiny landlocked country (48,845 sq km) that shares its borders with Austria (91 km) in the southwest, the Czech Republic (215 km) in the northwest, Hungary (515 km) in the south, Poland (444 km) in the north, and Ukraine (90 km) in the east.

Slovakia has a temperate climate, with cool summers and cold, yet humid winters. The average daily temperature in winter is 2 °C (35 °F) rising to 21 °C (70 °F) in the summer. The country is divided into two main regions: the central and northern part is covered with rugged mountains belonging to the western Carpathian Bow, which encompasses the Little Carpathians, the White Carpathians, and the Tatry (the highest Carpathian range). The southern part is made up of the Danubian Lowlands, a fertile region that extends to the River Danube on the Hungarian border. The Danube, located in the southwest, forms part of Slovakia's border with Hungary. Other important rivers include the Váh, Hron, Ipel' (Eipel), Nitra, Ondava, Laborec, and Hornád. There are many small glacial lakes in the High Tatry Mountains.

The country's population is approaching 5.5 million (but it is estimated that over one third of all Slovaks live beyond the borders of the current Slovak Republic). Slovaks are the most prominent ethnic group (85.7%), followed by Hungarians (10%) and Gypsies/Romany (1.6%, but this group is often under-estimated). Other minority ethnic groups include Czechs, Moravians, Silesians, Ruthenians, Ukrainians, Germans, and Poles. All enjoy full protection of their culture, language and history under the constitution and special laws. The dominant religion is Roman Catholicism (60.3%), but Protestant and Orthodox churches are common. The Jewish community was decimated during World War II.

Slovakia's administrative structure has eight regions, 79 districts and 2,878 municipalities (including towns and cities). The capital, Bratislava (0.45 million inhabitants), is the political, economic and cultural centre of the country and also a major port on the Danube. Other major cities include Banská Bystríca, Košice, Žilina, Nitra, Trnava and Trencin. The official language is Slovak, which belongs to the West Slavic subgroup of languages and is closely related to Czech, but other minority languages are widely spoken in their respective regions. Where minorities exceed 20% of the local population, their language may be used as the official language, alongside Slovak.

The currency is the crown or koruna (SKK); 100 haliers are 1 koruna. Since 1 October 1998, the koruna exchange rate has been set by a managed floating system, which replaced the former fixed exchange rate regime (the peg to a basket of 60% Deutsch Marks and 40% US dollars).

Means of communication

Slovakia has a developed system of mass communications, which includes two state-owned television stations and two privately owned (with extensive coverage). Major newspapers and business journals are *Narodna Obroda*, *SME*, *Hospodarsky Noviny*, and *Trend and Profit*. The only English-language newspaper is the *Slovak Spectator*.

9.2 Historical background

The Slovaks are one of the oldest nations in Central Europe. Archaeology indicates the existence of man in the area from the Middle Palaeolithic period (200,000–35,000 BC) and the territory of Slovakia was a significant European centre of bronze production in the Bronze Age. After the ancient Celtic settlement (dating from 4000 BC) and the Roman period, the area now known as Slovakia was occupied by Slavic tribes in the fifth and sixth centuries AD. These tribes began to be politically organized in the seventh century when they established Samo's Kingdom. The latter became part of the Slavic Empire of Great Moravia in the ninth century. The empire encompassed the lands of modern Slovakia and Moravia, as well as parts of Hungary, Austria, Bohemia and the southern part of Poland. The area rapidly became the target of the early Christian Church, led by the Frank clergy and missionaries from Byzantium, to convert the local tribes. After the death of King Svatopluk, the Great Moravian Empire began to disintegrate under the pressure of nomadic Hungarian tribes (Magyars). In the year 1000, Slovakia was incorporated into the Hungarian Empire, which was a multi-ethnic, political unit organized by King Stephen I of the Arpad dynasty. Subsequently, in 1526, Slovakia resisted Turkish occupation (except for the southern regions) and became a part of the Hapsburg Empire. As a consequence, it was turned into the principal battleground of the Turkish Wars and paid a heavy tribute for the defence of the Habsburg monarchy, and the rest of Europe, for that matter, against Turkish expansion.

Certain signs of national and political Slovak life appeared only at the very end of the nineteenth century, with the Congress of Oppressed Peoples of Hungary, held in Budapest in 1895. It resulted in the end of the coercive Magyarization policy and in the emergence of several nationalist cultural movements. In May 1918, Czech and Slovak patriots signed the so-called Pittsburgh Declaration that pledged co-operation leading to the establishment of a common state. In October 1918, Slovakia declared its independence and its incorporation into the new Republic of Czechoslovakia. The latter included the Czech lands of Bohemia and Moravia, a small part of Silesia, and Slovakia. A parliamentary democratic government was formed, with its capital in the Czech city of Prague. During the inter-war years, the Czechoslovak government's efforts to industrialize Slovakia failed, mostly because of the worldwide economic slump of the 1930s. This created profound discontent among Slovaks, who were economically and politically dominated by the Czechs, and gave rise to important extremist nationalist movements.

Indeed, Czechoslovakia was plagued with minority problems. The most important one involved the country's large German population. In 1938, the Czechoslovak government was forced by the Munich treaty (signed by Germany, Britain, France and Italy) to cede territory to Germany. On 14 March 1939, Slovakia declared its independence and created the Slovak Republic. Later the Germans occupied Czech lands, but Slovakia came under strong German influence and protection. During 1942–44, despite the efforts of several underground resistance movements, about 70,000 Slovak Jews and other 'undesirables' were carried off to concentration camps. This issue became grounds for further tension between Czechs and Slovaks that has lasted to this day.

When peace was restored after World War II, the Czechs and Slovaks held elections. The Democratic Party won the elections in Slovakia, but the Communist Party won 38% of the vote in Czechoslovakia. Communists eventually seized power in February 1948 and brought Czechoslovakia into the eastern bloc as a vassal of the Soviet Union. The strict communist rule was only briefly interrupted in 1968 when Alexander Dubcek, a Slovak, became party leader and proposed political, social and economic reforms. The so-called 'Prague Spring' was brought to an end by the 'fraternal' occupation of Czechoslovakia by the armies of the Warsaw Pact and the establishment of a pro-Soviet regime. As a result, nearly all of the reforms that had been introduced were revoked and another Slovak, Gustav Husak, replaced Dubcek as party leader.

Soviet influence collapsed in 1989 after a series of peaceful mass protests called 'the velvet revolution'. Czechoslovakia regained its freedom and the country elected the prominent Czechoslovak liberal, Václav Havel, to effectively end communist rule. Three years later, Slovak nationalists initiated a move to split Czechoslovakia into two separate nations. Czechs supported the idea because they resented the burden of subsidizing economically weaker Slovakia. As a result, on 1 January 1993, the Czech Republic and Slovakia peacefully separated to become sovereign independent states. Both attained immediate recognition from the USA and their European neighbours.

However, Slovakia had more difficulty than the Czech Republic in building a modern market economy. Headed by the populist leader, Vladimir Mečiar, Slovakia was soon the target of international criticism for its lack of respect for minority rights and the democratic process. Power was handed to an incompetent group of Mečiar's political clients. Opposition parties suffered from discriminatory practices, and their leaders were detained or kidnapped. Dissenting intellectuals and journalists were intimidated and laws were simply ignored.

Mečiar's government was finally replaced after the 1998 elections by a new centre-right coalition more committed to democracy and market reform and willing to catch up with Slovakia's Central European neighbours in the race to join the European Union (EU). The coalition has made impressive strides in advancing Slovakia's political and economic transition.

9.3 Political environment

Slovakia is a parliamentary democracy with a one-chamber parliament called the National Council (*Narodna Rada*), which is the supreme legislative body and the key rule-making institution. Its 150 members serve a four-year term. They are elected by direct universal suffrage in a secret ballot based on party lists within each administrative region. Seats are awarded to political parties in proportion to votes received. The president is directly elected by absolute majority vote for a five-year term.

He is the head of state, but has limited powers. He usually appoints as prime minister for a four-year term the leader of the majority party or majority coalition. He also appoints cabinet members on the recommendation of the prime minister.

Since independence, Slovakian politics have been characterized by a complex system of coalitions of parties that reflected the social-cultural character of the country. The Movement for a Democratic Slovakia (HZDS), the nationalist Slovak National Party (SNS), the far left Association of Slovak Workers (ZNS) and the small Slovak Peasant Party (SPP) backed up the 1994 government led by Vladimir Mečiar (HZDS). After the 1998 elections, the Slovak Democratic Coalition (SDK), the Party of the Democratic Left (SDL), the Party of the Hungarian Coalition (SMK), and the Party of Civic Understanding (SOP) formed a coalition to exclude Mečiar from power, resulting in the nomination of Mikulas Dzurinda (SDK) as prime minister. In May 1999, Rudolf Schuster (SOP) was elected president of Slovakia, in the first public vote for president in the country's history.

There is a consensus among all the current government parties in favour of EU and NATO membership and a shared wish to exclude former prime minister Mečiar from power. However, left-wing forces, particularly the Party of the Democratic Left (SDL), remain opposed to many of the government's measures, including privatization of the utilities, public-sector reform and rationalization of state administration. The HZDS (still led by Mečiar) remains the most popular opposition party with consistent poll ratings of 25–30%. In addition, Slovakia has over a dozen other active political parties, many of which are also coalitions. Since belt-tightening has proven unpopular domestically, the September 2002 parliamentary elections are likely to produce a shake-up of power with the majority of votes going to autocrats and economic populists centred on the HZDS and SNS. The Slovak Democratic and Christian Union (SDKU) and SDL are predicted to follow behind with 30–40% of the votes. Former nationalist prime minister Mečiar's efforts to return to office, if successful, would probably alter the course of future Slovakian economic development.

The country is a member of the United Nations (UN), the Council of Europe (CE), Organization for Economic Co-operation and Development (OECD) and the Central European Initiative (CEI), a group promoting regional political and economic co-operation. In February 1994 the Slovak Government signed the Partnership for Peace accord with Western nations, considered a precursor to joining the North Atlantic Treaty Organization (NATO). In October 1993 the country became an associate member of the EU, and in 1995 it applied for EU membership. Formal negotiations began in 1999.

9.4 Economic environment and infrastructure

Macroeconomics

In the space of a few years, Slovakia has made considerable progress towards achieving macroeconomic stability as it made the transition from a centrally planned to a modern market economy. Under the Mečiar government, GDP growth rates and macroeconomic performance indicators rose steadily, but (a) much of this growth was attributable to high government spending and excessive borrowing rather than productive economic activity; and (b) public and private debt and trade deficits soared; and (c) privatization was tarnished by corrupt insider deals.

In May 1999, the Dzurinda government approved a wide-ranging package of austerity programmes to cut state spending, lower social benefits, and deregulate various prices (such as those for electricity, natural gas and public transport) to lower the budget deficit. As a consequence, GDP growth recovered (3.3% in 2001) and is now on track to reach around 4% in 2002. Investment and domestic consumption are the main boosters for economic growth.

However, this growth has been accompanied by several deepening economic imbalances. The end of Mečiar's unsustainable public spending boom, monetary tightening and industrial restructuring have inevitably hiked up unemployment to around 20%, with rates reaching 28% in eastern parts of Slovakia against 7% in Bratislava. This high level of unemployment calls for increased labour market flexibility, as well as better incentives to seek and provide employment (in particular, removing disincentives to work stemming from the welfare system), but the government already faces considerable public discontent over rising consumer prices, reduced social benefits, and a drop in living standards. The IMF has criticized the slowdown in the pace of structural reforms.

The increase in the external current account deficit in 2001 and the projected size in 2002 (US$ 2 billion, or 9% of GDP) also threaten growth. The inflow of FDI as a result of forthcoming privatization should cover the huge current account deficit and mitigate risks in the immediate future. However, some privatizations may be delayed, or a possible change of government following the autumn elections in 2002 could make Slovakia less attractive to foreign investors. This underscores the urgent need to take additional fiscal measures that would contain the pressures on the external accounts. Despite certain improvements in tax collection, the government has struggled for the past several years to meet reduced fiscal deficit targets. This has left public finances vulnerable to structural and cyclical imbalances, while high unemployment and depressed wage growth continue to limit the upside of income tax receipts.

The National Bank of Slovakia has continued to loosen monetary policy in response to positive foreign trade results and weak domestic demand. However, the koruna is more sensitive to political uncertainty than macroeconomic news and should, therefore, weaken in 2002 in the run-up to the parliamentary elections.

Industry

The Slovak economy is still characterized by heavy industry and the processing of raw materials and agricultural commodities. Many enterprises are just beginning to restructure and need to modernize their equipment and methods. Slovakia's natural resources include brown coal and lignite, small amounts of iron ore, copper and manganese ore, and salt. Primary industries are in metal and metal products, food and beverages, electricity, gas, coke, oil, nuclear fuel, chemicals and man-made fibres, machinery, paper and printing, earthenware and ceramics, transport vehicles, textiles, electrical and optical apparatus, and rubber products. Industrial performance continues to diverge, with foreign-owned engineering and export-oriented sectors recording strong growth, while domestically owned companies suffer from depressed domestic demand and capital shortages as the major banks are restructured.

Strong manufacturing growth sharply contrasts the trend in individual subsectors. The hardening of budget constraints on firms with the restructuring of the country's major banks has exposed a lack of competitiveness that burdens much of the manufacturing sector. Reflecting this trend, output of transport equipment, which is dominated by Volkswagen's Bratislava plant, soared by 89% year on year in July. Other export-oriented subsectors with heavy foreign participation, including wood and paper products, rubber and plastics, petroleum products and electrical and optical equipment, performed less spectacularly, but have consistently outpaced domestically oriented industries, such as food and textiles.

Energy

Slovakia suffers from a lack of its own primary energy resources and must import about 88% of its total energy needs. Solid and liquid fuels represent about 40% of the energy demand. Oil is almost entirely imported from Russia through a long-term supply contract that expires in 2008, while the import of coal is divided between Russia, Ukraine, Poland, and the Czech Republic. Gaseous fuels (mostly natural gas) represent about 35% of energy demand and are almost entirely imported from Russia. The Slovak gas transmission system consists of 6,000 km of long-distance transit pipelines (including four international transit pipelines of more than 2,000 km) and almost 21,000 km of smaller pipelines in the local distribution network. This promotes Slovakia to the rank of a key player in the European natural gas market. Transport and distribution/sale of natural gas within the country is controlled by the state-owned enterprise Slovenský plynárenský priemysel (SPP), which is due to be privatized in 2002.

The Slovak market for electric power generation is small when compared to other Central European countries. Slovakia currently has six operating nuclear power reactors at two nuclear power plant sites. The nuclear plant at Jaslovské Bohunice is of a Russian design considered inherently unsafe by nuclear experts, but it has been extensively upgraded and is now considered both by the International Atomic Energy Agency and the Slovak Nuclear Regulatory Commission to be safe. In 2006 and 2008, two blocks of the older type will be phased out in Jaslovské Bohunice. Hydro energy is one of the pillars of Slovak energy production. The hydro energy potential is utilized up to 58% in the country and the trend is to increase the level of its utilization, as well as preparing the transformation, restructuring and privatization of the electro-energy sector. It is expected that generation will be separated from transmission and each power plant will be sold separately. As a consequence, state subsidies in the energy sector are gradually being reduced.

Agriculture

Once a dominant force of the Slovak economy, agriculture now represents a mere 4.5% of GDP and 8% of total employment. About 43% of the total land area is cultivated and focuses primarily on meeting domestic demand. The country's major agricultural products include grain, potatoes, sugar beet, hops, fruit, pigs, cattle, poultry and forest products.

Slovakian agriculture has undergone a major reform that covered two essential aspects: the effective privatization of the land, and the gradual transition to a market economy. The restoration of full ownership rights to land, the creation of new ownership rights to agricultural property (dividing the property of co-operatives into shares) and the transformation and privatization of state farms, agro-processing and services have been largely completed. However, these reforms did not result in the emergence of privately owned farms to any significant extent. Larger landlords established viable farms right at the beginning of the transition, but very few new entrants appeared at a later stage. The major reasons are an excessive fragmentation of ownership, high transaction costs on a dormant land market, a lack of loan capital during the entire period of transition and the limited experience of farm management among former agricultural workers. In addition, the Slovak agricultural sector now needs time to adapt to the new market situation. However, it will take longer to turn obsolete production facilities into efficient enterprises. Reducing costs and improving efficiency will be crucial to maintain market share against growing foreign competition.

Today, agricultural policy is heavily influenced by EU accession requirements as Slovakia strives to introduce measures that are consistent with the common agricultural policy (CAP). Slovakia has made considerable progress in veterinary issues and in the phyto-sanitary field. State subsidies have fallen dramatically and agricultural prices have been essentially deregulated, with the exception of milk. There is still some so-called intervention purchasing, where the price is below a certain level, to redress the imbalance between supply and demand.

Financial sector

Since the foundation of the Slovak Republic, there has been a two-level banking system, consisting of the National Bank of Slovakia (NBS) and a network of commercial banks and state financial institutions. The NBS is independent of the government and acts as the central bank of the country. It is responsible for monetary and foreign exchange policy, as well as the regulation and supervision of the banking sector. In particular, it sets minimum capital and reserve requirements and grants commercial bank licences. The sector counts 33 banks operating in Slovakia, including two branches of foreign banks and 11 representations of foreign banks. Most of the commercial banks are registered as joint-stock companies with headquarters in Bratislava and have foreign capital participation. Only two are state-owned institutions. According to the Banking Act, commercial banks may offer a wide range of services, including investment banking and broking activities, as well as traditional commercial transactions and lending. In reality, high interest rates and a lack of available financing for small and medium-sized enterprises restrict the services Slovak banks can provide for the market. In addition, foreign banks have concentrated on providing international payment services and services to Western clients, and there has been relatively little lending by foreign banks to Slovak companies, with the exception of some leading Slovak firms. This explains why loans and deposits are still concentrated in the banks where the state has major shares. Therefore, the banking system has yet to become fully independent of government coercion and control, but the privatization of these banks was a long-standing politically sensitive issue for a long time. It has now been resolved.

The Bratislava Stock Exchange (BSE) is a joint-stock company owned by banks, traders in securities, and the National Property Fund of the Slovak Republic. It organizes securities trading on three markets: a listed companies market, a registered companies market and a free market. Companies whose shares or bonds are traded on the BSE listed-companies market are obliged to publish their economic results once a quarter. Companies from the registered-companies market should publish their economic results every six months. No strict conditions are applied to securities traded on the free market. All securities must be registered in the Central Securities Registrar, a legal entity established by the Ministry of Finance. In addition, RM-System Slovakia, a private company, has established an electronic trading system for listed securities, and which is based on the NASDAQ model.

Despite low valuation levels, trading on the BSE is still quite inactive, and the market is dominated by state-bonds trading. The initial waves of voucher privatization resulted in a domestic loss of trust in the market, as well as in the restriction of the development of the equity capital market. Furthermore, large foreign investors seem to have stayed away from Slovak shares. Consequently, in 1999, the new government amended the Securities Law and passed a new Collective Investment Law in an attempt to revitalize the capital market.

Telecommunications

The development programme of the telecommunications sector has achieved spectacular results in Slovakia. Its structure has changed fundamentally with: (a) the separation of postal and telecommunications activities which took place on 1 January 1993; (b) the creation of a new regulatory agency; (c) the enactment of a new Telecommunications Law in May 2000; and (d) the privatization of Slovak Telekom in July 2000.

In just a few years, telephone service has been transformed from an outmoded analogue network into a modern digital network. Consequently, the number of installed telephone lines has more than doubled since 1992 and is now over two million. In addition, there are also more than 1.7 million mobile telephones. The two mobile operators – Globtel (64% owned by France Telecom, 980,000 customers) and Eurotel (60%

owned by Slovak Telekom and 40% by MediaOne and Bell Atlantic, 740,000 customers) have made Slovakia one of the fastest growing markets in Europe. However, fierce competition between the two providers has kept prices low. Slovak Telekom has a monopoly of voice services until the end of the year 2002, but there is open competition in data services. Internet service providers (ISPs) need to register and obtain an operating licence. There have been 74 ISP licences issued in total, but there is now a concentration of the Internet market, with larger companies buying out many ISPs and many local providers merging with bigger ones.

Transportation

Slovakia has a moderate transportation infrastructure. There is a good network of roads, but only two-lane highways or local roads cover most of the country, with 450 km of multi-lane highways extending from Bratislava to neighbouring borders and cities. The government intends to build an extensive network of new roads, including 660 km of multi-lane highway by 2005. About 70 million passengers and 50 million tons of goods are transported annually by rail. Many important industrial complexes have their own railway lines. The government also plans to modernize the rail track to increase speeds to 140 kmh (120 kmh in mountainous areas). Water transport is also important, as Slovakia has the unique advantage of being connected to the Western European waterway systems as far as Rotterdam and to the Black Sea, via the Danube. Finally, its major airport is located in Bratislava. However, there are few international flights to Bratislava and many business travellers use Vienna's Schwechat airport, which is only 40 km from Bratislava. Although there are other airports in Košice, Poprad, and Sliac (near Zvolen), domestic travel is infrequent and unreliable.

Environment

Slovakia is party to many international environmental agreements. Its major environmental issues are air pollution from metallurgical plants that pose risks to human health and acid rain that is damaging the forests. Austrian environmentalists strongly oppose Slovakia's two nuclear power stations at nearby Mochovce.

9.5 Legal environment, regulations and the judicial system

Slovakia's civil law system is based on Austro-Hungarian codes modified to comply with the obligations of the Organization on Security and Co-operation in Europe (OSCE) and to expunge Marxist-Leninist legal theory. The legal system consists of 43 district courts, four regional courts, and a Supreme Court, all under the jurisdiction of the Ministry of Justice. In addition, there is a Constitutional Court, independent of government control. Judges are appointed for an initial four-year term and are subsequently either appointed for life or removed from office. Once appointed for life, judges may be removed only for due cause.

The legal system recognizes property and contractual rights, but arbitration decisions are prolonged, thus making the system unattractive for dispute resolution. The courts recognize and enforce foreign judgments, subject to the same delays. A bankruptcy law exists but is not very effective. A number of bankruptcy cases have been filed, but few have been resolved and requirements for debtor-initiated bankruptcies are unrealistic. The Slovak Chamber of Commerce and Industry also has a Court of Arbitration for alternative dispute resolution. Most cases involve disputes between Slovak and foreign parties. Slovak domestic companies generally do not make use of arbitration clauses in contracts.

Crime and corruption

Slovakia is generally a safe place in which to conduct business, despite the rising presence of organized crime (not aimed at foreign investors). However, corruption is widespread in Slovakia, notably in areas such as healthcare, customs, education, the police and in the courts. Most bribes are small, but some can be quite large (particularly when expressed as a percentage of revenues). The new government recognized the harmful effects of corruption and placed anti-corruption measures high on the official agenda. A milestone was reached in late 1999 with the establishment of the Anti-corruption Steering Committee led by the deputy prime minister, the development and public dissemination of the National Programme for the Fight Against Corruption, and the significantly increased sentences for bribery and abuse of power adopted in an amendment to the Criminal Code in June 2001.

Taxation, accounting and auditing rules

The corporate income tax rate is 29%, with a reduced rate at 15% in agriculture. There is no special tax rate for capital gains, which are taxed at the normal corporate tax rate. Dividends are subject to a 15% withholding tax. Personal income tax is charged at progressive rates, which vary between 12% and 42%.

Slovakia is in the process of adapting its auditing standards to international norms. The Accounting Law is based on EU directives, and the first 35 Slovak auditing standards are based on the International Accounting Standards.

Laws on establishing and conducting business

There are no formal performance requirements for establishing, maintaining or expanding foreign entities. Foreign and domestic private entities are entitled to establish and own business enterprises and engage in remunerative activity in Slovakia. Local firms are free to contract directly with foreign entities.

Business organizations available to foreigners

The Slovak Commercial Code specifies the following as acceptable forms of businesses: joint-stock company, limited liability company, limited partnership, unlimited partnership, branch office of a foreign company, co-operative, silent partnership, and association. The most common foreign entity is the limited liability company (s.r.o.), because of its lower capital requirement (200,000 SKK). Apart from branch offices, silent partnerships and associations, all of the above-mentioned structures are legal entities and must be listed in the Slovak Commercial Register. The following procedures and documents are required for registering: (a) lease contract for the premises, (b) approval of the office/company's location by local authorities, (c) Slovak bank account, (d) trade authorization from the local trade authority, and (e) satisfaction of minimum capital requirements.

Restrictions on foreign investments (and entry requirements)

The Dzurinda government has made important improvements to the legal and control framework to encourage foreign direct investment (FDI). There is no formal screening process for FDI, no discrimination against existing FDI and no minimum performance requirements.

Investment incentives

The Dzurinda government's policy to promote FDI was to create substantial incentives, including tax holidays for strategic foreign investors, and customs relief for certain investment goods. The government may offer foreign investors a five-year tax holiday (for up to 75% of taxes) if an investor puts more than SKK 200 million (roughly US$ 6.6 million) into a 'strategic industry'. This offer also requires that the company increases its Slovak exports by 25% annually during the five years.

Protection of property rights

Protection of property rights fall under the jurisdiction of two agencies. The Industrial Property Office has responsibility for most areas, while the Ministry of Culture is responsible for copyrights, including software. Slovakia is a member of the World Intellectual Property Organization (WIPO), is a founding member of the World Trade Organization (WTO), and has a membership application pending with the European Patent Office. It adheres to major intellectual property agreements including the Bern Convention for Protection of Literary and Artistic Works, the Paris Convention for Protection of Industrial Property, and numerous other international agreements.

There have been no expropriation cases in Slovakia, nor are any foreseen. The constitution and the law, including the Commercial and Civil codes, permit expropriation only in exceptional cases of public interest, and compensation must be provided. The law also provides for an appeal procedure.

Visa requirements

Visitors to Slovakia staying more than 30 days are required to obtain a residence permit prior to entering the country. It should be noted that foreign visitors are required to have a medical insurance valid in Slovakia and at least US$ 50 per day for their stay in Slovakia. Foreign nationals heading offices in Slovakia must have a long-term residence permit. These permits are granted for a maximum of one year with the possibility of a recurrent extension.

9.6 Business environment

Privatization

The privatization process in Slovakia started in 1991 and was divided into restitution, small-scale privatization, and large-scale privatization. The restitution laws returned the property expropriated by the communist authorities to the original owners or their heirs. The small-scale privatizations involved primarily the sale by auction of small retail units in trade and service sectors, and small-sized industrial and construction units. The large-scale privatizations are still going on and can be divided into three waves. The first wave was essentially a voucher privatization process directed towards Slovak citizens. It resulted in a dispersed ownership structure, as 2.6 million citizens out of 5 million participated in the process. The second wave covered 1994–98. It essentially relied on direct sales and public tenders, with only a few auctions.

The poor quality of all these privatizations (fraught with corruption, non-transparency, and inefficiency) led to a lack of corporate restructuring, inadequate resource reallocation within and between companies, and little improvement in profitability. In particular, The Mečiar government barred by law the privatization of 'strategic' companies, including natural monopolies, defence firms, banks, and a few other companies. By contrast, the Dzurinda government recognized the need to introduce more market-oriented management to these strategic firms. In late 1999, the third wave of privatizations started. It focused on the bigger companies and is still going on. For instance, in March 2002, the government approved the sale of 49% of its stockholdings in Slovenský plynárenský priemysel, the state-owned gas company, to a foreign consortium at the price of US$ 2.7 billion (13% of GDP).

Despite the earlier problems surrounding privatization, more than 85% of Slovakia's GDP is now produced by the private sector, including over half of industrial production, one of the highest rates of privatization in the former eastern bloc – and significantly higher than in neighbouring Austria.

Foreign direct investment (FDI)

Slovakia ranks far behind its Central European neighbours in terms of foreign direct investment (FDI), essentially as a consequence of the early government's economic policy and significant barriers presented to foreign companies seeking to participate in the privatization process. However, the generally improved political outlook and the attractive package of incentives for foreign investors (including tax breaks and the elimination of tariffs on imports of new manufacturing machinery) has resulted in a sharp increase in FDI in recent years.

The FDI flow into the country accounted for 11% and 5.5% of GDP in 2000 and 2001 respectively. The higher figure in 2000 corresponds to the privatization of Slovak Telekom. Cumulative FDI reached 27% of GDP, 76% of which was from the EU, and 55% of the total was invested in the manufacturing sector at the end of 2001.

Free economic and trade areas

There is a 12-hectare free-trade zone (FTZ) in Košice. Government plans exist to expand the zone and intensify co-operation with its Hungarian and Ukrainian neighbours. The government also plans to build a second, larger FTZ in Bratislava. The existing zone is not a significant factor in the Slovak economy and has not yet played an important role in attracting FDI.

Major booming sectors

Slovakia has several sectors with high growth opportunity. These include infrastructure, information technology, pharmaceuticals, industrial equipment, audio-visual equipment and services, chemicals, business services and tourism. Capital goods, information and communication systems, financial services, environmental products and services, management skills, production processes, and access to Western marketing networks and know-how are among the areas offering potential for foreign businesses.

Major trading partners

Slovakia's major trading partners are in the EU, and more specifically Germany (16.8%), Italy (9.2%) and Austria (8.3%) for exports, and Germany (25%) and Italy (6.2%) for imports. The Czech Republic is also a major trading partner with 17.4% of exports and 14.7% of imports. The Czech Republic holds a pre-eminent share of Slovak trade because of the unique nature of their relationship. German and Austrian companies enjoy the advantages of proximity and historical familiarity with the Slovak market. Imports from Russia are also significant (17%), but consist mainly of fuels and raw materials. Moreover, Slovakia is trying to develop its markets in the east, although the economic crisis in Russia and Ukraine is making it difficult to increase exports to those regions. Major export products are machinery and transport equipment (37%), intermediate manufactured goods (30%), miscellaneous manufactured goods (13%), chemicals (9%) and raw materials (4%). Major import products are machinery and transport equipment (40%), intermediate manufactured goods (18%), fuels (11%), chemicals (11%), and miscellaneous manufactured goods (10%).

Free trade agreements

Among the most important agreements concluded by the Slovak Republic is the agreement establishing the customs union between the Slovak and the Czech Republics that was signed in 1992. Slovakia is also a member of the Association Treaty with the European Union (1992), EFTA (European Free Trade Agreement) (1992), and CEFTA (Central European Free Trade Agreement) (1993). In addition, it has signed numerous bilateral free-trade agreements.

Tariff system

Levels of import protection are currently relatively low. However, when the economy reached the bottom of its economic crisis in early 1999, the Dzurinda government instituted an austerity package and temporary protective measures (e.g. customs, non-tariff and licence policies). The new government has agreed to reform the cumbersome product certification system that is an obstacle to imports.

Slovakia is a member of the WTO and is bound by the GATT Agreement on Implementation of Article VII GATT 1994. The basis for calculating import duties is the customs value of the goods, including transportation costs and insurance from the point of loading to the border of the country. The rules appear to provide a uniform and neutral system of valuation.

Value added tax (VAT)

The customs authorities collect customs duties and are simultaneously administrators of the value added tax (VAT) for imports. The basic VAT rate is 23% and the reduced rate for specified goods and services is 10%. There have been periodic proposals to lower the basic VAT to 22% and to raise the decreased rate to 12%. Excise duties are imposed on spirits and alcoholic beverages, hydrocarbon fuels and lubricants and tobacco products. Slovakia does not impose export duties.

Major customs documentation for importing and exporting

Slovakia's documentation requirements are being harmonized with EU standards and trade documentation is similar to that of EU countries.

9.7 Etiquette and cultural issues

Business practice and etiquette in Slovakia is a mix of Western Europe and the United States on the one hand, and Eastern Europe and Russia on the other hand. It blends formal and direct business styles. Older business people tend to be more formal, as a legacy of communist times. Many members of the younger generation – especially those under 30 – have adapted quickly to the new market system and are eager to succeed and embrace capitalism. Doing business with them is very similar to doing business with Western Europeans or Americans.

Culture/negotiating style

Decision-making in a Slovak company is often restricted to very few, if not just one person. Even relatively minor decisions may require the approval of a high-level official. Decision-making in older, state-run companies can be problematic. Western managers have encountered factory workers trained under the communist system, who are afraid to take initiative. They prefer to forfeit decision-making power to the boss. Many Western companies in Slovakia have overcome this attitude through intensive training, but it still exists in some companies. However, initial business contacts should not be limited to senior management. The support of middle management and labour is critical to the success of negotiations. Foreign business people are advised to visit trade fairs and participate in trade conferences to establish contacts and to gain valuable background.

Negotiations in Slovakia are often a long, methodical process. The pace of business is slower but initial meetings may be businesslike and matter-of-fact, and several meetings may be necessary before Slovak partners feel comfortable. They are unlikely to move quickly to closure. Slovaks are non-confrontational and believe it is impolite to say 'no'. They are more likely to say: 'it is difficult' or 'we will see'. In response, foreign business people should cushion a negative response.

Slovaks take a long-term view of relationships. Successful business depends on building trust between partners. It is normal to engage in general social conversation before getting down to business. Launching directly into the basics may impede the development of a good personal relationship with the Slovak partner. They will generally ask about your flight, your accommodation, your home country or state, and what you have seen in their country. It is appropriate for the foreign business person to ask similar questions in return. Foreign companies operating in the country must take a similar, long-term view and be prepared to invest time in building relationships and investing capital into the country. Business people should avoid appearing impatient when dealing with Slovak partners because this will cause resentment.

If a Slovak partner seems anxious to quickly forge ahead, he may have the impression that the foreign partner is the one who will be advancing hard currency for the enterprise. Be cautious and make sure that you and your attorney have researched the deal thoroughly. Business correspondence in English is acceptable, but will make a more favourable impression if letters are written in Slovak. Correspondence should be addressed to a firm or company rather than to an individual executive.

After an initial meeting, delivering a written summary of goals, objectives, and points of agreement or disagreement will minimize misunderstandings between business parties. It is advisable to hire a Slovak business lawyer with a command of your native tongue to guide you through the maze of new regulations.

Greetings, gestures, and conversation

Business appointments should be arranged as far in advance as possible and confirmed in writing. Remember that it is very difficult to conduct business on Fridays because for many managers the day ends after lunch. Both business and social meetings begin punctually, and all parties are expected to arrive on time. Business dress for men and women is conservative. Even in very warm weather, the more formal business executives do not remove their jackets. It is preferable to have someone introduce you, particularly in formal situations. In casual settings, however, it is acceptable to introduce yourself. If you are in a position of making introductions, always give the name of the younger or lower-ranking person first.

It is customary to shake hands, firmly but briefly, upon arriving and departing from any meeting, business or social. Women and elderly people should be allowed to offer their hand first for the handshake. If a number of people are introduced at the same time, take turns shaking hands. Do not reach over someone else's handshake and do not keep your left hand in your pocket while shaking hands.

Generally, Slovaks are formal and address each other by their title and surname. Only close friends and family members use first names. Allow your counterpart to suggest the use of first names, before you try to do so. Slovaks have a high regard for professional titles and positions (for example, director or 'rediteli', doctor or 'doktore', engineer or 'inzenyre') and include them on their business cards. People without professional titles should be addressed as Mr ('Pan'), Mrs or Ms ('Pani'), or Miss ('Slecna'). Those with professional titles are addressed as 'Pan', 'Pani', or 'Slecna', plus their professional title and surname.

Business cards may be printed in English or Slovak. Be sure to take an ample supply of cards in order to offer one to each business person you meet. Also include the founding date of your company, if it has been established for a number of years. Remember that giving presents is deeply ingrained in the Slovak culture and token gifts should be taken for all social and business occasions.

Business entertainment is not as common as in other countries. However, the business luncheon is gaining acceptance. One local custom foreigners should observe occurs during a toast. When making a toast, be sure to look the person you are toasting in the eye. Some foreigners are unaccustomed to this practice, and tend to look at the glass instead of the person. Failing to make eye contact is considered rude. Meetings with Slovak business representatives typically include a welcoming toast of an alcoholic beverage, such as *slivovitz* (plum brandy) or *borovicka* (similar to gin).

10
Slovenia

Slovenia was the wealthiest and most export-oriented of the former states of Yugoslavia. When it declared its independence from Yugoslavia on 25 June 1991, it managed to maintain relative stability while its neighbours witnessed conflicts of unimaginable atrocities that swept across their landscape. Consequently, Slovenia experienced one of the most fluid transitions from a communist centrally planned economy to a market economy. Hence its motto, 'A Green Peace of Europe'.

10.1 Basic facts

With its 20,253 sq km, Slovenia is one of the smallest countries in Europe. It lies in an enviable geographical position where the Alps meet the Adriatic, where the Hungarian plain slopes to the sea, and where the German, Slavic, and Latin worlds collide. Slovenia shares borders with Italy, Croatia, Hungary and Austria. To the west, it also has a small coastline (47 km) on the Gulf of Venice in the Adriatic Sea. Mountains, lakes, rivers and thick forests dominate the country. The highest mountain (2,864 m) is called Triglav, which means 'three-headed'. The climate varies from warm along the Adriatic coast to moderate on the eastern plateaus. The total population numbers around two million inhabitants and is relatively homogenous, with 88% Slovenes, 3% Croats, 2% Serbs, 1% Belarusians and a few other minorities. About 70% of the population consider themselves to be Roman Catholic, 3% are Eastern Orthodox, with small Muslim, Protestant and Jewish minorities. It should be noted that these statistics have fluctuated over the years due to refugee flows across the border.

The country is divided into four main geographic regions – Gorenjska (Julian Alps), Zagorska (Danubian Plain), Primorska (Adriatic coastline and Littoral) and Dorenjska (Ljubljana Basin and the Dinaric Mountains). Ljubljana (270,000 inhabitants), the capital of Slovenia, is located in the heart of the country, along the banks of the Ljubljanca River, within a two-hour drive of all the state borders. The second largest city is Maribor (population 92,000), which is on the Drava River, close to the Austrian border.

Slovene is the official language and spoken the most. It is closely related to Croat and Czech. Despite the small size of Slovenia, dialects are numerous and differ greatly. Along the border regions the respective Italian, German, Hungarian and Serbo-Croatian are prevalent. In addition, English is widely understood throughout the country. The education system is very good, with 99% literacy rate for citizens above the age of 15 and 80% of the population having completed secondary school by the age of 22.

The currency is the Slovene tolar (international symbol: SIT); 100 stotin are 1 tolar.

Means of communication

Unlike its neighbours, historically Slovenia's media were relatively free for a socialist country and access to Western media was not a problem. Consequently, Slovenian media today are editorially independent in general, although some of them are government-subsidized. There are several daily newspapers, for example *Delo* (circulation 93,000), *Vecer* (62,000), and *Dnevik* (66,000), which are supported by private investment and advertising and are distributed privately by independent vendors. The largest broadcaster is Radiotelevizija Slovenija (Slovenia Radio-Television), which operates three radio stations, two television channels and relies on government funding. There are also seven other television channels, four of which are independent private stations, and nine major commercial radio stations.

10.2 Historical background

Once part of the Roman Empire, the territory of modern Slovenia initially consisted of four distinct areas, namely Styria, Carniola, Carinthia and Gorizia. South Slavs invaded them in the sixth century AD and established the Slavic Duchy of Carantania, the first Slovene state, in 623. It became part of the Frankish Empire in the 700s. Later, upon the division of Charlemagne's empire (843), the region passed to the Dukes of Bavaria. German missionaries converted Slovenes to Catholicism and German nobles turned them into serfs. In 1335, the provinces of Carinthia and Carniola became hereditary possessions of the Habsburgs. Despite new found prosperity, Germanization drove several Slovenes to preserve a heightened sense of national identity. In particular, many intellectuals educated in Vienna and Paris preferred to write in Slovenian rather than German and initiated the notion of greater autonomy and even of an independent nation.

With Napoleon's victory over Austria, the French ruled the region. They restored the use of Slovenian in schools, incorporated local Slovenes into the reformed government and created the linkage between Slovenes, Croats and Serbs by uniting the Slovenes and South Slavs within the Illyrian provinces. The Habsburgs regained the ascendancy in 1813, but the pride and usage of Slovenian had already taken root. Later, in 1867, when the Habsburg Kingdom became the Dual Monarchy of Austria and Hungary, the Slovenes fell under the jurisdiction of the Austrian Crown. However, it was not until 1907 that Slovenes gained the right to vote.

Following the destruction of the Austro-Hungarian Empire in World War I, Slovenia was annexed to the Kingdom of Serbs and Croats (renamed Yugoslavia in 1929), and in 1919 Austria formally ceded the territory by the Treaty of Saint-Germain. Unfortunately, it was so diverse in terms of ethnic groups, religion, language, and political views that democracy never managed to become entrenched and dictatorship emerged as the only option.

During World War II, Germany, Hungary and Italy occupied the region and the communist-backed Liberation Front became the pillar of the partisan struggle against the occupation. After the war, Slovenia once again joined its neighbours in creating the Federated People's Republic of Yugoslavia, which changed its name in 1963 to the Socialist Federal Republic of Yugoslavia. The process of nationalization began, gradually bringing private business, industry and land ownership under state control.

During the 1980s, Slovenes were bitterly disappointed by the federal system's faults. Against a background of crumbling communist power throughout Eastern Europe, Slovenia held multi-party elections in April 1990. The winning coalition called for independence, which was approved by 90% of Slovenia's population in a referendum. In June 1991, following Serbia's refusal to transfer the country's rotating presidency to the Croatian representative, Slovenia declared its independence. A 10-day war ensued, in which Slovenian troops repelled the Yugoslav forces, thus enabling Slovenia to secure true independence as well as international recognition as a separate republic. A new Slovenian constitution was adopted on 23 December 1991. The first presidential and parliamentary elections were held in December 1992.

10.3 Political environment

According to its 1991 constitution, Slovenia is a parliamentary democracy and constitutional republic. The power of the state is divided into three branches: the legislature, the executive and the judiciary. The legislative branch includes two bodies: the National Assembly (*Državni Zbor*) and National Council (*Državni Svet*). The National Assembly takes the lead on virtually all legislative issues. It has 90 members elected by popular vote (through proportional representation) for a maximum term of four years. The next election will be in October 2004. The National Council is an advisory body with very limited legislative powers, composed of representatives from economic, social, professional, and local interests. Its 22 members are directly elected and 18 appointed for five years by an electoral college. The next elections will be in late 2002.

The president is the head of state and commander-in-chief of the armed forces. He is directly elected by universal adult suffrage for a five-year term. The current president is Milan Kučan, who was re-elected in November 1997. The next election will be in November 2002. The prime minister is nominated by the president and confirmed by the national assembly. The current prime minister is Dr Janez Drnovsek. The council of ministers, or cabinet, is nominated by the prime minister and appointed by the national assembly. So far, Slovenia has enjoyed an exceptionally stable political scene, despite two changes of government in 2000.

The judicial branch is based on civil law and is composed of the supreme court and constitutional court. The supreme court is the highest criminal and civil court in the country. The national assembly elects its judges based on recommendations of the judicial council. The constitutional court settles all disputes between government entities and ensures that laws, decrees and regulatory acts issued by local authorities are consistent with the constitution, international treaties, and the general principles of international law. Its nine judges are appointed by parliament for a non-renewable nine-year term of office upon the recommendation of the president.

Slovenia counts 30 registered political parties, all of which contested the last general elections in 1996. However, the political scene revolves primarily around the Liberal Democracy of Slovenia (LDS), the Social Democratic Party of Slovenia (SDS), the United List of Social Democrats

(ZLSD) and the Slovene People's Party (SLS + SKD), which form the government coalition. Exact figures on total party membership are not readily available.

10.4 Economic environment and infrastructure

Macroeconomic tendencies

The macroeconomic climate in Slovenia is largely favourable as the country is in its 8th year of economic expansion. GDP growth slowed slightly in 2001 to about 3% from a record 5.2% in 1999 as domestic demand fell sharply and external demand weakened. Over the medium term, Slovenia's GDP is forecast to grow steadily at 4–5% per year. Inflation has been steadily declining, but remains in the 8–10% range. It is attributable to higher energy prices, the 1999 VAT introduction and to structural causes – until recently, there was a retrospective full-wage indexation. The tightening of monetary conditions allowed the Bank of Slovenia to announce an inflation goal of 5.8% for 2002. Slovenia aims to reach an inflation level in the 3–4% range by 2004, thus meeting the Maastricht criterion.

The Slovenian tolar has been stable *vis-à-vis* the Euro, the currency targeted by the Bank of Slovenia's managed float regime. Competitiveness remained strong and the current account deficit narrowed to about 0.4% of GDP in 2001. Fiscal deficits have also been relatively small. External debt amounted to slightly over 25% of GDP at year-end 2001, far below the 60% of the Maastricht criterion. The general government deficit represented 1.4% of GDP in 2001, due to higher-than-budgeted wage, consumption, and pension outlays. The budget for 2002 provides for a deficit of 2.5% of GDP, the increase being due only to a change in the method of calculation. Thus, Slovenia clearly continues to meet the respective Maastricht criterion (maximum 3% of GDP).

After a relatively long period of stagnation, the unemployment rate started to rise in 1999 and stabilized around 7% (ILO standards) in 2001. It is likely to remain high, since there is structural, long-term unemployment and a high proportion of unskilled and older workers among the unemployed (47% are unskilled and 47% are above the age of 40). Furthermore, Slovenian unemployment insurance creates perverse incentives for employment, as many recipients of unemployment compensation wait until their benefits are about to expire before taking a new job. The average gross monthly salary in Slovenia in 2000 was 191,669 SIT (approximately US$ 800).

Slovenia enjoys Central Europe's highest standard of living and per capita income (US$ 10,070, comparable to Greece and Portugal). However, this relative prosperity seems to have put the brake on the implementation of certain reforms, particularly on the privatization and foreign investment side. Consequently, the government consumes about 21% of GDP, the public sector accounts for around 45% of GDP, and foreign direct investment has been minimal because of the high level of bureaucratic red tape and the small size of the Slovene market. Fortunately, Slovenia's willingness to join the European Union (EU) in 2004 has recently provided the impetus for a recent increase in efforts to reform. These are now necessary to maintain its long-term competitiveness.

Industry

Industry represents 38.4% of GDP, including manufacturing at about 27.8%. Due to the small size of the domestic market, Slovenian industry is mainly oriented towards export. Its major outputs are metal works, electric power equipment, machine tools, textiles, wood products, paper, food processing, road vehicles, construction, chemicals and pharmaceuticals. The overall industrial production growth rate in 2000 was 6.2%.

Energy

Slovenia has few indigenous resources of oil and relies heavily on imports. Oil is imported essentially through the Adria pipeline (capacity of 15 million barrels per year) that links Slovenia with Croatia and Yugoslavia. The lack of sufficient storage capacity for oil is a clear problem in Slovenia.

Slovenia has proven brown coal resources, which are mainly used for heating and electricity generation. However, given its position as a transit country for pipelined gas, the country seems to be moving towards the use of imported gas. The latter is provided by Russia (60%) through a pipeline that crosses Ukraine, Slovakia, and Austria, and by Algeria (40%) by way of pipeline to Tunisia, then through the trans-Mediterranean pipeline system and Italy.

Electricity generation is fairly evenly split between thermal (43%), hydro power (31%) and nuclear (26%). The only nuclear power plant is the Krsko plant. It is located on the Sava River in western Slovenia and is jointly operated with Croatia. Wood is an important fuel for space heating, particularly in the residential sector. The government's primary focus is on greater energy efficiency with a substantially greater share of energy coming from renewable sources (e.g. hydro power).

Agriculture

Given the small surface of the country, Slovene agriculture represents merely 4% of GDP and employs about 4% of the workforce. It is characterized by the very small size of an average farm (3.2 ha) and its declining importance in macroeconomic terms – although it played and continues to play an important role in maintaining social and territorial equilibrium. Over 90% of agricultural land is privately owned. The major agricultural products are animal husbandry, fodder plants, corn, potatoes, industrial crops, garden products, fruit and wine. The food-processing industry likewise contributes about 4% to GDP and has a 3.2% share in the number of all the people employed. Food-processing is important and is a major importer of raw materials, since its capacity exceeds both the domestic production and the consumption of food products in Slovenia. The major productions are meat, milk, wheat, sugar and oil. Both agriculture and food processing are largely influenced by happenings in Slovenia's process of integration into the EU, as well as environmental protection issues.

Financial sector

Slovenia has a two-tier banking system, with the Bank of Slovenia operating as an independent central bank. Its primary tasks are to ensure the stability of the domestic currency and the liquidity of payments within the country and with foreign countries, as well as to curb inflation. The Bank of Slovenia also supervises the banking system, grants banking licenses and acts as the lender of last resort when necessary.

Slovenia's financial system counts a record number of 25 commercial banks, four savings banks, 68 savings and loan institutions, 42 broking houses, and 17 insurance companies. However, the banking sector is quite concentrated and underdeveloped, since the three largest banks control more than 50% of the assets. The two largest banks – Nova Ljubljanska banka d.d. (NLB), Nova Kreditna banka Maribor d.d. (NKBM) – have been state-owned since the 1993 bank rehabilitation programme. Most other banks are privately owned, with important equity participations and cross-shareholdings. Despite strong capital bases and robust loan portfolios, the banking sector has been over-regulated, which has restricted competition and limited domestic company access to credit. Most banks solely perform a narrow range of traditional activities, require 100% collateral on long-term loans and disregard profitable areas such as new consumer services or investment banking. This is likely to change in the future, as the banking sector is currently undergoing a consolidation process, with several banks engaged in merger talks and the state engaged in gradually privatizing NLB and NKBM, despite considerable opposition to foreign participation in the privatization process.

In order to gradually harmonize Slovenian regulations with those of the EU, Slovenia has recently changed significantly its legal framework governing the regulation and supervision of the banking sector. The new Banking Act allows foreign banks to open branch offices in Slovenia, but so far there are only three subsidiaries of foreign banks and one branch of a foreign bank, resulting in little impact on the structure of the banking system. Individuals and enterprises are also allowed to hold foreign currency accounts in domestic banks. Enterprises may also take loans abroad without incurring penalties. On 1 January 2001 a new deposit-guarantee scheme was introduced in accordance with the EC Directive on Deposit-Guarantee Schemes.

The insurance sector is also concentrated, with the three largest insurance companies controlling 80% of the total market. Life insurance has emerged as a high growth product, but continues to account for only a small share of the total premiums.

The Slovenian Securities and Exchange Commission regulates Slovenia's capital markets, under the authority of the Ministry of Finance. The Ljubljana Stock Exchange (LSE) trades equities, bonds and shares of privatization investment funds. Although it has seen impressive institutional developments over the past few years, its market capitalization remains limited (28% of GDP) and five companies generate around 70% of the turnover. With a few exceptions, Slovenian companies do not yet use the LSE as a means of raising new capital. Currently there are no controls on capital movements, with foreigners being able to trade in Slovenian bonds and equities without restriction.

Telecommunications

Slovenia is among the most developed transition countries in terms of its development of telecommunications networks and services. In anticipation of the liberalization of the market, Telekom Slovenije, the national telecommunications operator, invested US$ 700 million in expansion and modernization projects in order to bring its infrastructure up to Western European standards. Full digitalization of the long-distance fixed network (lines and exchanges) was achieved in 2000, and there are now more than 680,000 fixed-line subscribers. Telekom Slovenije still holds a monopoly on the fixed-line market, but the latter should be progressively liberalized in preparation for EU membership and the privatization process of Telekom Slovenije should be completed in 2003.

The number of mobile phone users continues to rise and now exceeds 55% of the population. The market is still dominated by Mobitel, which is part of the Telekom Slovenije group. However, Slovenia introduced competition in mobile phone operations in 1999 when SiMobil, a second mobile telephone operator, successfully launched services with an entirely new GSM network built by Siemens. The government also handed out licenses for the 1800 MHz mobile phone spectrum, to Mobitel, SiMobil and the US company Western Wireless. The Slovenian government is also expected to hand out licenses for third-generation mobile telephony (UMTS).

Postal facilities and services are of European standard. Internet use is well above the average for Central Europe, with about 20% of Slovenian households connected. The largest Internet service providers are SiOL, a subsidiary of Telekom Slovenije, and Telemach.

Transportation

Because of its location at the crossroads of trade routes linking east and west and north and south, Slovenia's transport infrastructures are key to the country's future. Therefore, the government has committed important resources in order to modernize and extend them.

It has a well-developed road network that includes 6,253 km of categorized state roads, 249 km of expressways and numerous border crossings into neighbouring countries. The country is currently in the process of building a modern expressway system to be completed by 2004. Upon completion, expressways will total around 660 km. The financing of this programme comes from a petrol tax (20% of the retail price of petrol) and motorway tolls.

Rail is a popular and convenient means of transport, with all necessary links to neighbouring countries. Slovene Railways (SZ), a state-owned public company with around 9,000 employees, operates railway transport and owns an upgraded network of 1,201 km of railway track, including 871 km of double-track lines. In recent years, there has been a noticeable trend towards switching transport from road to rail, for both economic and ecological reasons. Major cities also have efficient public transportation systems, essentially relying on buses.

The port of Koper, equipped with modern terminals and facilities, serves as a gateway to Central Europe for Austrian, Hungarian, Czech, German, and Slovak exporters. Other leading ports are Izola and Piran. Given the country's small size, interior air traffic is of lesser importance.

There are three international airports (Ljubljana-Brnik, which accounts for almost all airport traffic in Slovenia, Maribor-Orehova vas and Portoroz) and one national air carrier, Adria Airways.

Tourism

With more than 1.4 million visitors in 2001, tourism is one of the most promising and fast growing sectors of the economy. It employs directly and indirectly over 52,000 Slovenes. Direct income from the hotel and catering industry generates 3.4% of the GDP, while the tourism plus travel industry as a whole generates as much as 9.1% of GDP. Thus, the government has recognized the importance of the tourism sector and has taken a number of initiatives to aid the industry, particularly in terms of promoting and stimulating the development of related activities.

10.5 Legal environment and regulations

Crime and corruption

Slovenia has a low crime rate, and most street crime involves non-violent robbery. Assessing the corruption level of Slovenia is difficult, since, until recently, journalists were penalized for reporting on it. Nevertheless, despite some accusations of insider deals that surrounded the privatization process, there is no significant evidence of official corruption. Slovenian law makes corruption of private firms or public officials a criminal offence, and the state prosecutor's office has jurisdiction for the enforcement of anti-bribery regulations. Since June 2001, Slovenia is a full participant in the OECD Working Group for Combating Bribery in International Business Transactions, a necessary condition for acceding to the OECD Convention on Combating Bribery of Foreign Public Officials in International Business Transactions.

Judicial system, dispute settlement and bankruptcy procedures

As mentioned above, Slovenia has a well developed and impartial judicial system. Its five-tier court system (district, regional, appeals, supreme and administrative courts) operates as an independent branch of government and is not linked to any executive body. However, the judicial system is relatively slow, owing to the lack of judges (relatively low level of pay) and an important backlog of cases. There are currently plans to improve the situation by procedural reforms and systematic use of computers.

In addition to the court system, companies also have access to arbitration. With the consent of both parties, the Court of Arbitration under the

Chamber of Economy hears all domestic and international disputes where companies are involved. Its rulings are final and have the same power as a court ruling. In addition, Slovenia adhered to the 1958 New York Convention on Recognition of Foreign Arbitral Awards and the 1961 European Convention on International Commercial Arbitration. Bankruptcy procedures are well established in Slovenia and are heard by the competent district court. Bankruptcy may take one of three forms: forced settlement (requested by debtor and approved by creditors); bankruptcy administration (requested by debtor or creditors); or forced liquidation (requested by law).

Taxation, accounting, and auditing rules

All companies engaging in commercial activities in Slovenia and/or having their head offices in Slovenia are subject to corporate income tax. The latter is levied on their net profit at a single rate of 25%. Investment allowances may further reduce the actual tax rate. Companies located in special economic zones are taxed on their income at a reduced rate of 10% to the extent the income is generated from their activities in these zones.

Personal income tax is levied on individuals' income at progressive rates, with a minimum rate of 17% and a maximum rate of 50%. The average taxpayer is in the 35% bracket. Estimated tax advances are paid or withheld monthly. After an annual tax assessment, the difference is either paid to the tax authority or returned. In January 1997, a 30% capital gains tax was also introduced on sale of property, shares and securities within less than three years of purchase. Companies must withhold a 25% tax on their distributed dividends to a resident of Slovenia and 15% on dividends transferred abroad, unless otherwise provided for by a tax treaty. So far, 26 agreements to avoid double taxation have been signed. A new law on personal income tax is under preparation and is expected to become effective in 2003.

Slovenian companies are obliged to keep records according to a two-way accounting system that is mainly based on the Companies Law and on accounting standards issued by the Slovenian Institute of Auditors. The Slovenian Accounting Standards (SAS) were adapted from the International Accounting Standards (IAS) in 1993, but there are some differences arising from inflation adjustments and accelerated depreciation schedules. Although Slovenia is not a hyperinflationary economy, financial statements are adjusted for inflation; the resulting revaluations of assets are treated as income, and revaluations of liabilities and equity are treated as expense. Therefore, revaluations have a direct impact on the income statement. As a result, reported profits in SAS are lower than they would have been in IAS (i.e. without inflation adjustments). Therefore, well-capitalized companies may end up having understated ROE, ROA and net margins, while some other ratios will be overstated (P/E). However, one must be careful as inflation adjustments can help companies to increase their per-share book values without any actual profit or activity.

Laws on establishing and conducting business

Establishing a business in Slovenia is now easier than it was, despite an entrenched and sometimes inefficient bureaucracy. The registration process is rather simple and usually takes between three weeks and one month to complete. Interested parties are advised to consult the Chamber of Commerce and retain a local lawyer to speed up the registration process and interact with the local administration without experiencing unexplained delays.

Various forms of business organizations available to foreigners

The Foreign Investment Act permits foreign investors to establish any legal structure provided by the Commercial Companies Act. These include general partnerships (*samostojni podjetnik*, s.p.), limited partnerships (*komanditna druzba*, k.d.) and silent partnerships (*tiha druzba*, s.t.d.), limited liability companies (*druzba z omejeno odgovornostjo*, d.o.o., minimum capital of SIT 2,100,000), joint-stock companies (*delniska druzba*, d.d., minimum capital of SIT 4,100,000), limited partnership with share capital (*komanditna druzba na delnice*, k.d.d., minimum capital of SIT 4,100,000) and economic interest groups. In addition, commercial associations and co-operatives may also be formed in Slovenia. Common entry strategies deployed by foreign companies also include franchising and joint-venture/licensing.

Restrictions on foreign investments

For several years, foreign investment in Slovenia has been heavily restricted for fear that foreigners would buy up the country's most valuable assets, thus threatening Slovenian culture and the national interest. Progressively, the government has shifted its ideology and foresees foreign investment as a catalyst to savings, new technologies and innovative business practices. In 1999, most of the restrictions on foreign investment have been abolished (e.g. the requirement that the managing director of a business be a Slovenian national, or the 50% maximum foreign investment limit in some companies). As of today, there are only a few sectors that suffer from foreign direct investment (FDI) restrictions in Slovenia, and these include military equipment, mandatory pension and health insurance subject to budgetary financing. There are still a few remaining hurdles including a strict foreign take-over legislation for larger companies. Otherwise, foreign investors enjoy national treatment and there are no restrictions on repatriation of profits, provided all tax obligations have been met.

Investment incentives

Slovenian authorities are now offering a number of investment incentives (e.g. tax relief, investment allowances) in order to promote investments by foreign entrepreneurs in Slovenia.

Protection of property rights

Slovenia's intellectual property legislation is comprehensive and compatible with EU standards. The number of intellectual property complaints has been quite low. The 1992 Industrial Property Law grants and protects patents, model and design rights, trademark and service marks, and appellations of origin, while the Copyright and Related Rights Act deals with all fields of modern copyright and related rights law, including computer programmes and new technologies. Slovenia has also signed and implemented the WTO Uruguay Round Agreement on Trade-Related Aspects of Intellectual Property Rights (TRIPS).

There are currently no property disputes in Slovenia, with the exception of those linked to the communist expropriation after World War II. In theory, the government has the right to take away privately or corporately owned property, but must provide adequate compensation in kind or financial.

Entry requirements

A valid passport is required for entry into Slovenia. A visa is not required for a tourist/business stay of up to 90 days.

10.6 Business environment

Privatization

On gaining its independence in 1991, Slovenia began its transition by focusing on stabilization rather than on reforms. Therefore, the country has been relatively slow in privatization and restructuring has taken place only to a limited degree.

As an illustration, the 1992 Ownership Transformation Law stipulated that when a state entity was to become private, it was mandatory to transfer 10% of its total capital to the Slovenian Capital Fund, 10% to the Slovenian Compensation Fund for restitution of nationalized property and 20% to the Slovenian Development Fund for needed restructuring. The remaining 60% could be distributed to 'known owners', e.g. employees, management, relatives, or the public, against ownership coupons. These free coupons were distributed to all Slovenian citizens, who could use them to bid for shares in public auctions, deposit the coupons in investment funds, or redeem them in employee buy-outs. As a consequence, the dispersion of ownership of privatized companies resulted in ineffective shareholder control, slowing down consolidation and structural change.

Foreign ownership was not encouraged. In addition, newly privatized companies were protected from hostile take-overs by a two-year freeze on share-transfers. Therefore, although during 1993–98 around 1,600 companies were privatized, only 13% of them were effectively publicly sold. This situation has been one of the greatest hurdles for Slovenia in its case for accession to the EU. Therefore, the government has planned a more efficient and expedient privatization of the remaining state-owned enterprises, for example the two largest banks, the telecommunication operator, several insurance companies, the iron and steel company Slovenske Zelezarne and some transport infrastructure units, such as Ljubljana airport. However, there is opposition to foreign participation in the banks' privatization process and insurance company privatization is stalled by a court challenge.

Foreign direct investment (FDI)

Slovenia is considered to lag behind in emerging Europe with regard to foreign direct investment (FDI), which totalled only about 16% of GDP at year-end 2000 (compared to around 50% for Hungary and the Czech Republic). However, thanks to revised regulations governing FDI, foreign investment reached a record figure of approximately US$ 500 million in 2001. The main sources of FDI were Austria (41.8%), Germany (12.8%), France (11.6%), Italy (5.9%), and the Czech Republic (4.2%). FDI was most heavily concentrated in manufacturing (47.7%), and in financial intermediation (17.8%), trade (16.8%) and other business activities (11.2%). Among the larger deals, Société Genérale acquired a majority share in SKB Bank and Mobilkom acquired a majority stake in phone operator SiMobil.

Free economic and trade areas

There are two kinds of free-trade zones in Slovenia: free-customs zones (FCZ) and free economic zones (FEZ). A FCZ exempts its users from the payment of customs duties and other trade policy measures until goods are released into free circulation. There are currently six FCZ in Slovenia: Celje, Ljubljana, Maribor, Nova Gorica, Sezana, and Koper. A FEZ grants its users VAT exemption for imports, 10% corporation tax on profits (rather than 25%) and several additional tax concessions. There are currently two FEZ in Slovenia: Maribor and Koper. It should be noted that one or more domestic legal persons may establish a FCZ or a FEZ after obtaining governmental approval and the appropriate tax authority decisions.

Major booming sectors

The sectors offering prospects for significant sales growth Slovenia are automobiles and light trucks, defence industry equipment, electricity, financial services, telecommunications and information technology (hardware and software).

Major trading partners

In 2000, according to data supplied by the Statistical Office, Slovenia exported US$ 10.6 billion's worth (up 11% in real terms) and imported US$ 11.6 billion's worth (up 6% in real terms) of goods. Slovenia's trade was mainly with EU states (63.7% of exports, 67.8% of imports), particularly Germany (27.2% of exports, 19% of imports), Italy (13.6% of exports, 17.4% of imports), France (7.1% of exports, 10.3% of imports) and Austria (7.5% of exports, 8.2% of imports). Although Croatia figures as an important trading partner (7.9% of exports, 4.4% of imports), most of the trade is in fact related to the Krsko nuclear plant, which is jointly operated by the two countries. Slovenia also aims at establishing trade links with parts of the former Yugoslav market, CEFTA countries, the United States and states of the former Soviet Union.

Free-trade agreements

Slovenia was a founding member of the World Trade Organization (WTO) and has concluded free-trade agreements with EU, EFTA and CEFTA countries, the Baltic States, Croatia, Macedonia, Israel and Turkey (not yet operational).

Foreign trade regulations

Most imports are free of quantitative restrictions but import quotas are applied to a few categories of goods (e.g. textiles). Permits or licenses restrict importations in some sectors (e.g. drugs, chemicals, gold and precious metals).

Tariff system

Slovenia applies two classes of import duties. The lower class applies to the EU states and to the states that maintain preferential trade agreements with Slovenia. The higher class applies to other countries. Goods imported temporarily can be totally or partially exempt from customs duties according to relevant customs procedures. When Slovenia accedes to the EU, all tariffs will be eliminated according to EU bylaws, while tariffs for non-EU countries will become obsolete.

Value added tax (VAT)

Value added tax (VAT) was implemented on 1 July 1999, with a transition period until the end of 1999. VAT rates were increased in January 2002 and are now 20% (general) and 8.5% (reduced rate). Excise duties are levied on alcohol and alcoholic beverages, mineral oils, gas and manufactured tobacco.

Major custom documents for importing and exporting

The documents required for importing and exporting are in line with Western countries' requirements. They include transport and customs documents and quality and licenses if necessary. Labels must include the title of the product, address of importer, net quantity, as well as ingredients, nutritional information, storage instructions and other warnings whenever appropriate. Products must also meet the standards established by the Slovenian Institute of Standardization (SIST) or be certified by a foreign authority recognized by the SIST.

10.7 Etiquette and cultural issues

Slovenian managers are well versed in Western-style customs and business practices, with a tendency towards formality. Therefore, formal dress and punctuality is the norm for business and social meetings in Slovenia. It is customary to greet Slovenians with a handshake and address them by their surname. As in Austria and Germany, titles are widely used, including on business cards. Slovenes are a rather reserved people and dislike an aggressive approach by foreign business associates. For them, meetings and discussions are important in developing a business relationship. Decision-making is usually concentrated among senior management in a company, with a very limited delegation of authority. Therefore, negotiations should always include senior managers or key decision-makers. It is also a good idea to use a local agent, since Slovenia is a very relationship-oriented society. The Slovenian Chamber of Commerce is also an excellent source for obtaining more information about potential partners.

11
Turkey

11.1 Basic facts

For centuries, Turkey has embodied a natural bridge between Europe
and the Middle East and served as the passage between the Mediterranean and the Black Sea. In size, Turkey is slightly larger than the US
state of Texas, with a total area of 814,578 sq km. Its population is
around 66.5 million, with an annual growth rate of 1.5%. Istanbul,
its most prominent city, is home to 10 million people and Ankara, the
capital, has a population of 3.7 million. Other large cities include Izmir
(3.2 million) and Adana (1.7 million).

Turkey has borders with eight countries: Bulgaria and Greece in the
west, Georgia, Armenia, Azerbaijan and Iran in the east, and Syria and
Iraq in the southeast. Despite such geographic diversity, the population
is relatively homogeneous, with 80% Turkish and 20% Kurds. The official language is Turkish, although ethnic minority groups speak Kurdish
and Arabic. Turkey is a secular state, with 99.8% of the population
adhering to Sunni Islam as their religion. Christians and Jews make up
the remaining 0.2%. Life expectancy at birth for the total population
is about 72 years, averaging 68.89 years for men and 73.71 years for
women. The infant mortality rate is 47.3 for every 1,000 live births. The
literacy rate over the age 15 is 85%, with men averaging 94% and
women 77%.

Depending upon the geography and the season, the climate varies
considerably. In the coastal areas the climate is quite moderate. However, inland, particularly in mountainous areas, the climate is much
harsher, with very hot, dry summers and cold, wet winters. Generally,
temperatures in the northeast fall below −35 °C in winter, while the
southeast may experience desert-like temperatures as high as 45 °C

during the summer months. Turkey is susceptible to recurrent earthquakes and seismic activity as it lies along an important fault line.

11.2 Historical background

Turkey has been home to many of the oldest recorded civilizations. Through migration and military conquest, numerous peoples – Hittites, Lydians, Greeks, Romans, Ottomans, Europeans and Turks – have inhabited Turkey. The Ottoman Empire had perhaps the greatest influence on the historical development of modern Turkey. Beginning in the fifteenth century under the rule of Sultan Osman, the Ottoman Empire established itself as a dominant power that lasted for 200 years, and in the seventeenth century fell into a slow decline as it began to suffer military defeats. The Russian Tsar, Nicholas I, referred to the declining empire as 'the Sick Man of Europe'. It was not until the nineteenth century that the Ottoman Empire instituted new reforms and adopted Western ideas. Seemingly on the road to recovery, the Ottoman Empire was yet again defeated in World War I and found itself divided into three protectorates – Greek, French and British.

On 29 October 1923, Turkey gained its freedom as a result of the War of Independence led by Mustafa Kemal 'Atatürk'. Kemal was elected president and led the country for 15 years until his death. Under his leadership, Turkey became a republic and underwent profound changes. A new constitution was introduced; the legal, administrative, and educational structures were changed; a single-party system was adopted and a secular state was established; polygamy was outlawed, and women were given the vote and could be elected to office.

Following World War II, Turkey witnessed the development of a multi-party system, and suffered three military coups/regimes, and general political instability. In the 1980s, the country pursued a market-driven economic policy and launched a process of liberalization and privatization. A written constitution, providing for a parliamentary system, was adopted in 1982.

11.3 Political environment

In 1982, the Turkish parliament ratified a new constitution, which redefined the country's political system as a secular, parliamentary democracy with three distinct branches – executive, legislative and judicial – with universal suffrage from the age of 18. The president, the parliament, the military, and the major political parties are the most influential forces in the country's political and economic spheres. However, the labour unions, the private sector and the Kurdistan Workers' Party (PKK) may also directly influence Turkey's political and economic stability.

The executive branch includes two key leadership posts, the president, who serves as head of state, and the prime minister, who heads the national government. This branch also has a council of ministers (or cabinet), which serve as advisers. The president, chosen by the 550-member parliament (Turkish Grand National Assembly), serves for a single seven-year term and cannot be re-elected. Ahmet Necdet Sezer was elected president in May 2000. The next presidential elections will take place in May 2007.

The 550 members of parliament (Meclis) are elected for a five-year term in national elections. Seats are allocated on the basis of proportional representation. However, only parties which win 10% or of the votes qualify for seats. The last elections were held in March 1999, when Bulent Ecevit of the DSP (Democratic Left Party) was elected to head a three-party coalition, which included the MHP (Far Right Party) and the Anap (Centre Right 'Motherland' Party). The next elections are scheduled for April 2004.

The leading political parties in Turkey include the Welfare Party (RP), the centre-right: the True Path Party (DYP) and the Motherland Party (Anap), the centre-left: the Democratic Left Party (DSP) and the Republican People's Party (CHP), – the nationalist right: the Nationalist Action Party (MHP), and the independent pro-Kurdish People's Democracy Party (Hadep).

The judicial system is based on a court system, which includes state security courts, the Constitutional Court, High Court of Appeals, and the Council of State and High Council of Judges and Prosecutors. State security courts handle offences that threaten the democratic freedom and values of the state. The Constitutional Court is responsible for reviewing legislation. The High Council of Judges and Prosecutors oversees the courts. Freedom of speech and religion and the right to strike are recognized by the State.

The legal system in Turkey, which maintains an independent judiciary, was modelled on various continental European systems. Civil, administrative and military matters are each treated separately. The Turkish Army is the self-appointed guardian of secularism in Turkish society. Although it has no official political role, for better or worse the military has assumed the responsibility of maintaining the separation of 'church and state'. International organizations, such as the International Monetary Fund (IMF), the World Bank, and the

European Union (EU), play an indirect role in influencing government policies.

11.4 The Cyprus Question

In 1960, the United Kingdom granted Cyprus its independence, under which Turkish Cypriots and Greek Cypriots enjoyed equal political power. The issue of Cyprus came to a head in 1963 when the Greek Cypriots ousted the Turkish Cypriots from all governmental positions. Since that time, the Turkish government has recognized only the Turkish Republic of Northern Cyprus, which its forces invaded in 1974 allegedly to protect Turkish Cypriots. Since then, the Greek Cypriots have made several attempts to gain control of all of Cyprus. Although the UN has initiated several rounds of talks to address and ultimately resolve the Cyprus issue, the talks have produced no positive results. However, ambitions to join the EU have caused the two states, supported by Greece and Turkey, to move towards a degree of conflict resolution and talks resumed in January 2002.

The Kurdish terrorism/independence movement

Since 1984, the Kurdistan Workers' Party (PKK) has been at the centre of terrorist acts, primarily targeting southeastern Turkey, where it hoped to establish an independent state. It has focused its attacks mainly on Turkish security forces, state facilities and anti-PKK government supporters. In retaliation, the Turkish government has initiated several air and ground strikes against the Kurdish separatists. The 15-year battle has resulted in over 30,000 deaths, including scores of civilians. In April 1999, Abdullah Öçalan, the Kurdish separatist leader, was captured and given a death sentence. The arrest marked the beginning of the government's 'counter-attack' to restore security to the southeastern part of the country. However, Öçalan's death sentence was controversial, especially since it could jeopardize Turkey's accession to the EU, which strictly opposes the death penalty. Besides, many observers believe that carrying out the death sentence would only incite more violence among Kurdish separatists.

Human rights

Turkey has frequently been under public scrutiny because of its human rights violations. Although the current constitution serves to protect the civil liberties of all Turks, police abuse, such as torture, killings and delayed trials, are common. There are limitations to freedom of speech, such as the media's constraint in its portrayal of the military, the president or parliament. In addition, Kurdish separatists located in the Eastern parts of the country have been subjected to deadly violence.

11.5 Economic environment

Turkey is considered the 16th largest economy in the world, with national income totalling approximately US$ 410 billion. According to World Bank figures, the country's GDP was slightly below US$ 200 billion and GNP per capita slightly above US$ 3,000 in 2000. The United States Department of Commerce and the Export Forum of the United Kingdom have designated Turkey as one of the ten biggest emerging markets. Turkey's main economic partner is the EU, with the UK accounting for 7.1% of exports. The share of Turkey's exports is 17.1% to Germany, 7.8% to the United States, 7.4% to Italy, 7.1% to the UK, and 5.7% to France. Top exporters to Turkey include Germany, Russia, Italy, France, USA and the UK. The UK exports about US$ 2.3 billion to Turkey, which recently became a member of the new G-20 Group. Turkey's foreign debt in 2001 was about US$ 116 billion.

The 1980s saw dramatic changes in Turkey's economy. Its protectionist, state-controlled economy was transformed into a market-driven economy that contributed to a rise in exports, a drop in taxes, privatization of various sectors, and global economic integration. As a result of these changes, Turkey's annual growth rate was the highest of any OECD country. The early 1990s witnessed a further period of transition. Indeed, in that period, Turkey experienced economic growth, combined with greater political freedom. Unfortunately, by 1994 the country was suffering the effects of a financial crisis that led to a recession. In 1995, the authorities decided to revise the constitution and by 1996, the country had signed customs union agreements with the EU. It had also obtained an IMF loan agreement, which fostered growth and prosperity. However, as a result of EU trade liberalization, Turkey incurred a high level of national debt and a widening trade deficit. In December 1999, its candidacy for eventual membership of the EU was unanimously approved by the European Council at its meeting in Helsinki.

The nature of Turkish politics threatened to hold back the country on its path to becoming a fully developed market. Poorly run state-controlled industries contributed to high inflation and a growing current account deficit were key factors in inciting the January 1994 financial crisis. As a result, the Turkish lira depreciated dramatically. The reaction of the Turkish government was to implement a strict economic programme designed to privatize loss centres, modernize the social security system, and implement efficient tax collection methods. However, the results of this programme were dismal. GNP plummeted to 6% and spiralled to 150%. The only positive result was the increase in exports due to the currency depreciation, which created a surplus in the current account balance.

During the mid-1990s, Turkey's economic volatility continued. In 1995, GNP rose 8% and inflation was about 80%. Economic observers remained cautious due to the political instability and the continued rise in the budget deficit, a result of increased government borrowing to pay its debts. Inflation rates continued to fluctuate and the balance of payments was showing a deficit. However, the high level of foreign exchange reserves in the mid-1990s lessened the probability of another financial crisis.

On 1 January 1996, Turkey signed a customs union agreement with the EU. This provided for the free movement of certain goods between the EU and Turkey, which were exempt from customs duties or quota restrictions. It was a positive step towards Turkey's goal of a free-market economy.

In August and November 1999, the country fell victim to two disastrous earthquakes. The August earthquake occurred in the Marmara region, the most densely populated area and the region considered the 'industrial heartland' of Turkey. The earthquake measured between 7.4 and 7.8 on the Richter scale, killed over 17,000 people and left 200,000 homeless. The international community responded quickly by providing over US$ 20.6 million in relief funds. In November 1999, a second earthquake struck in the northwestern province of Bolu, 100 km east of Izmit. The death toll reached 845 and more than 5,000 people were injured. The total loss was estimated at US$ 5.5 billion. An agreement between the Turkish government and the European Investment Bank granted Turkey US$ 600 million in loans primarily to restore its infrastructure. Any moneys remaining were to be allocated to refurbishing small and medium-sized enterprises.

Turkey still faces several economic adversities, including the volatility of the lira, high inflation, and domestic debt. In an effort to bring the country out of recession and to boost the banking sector, the government has passed legislation to attract capital to the banks through the issue of convertible bonds. The government is committed to abide by the IMF contentions and is in line to receive additional funds, including US$ 12 billion under a three-year agreement.

Although the government has made some headway in reviving the economy, much remains to be done. By the end of 2001, real GDP had fallen by 7%, industrial output was down 9.2%, the unemployment rate reached 8%, and inflation was over 67%. The foreign trade deficit declined dramatically during 2000–01, showing a deficit of US$ 7.5 billion in 2001 compared to US$ 19.1 billion in 2000. The current account showed a surplus of US$ 2.5 billion, largely due to the smaller deficit and to the increase in tourism, which was up by 17%. The Istanbul Stock Exchange also responded well to the IMF agreement.

In 2001–02, Turkey faced a major economic crisis due to mismanagement, resistance to implementing necessary reforms, and a measure of political bickering. In fact, the financial crisis was triggered by a public squabble between prime minister Bülent Ecevit and president Ahmet Necdet Seze. The crisis compelled the government to renounce the crawling-peg exchange-rate system. Fortunately for Turkey, a multi-billion dollar, IMF-led international support programme was put in place just in time to save the country from a situation similar to what has recently taken place in Argentina. The strengthened US$ 19 billion IMF stand-by programme was put together to deal with the fundamental structural problems that have thwarted better economic results. Undoubtedly, both Turks and outside observers concur that the country needs to strengthen its banking system and eliminate the prospect of a new round of flawed loans on such a scale as to provoke systemic risk and macroeconomic instability, as happened in recent years. Since his appointment in March 2001, all hopes have been put on Kemal Dervis – the economics minister and highly regarded economist and former World Bank vice-president for the Middle East and North Africa – to implement the consolidated IMF programme. Given the likely resistance from various political quarters in Turkey, it is difficult to predict how successful he will be. But, there is no doubt that Turks are aware that with this IMF-backed programme, the country has a genuine opportunity to reform its economy and lay the foundation for a steadier and more sustainable growth path. No doubt such success would also improve Turkey's chances of accession to the EU.

Infrastructure

Turkey has one of the heaviest transportation infrastructures in the Near East and this facilitates passenger and commercial travel throughout the country. Twenty-two public airports support domestic travel and five of them serve international destinations. Istanbul, Izmir, and Ankara serve as international gateways. Turkey has 21 international ports with a total of 548 vessel berths.

The road system handles 85% of cargo traffic and 94% of passenger traffic. There are almost 400,000 km of highways, one-third of which are paved. A major toll highway, close to completion, will link the capital, Ankara, to Istanbul. The railway system provides train service between the most Western points to the eastern borders. One 'high speed' train runs between Ankara and Istanbul. Turkey is also served by several major courier services, including DHL, Federal Express, UPS, and Air Express International.

Labour

In 2000, the Turkish workforce was made up of 22 million people, with 40% employed in the service sector, 35% in agriculture, and 25% in the industrial sector, including construction. Approximately 1.5 million Turks work abroad, mostly in Germany. Unemployment in 2000 reached 6.6%. Although women account for a little less than half of the population (31.4 million), they make up only 25% of the workforce, of whom 60% work in the agricultural sector. The average annual growth in the workforce is 2.4%.

Telecommunications

There are 19.5 million fixed telephone main lines in use, in addition to 12.1 million mobile phones. In 1996, 26% of the population subscribed to a telephone line; in 2000, that number practically doubled, reaching 50%. Turkey is experiencing a rapid expansion of fibre-optic cable lines and digital microwave radio relays to meet the increasing demand for mobile phone service. There are 22 Internet service providers and approximately two million Internet users. The principal media include newspapers, television (69 broadcasting stations), and AM/FM and shortwave radio stations. About one third of the total Turkish population owns television sets.

Transportation

As indicated earlier, there are 382,397 km of highway in Turkey, with only 95,599 km paved, including 1,560 km of expressways. There are 10,413 km of railways. Inland waterways account for 1,200 km. Major ports, such as Gemlik, Hopa, Iskenderun, Istanbul, Izmir, Kocaeli (Izmit), Icel (Mersin), Samsun, and Trabzon, have 548 vessel berths. Although there are 117 airports, only 81 have paved runways and only 16 are considered major. In addition, the country possesses two heliports.

Agriculture and industry

Turkey is a major producer of agricultural products, including cotton, sugar, beets, hazelnuts, wheat, barley, olives, fruit, certain animal products, and tobacco. Agriculture accounts for 15% of GNP. The output of the agricultural industry has made the country self-sufficient in terms of food production. Moreover, Turkey is rich in natural resources, which include coal, chromium, mercury, copper, iron ore, sulphur, boron and oil. Hence, the major industries found in Turkey are textiles, food processing, mining, steel, chemicals, petrochemicals, construction, lumber and paper. The chief exports are clothing and other finished textile products, electrical and non-electrical machinery and appliances, vehicles, iron and steel, and fruit and vegetables, valued at US$ 15.2 billion.

Core industries

There are 21 automobile and lorry manufacturers currently operating in Turkey, primarily as joint ventures or wholly owned subsidiaries, resulting in low demand and saturation of the domestic market. By contrast, vehicle exports increased by 60% as of 1999. The primary export destinations include Germany, USA, the UK, Italy, France and the Netherlands. The transport sector has remained a priority for the government. This was particularly highlighted in 1994 when, because many state projects were put on hold, the planning and construction of airports, ports and highways was reinstated.

Textiles are Turkey's largest manufacturing industry. It represents the largest export sector, where increased growth has resulted from the customs union agreement signed with the EU and the 'global phase-out of textile quotas called for in the Uruguay Round'.

Major booming sectors

Energy, telecommunications and tourism are the country's main growth industries. The automotive industry, transport and textiles remain the core of the Turkish economy. Its energy market is the fastest growing in Europe and represents a US$ 8–US$ 10 billion annual market. The demand for electrical energy has been growing at about 8% a year. According to Turkish officials, by 2010 oil consumption will approach 45 million tons. Several pipeline projects are underway and expected to meet this demand and the government has committed an investment of close to US$ 60 million over the next ten years for this sector. In 2002, Turkey expects to have 20 million telephone subscribers, a 64% increase over 1993. The telephone line density, it is estimated, will rise to 25 per 100 persons, from 21 per 100 in 1993. It is expected that the system will be 80% digital.

Turkey has seen a boom in its tourist industry. The diversity and richness of the country offers something for every visitor, from swimming in the Mediterranean to skiing in the mountains. The country has been engrossed in developing hotels and resorts to keep abreast of tourist growth. The industry saw a 39.3% increase in its tourist arrivals during 1999–2000, from 7.5 million to a record 10.4 million foreign visitors. The 11 September attack on the United States caused a slight decline in the months that followed. However, 2001 still saw one million more tourists than the previous year. Germany provides the largest tourist market in Turkey, and the UK is second.

In 1991, the Environment Ministry was established, and this brought about an increased recognition of environmental issues. Regulations on issues such as sewage, medical waste and power plant emissions, have also contributed to a growing awareness of the importance of the environment.

Trade

During the past six years, Turkey has signed or has been in the process of elaborating free-trade agreements (FTA) with 52 countries. Twelve of these are now in force with Israel, Romania, Lithuania, Hungary, Estonia, the Czech Republic, Slovakia, Bulgaria, Poland, Slovenia, Latvia and Macedonia. In addition, Turkey has established strong trade relations with the United States and the EU, with which it has signed FTAs. Negotiations with Morocco, Egypt, the Faroe Islands, Palestine and Tunisia are under way. In 1985, in an effort to promote export and import activity, Turkey passed the Free Zones Law. Today, there are eight free-trade zones (FTZ) in the country and these foster the freedom to trade and perform various business activities exempt from customs or trade regulations. Five additional FTZs are in the process of being approved. Additionally, 20 organized industrial zones are in place for the promotion of industrial activities.

As of August 1999, UK companies had set up 391 joint ventures in country. The UK was the sixth largest foreign investor in Turkey with an estimated US$ 1.8 billion in foreign capital invested. Other leading foreign investors were France, USA, the Netherlands, Germany, Switzerland, Italy and Japan. British and Turkish trade relations are rooted in history. Trade volume has increased by 1,000% over the last 25 years, from US$ 414 million to US$ 4.1 billion.

Crime and environment issues

Drug trafficking is frequently tied to countries where terrorist activities are present and Turkey is no exception. The Kurdish PKK has allegedly been involved in drug trafficking and has also been accused of using drug profits to finance its terrorist activities against the Turkish government. The country's geographical location has made it a major channel for trafficking illegal drugs. In 1996, Turkey passed a Law to Prevent Money Laundering in an effort to control and 'crack down' on drug trafficking. It stipulates zero tolerance for the possession, dealing in and use of illegal drugs and provides for the enforcement of strict penalties in the form of heavy fines and/or jail sentences.

Environmental issues include air and water pollution, particularly from chemical and toxic wastes, deforestation in urban areas, and earthquakes, primarily in the Northern part of the country.

Incentives for foreign investments

Foreign investors have relative freedom in investment activities in Turkey. All rights, incentives, exemptions and privileges available to national capital and business are available to foreign business and capital. 'Foreign firms are eligible to participate in government financed and/or subsidized research and development programmes on the same basis as nationals.' Foreign companies may hire expatriates as managers or technical staff. There is no requirement to hire local workers. Obtaining visas or work permits is a relatively easy process.

Investment incentives, identified in specific regulations, include exemptions on corporate and value added tax, customs fees, and duties, as well as soft loans for research and development investments. To increase exports, Turkey has set up eight FTZs. Furthermore, the government has offered additional incentives (accelerated depreciation, tax credits) to encourage foreign and local investments in Turkey's underdeveloped regions and industries. Manufacturing, export and tourism are sectors that the government has targeted as the primary areas for investment.

11.6 Legal environment and regulations

Foreign firms may generally retain 100% ownership of their companies. However, in the radio and broadcasting industry this is limited to 20% equity ownership, and 49% in the aviation and maritime transportation industry. Acquiring and disposing of interest in other companies is permitted. Under the Foreign Investment Law No. 6224, there is no restriction on the repatriation of capital, profits, fees, and royalties. However, the financial services sector, including banking and insurance, and the petroleum sector, require permission from the government to start up a business. Mining and processing of borax, uranium, and thorium is limited to the state. The postal system is also government-owned.

Due to high inflation rates and fluctuations in the relative value of the Turkish lira (TL) – which is fully convertible – US dollars and German marks (now implicitly expressed in Euros) are used as the primary monetary denominations in international transactions. Foreign firms may retain their own currency when establishing a company in Turkey; conversion into Turkish lira is unnecessary. Banks borrow and lend in foreign currencies on the foreign exchange market. As a result of recent devaluations, the Turkish lira exchanged at 164,000 to the US dollar in May 2002. This constitutes a sharp drop from a year earlier when the dollar was worth only 679,051 TL.

The Turkish authorities have gradually eased legislation governing foreign investment, thus creating a rather more liberal and favourable investment environment. Today, Turkey complies with WTO rules pertaining to intellectual property laws and has made improvements in its tender law for greater transparency. Unfortunately, the court system remains overstrained and sluggish, even if the judiciary is believed to be quite unbiased in commercial affairs. Furthermore, at the beginning of 2000, the country adopted a law that permits international settlement of disputes between the state and foreign investors; hitherto, the law was restricted to Turkish courts.

Because of its ineffectiveness and its excessively centralized administration, the Turkish authorities have made tax system reform a priority. In order to attract foreign direct investment (FDI), the authorities have reduced corporation tax rates. They have also launched an array of incentives to induce foreign investors to come to Turkey. Unfortunately, despite the government's willingness to facilitate the tax system, the tax structure remains convoluted and, hence, needs to be made simpler. The government has announced that a new set of tax reforms will be introduced before the end of 2002.

Competitive environment

There are over 5,000 foreign firms in Turkey with total cumulative investments approximating US$ 13 billion. The EU has 2,420 companies operating in Turkey, the largest share in terms of number of companies. Of all the EU member states, Germany has the highest number of companies in Turkey, with 919 firms; the Netherlands is second with 313 firms, the UK third with 330 and France fourth with 248. The Netherlands has the highest capital inflow into Turkey, followed by France, the USA, and Germany.

Several well-known global companies have invested in Turkey, particularly in the banking, consumer goods, automobile, and pharmaceutical industries. These include American Express, Citibank, Dresdner Bank, Saudi

American Bank, Alcatel, Bayer, Castrol, Ciba-Geigy, Ciment Français, Coca Cola, Colgate-Palmolive, Conrad, Daimler-Benz, Dupont De Nemours, General Electric, General Motors, Henkel, Ford Motor Co., Lockheed, Gillette, Goodyear, Hilton International, Hoechst, Honda, Kumagai Gumi, McDonald's, Nestlé, Mobil, Nabisco, Philips, Philip Morris, Pfizer, Pirelli, Procter and Gamble, and Renault.

Pricing

Undoubtedly, Turkish consumers value quality, and pricing reflects this reality. Foreign firms must understand the pricing structure to remain competitive. The European Free Trade Association (EFTA) and EU countries do not have to pay duty on imports.

Advertising

Advertising is most effective by publicizing one's product and/or service through trade associations and the national chambers of commerce and industry, and in industry publications, on television and in newspaper advertisements. Foreign investors may consider major newspaper publications, such as *Dunva, Cumhuriyet, Hurriyet, Milliyet* and *Sabah,* as well as weekly periodicals, such as *Anka Haber, Barometre, Briefing and Ebareport,* and monthlies including *Bilgisayar, Bt/haber, Finans Dunvasi, Turkey,* and *Yazilim, Donanim.*

Promotion

Trade shows, seminars, and exhibits are widely used to introduce and promote products in the country. Most of these events take place in the bigger cities. Foreign and domestic firms have the opportunity to evaluate and meet current competition. Brochures with details of these events are widely available. Foreign companies that wish to advertise by such means can contact qualified distributors and/or agents, which are vital in assisting foreign firms to establish themselves in Turkey. Specifically, they serve as the indispensable intermediary between the firm and the government bureaucracies. Foreign companies looking to do extensive business with government agencies should consider agents from Ankara or Istanbul firms. Developing personal contacts and relationships are essential to the marketing process. There are also some outstanding market research firms, such as Beliçim in Istanbul.

Privatization

The 1980s represented a period of economic reforms. The private sector replaced government's central role in the economy. Today, the private sector is Turkey's driving economic force. In 1994, a privatization law was adopted and by 1995, the government had sold more than US$ 500 million in assets. However, this was far below the US$ 2 billion target. Privatization has remained moot since then due to political instability and frequent policy changes continue to affect certain private business sectors.

State-owned enterprises have continually been a burden for the Turkish economy. Increasing budget deficits have done little to increase the public's confidence in the government and to enable Turkey to regain its economic footing, experts feel that the country needs to remove inefficiencies and tighten its tax administration to reduce tax evasion. The sale of Turk Telecom is still planned for 2002, although the sale of the national carrier, Turkish Airlines, has been delayed. Since 1986, foreign companies have been able to take part in the private sector through government block sales in selected industries, including cement, iron and steel, appliances, automotive, telecommunications, textiles, and aviation sectors. Public offerings are another method that the Turkish government has used to privatize specific economic enterprises.

11.7 Conducting and implementing business

Mode of entry

The Under-Secretariat of the Treasury (UFT), General Directorate of Foreign Investment (GDFI), is the agency responsible for granting permission to foreign investors interested in establishing a company or branch office or investing in an existing company in Turkey. The Foreign Investment Law of 1954 has guided foreign investment activities in Turkey. In the 1980s, in the light of Turkey's need to expand its economy, the Law was revised to encourage FDI. Besides, a recent amendment has made it possible for foreign companies to obtain loans from abroad without GDFI approval. The process may take up to 3–4 weeks.

Business structures

Possible business structures include the Anonim Sirket (AS), a joint-stock company, a Limited Sirket (LS), a limited liability company, and branch.

The AS is the better structure for firms with larger projects. It enables the firm to attract a greater number of stockholders and secure bank support. Insurance companies and banks are examples of AS. In general, the AS requires a minimum capital of TL 5 billion with 20% paid-in capital contributed to a legal reserve, a minimum of five founders, and an annual shareholder meeting and annual audit. The board of directors heads the AS issued shares may include ordinary, preferred, multiple-vote, and non-voting shares.

The LS is more applicable to sales and distribution companies. In general, LS entities have smaller administrative costs and fewer constraints. Specifically, the LS requires a minimum capital of TL 500 million with 20% paid-in capital contributed to legal reserves, and no less than two founders but no more than 50. Annual audits are required only if there are more than 20 partners. Participation shares are the only type of share issued.

Branches are subject to similar requirements to the AS or LS. In addition, an authorized commercial representative, resident in Turkey, must manage the branch.

Licensing

Licensing is under the direction of the Under-Secretariat for the Treasury, which oversees the licensing agreement between the Turkish company and the foreign investor. The required registration indicates that the licence will provide training, services and/or goods and expertize and defines regulations concerning the quality of manufacturing, factory capacity, copyright and other such issues. As licensing has grown in recent years due to privatization and an increase in FDI into Turkey, a number of foreign companies have entered into various licensing agreements, such as Yatap and Dupont, LM Ericsson of Sweden and Ericsson Cukurova Telekomunikasyon, and Yalim Serbest Musavirlik and Andersen worldwide.

Acquisitions

Acquisition of a Turkish company no longer falls under the guise of foreign investment. As a result, acquisitions have become more frequent in recent years with the opening of the Turkish markets – Siemens acquired 60% of Profilo, a Turkish holding company, for close to $100 million and Nestlé purchased 25% of Mis Sut, a Turkish dairy company.

Franchising

The UFT and GDFI are strong supporters of franchises, as these provide opportunities for local employment, transfer of technology and expertize, and create healthy competition in a free-market economy. Under the master franchise agreement, the foreign investor may repatriate royalty revenue minus a 10% tax deduction.

McDonald's was the first franchise in Turkey. Since that first entry in 1986, franchises have boomed in urban areas and spread into the smaller cities and towns, particularly in the fast food and clothing sectors. The Turkish Franchising Association (UFRAD), founded in 1991, is an association of franchisors in Turkey. There is currently no specific regulation of franchise sales or the franchise relationship in Turkey and there is no government legislative body, department or agency that is considering the specific regulation of franchise sales or the franchise relationship. There are no laws that make it difficult for a foreign franchisor to use one or more forms of transnational franchising in Turkey.

11.8 Business customs

Greetings are the first step towards building a business relationship. Foreign business people may shake hands with both men and women. Using a title to address one's counterpart shows a sign of respect, particularly when it is someone older. The visitor may witness a more 'traditional' greeting between Turkish men that involves shaking the right hand and kissing both cheeks. The left hand is not and should not be used in greeting, gesturing or eating, as it is considered unclean in Muslim societies. Business meetings will usually be conducted in English or German and to a lesser extent in French.

The foreigner should dress appropriately and formally. One's attire is very important, as it will indicate the value the individual places on the business at hand. Men should wear a jacket and tie with a long sleeved shirt, and women should wear a conservative dress and stockings. Crossing one's legs when seated is inappropriate and showing the bottom of one's foot is considered offensive. Although Turkey is a liberal society, touching or showing affection in public is still not acceptable.

Lateness or cancelled meetings are not uncommon and keeping a guest waiting is customary. Although tardiness is excusable, foreigners should avoid being late. Meetings will typically start by inquiring about one's health and trip. As in near eastern societies, it is rude to begin talking about business straight away. Personal relationships are vital in doing business in Turkey. It is whom you know rather than what you know that matters.

General culture

The Turkish culture is a rich mixture of tradition and modernity. Much of the traditional artwork, such as carpet weaving and ceramics, has been preserved and remains an integral part of the country's heritage.

Since the reform movements of the 1920s, Turkey has been influenced by various Western cultures in its art, music, literature, and drama.

Although a secular state since the 1920s, Islam accounts for 98% of the population. Christianity and Judaism comprise the remaining 2%. The major holidays include New Year's Day, National Day (29 October), Ramadan, Sugar Days (a feast celebrating the end of fasting in the month of Ramadan), Ataturk's Day (19 May), and Children's Day (23 April).

Ramadan is the principal religious period of Islam, which lasts for 29 or 30 days (depending on the lunar calendar). During this period, fasting is required of all Muslims from sunrise to sunset. It is not appropriate for foreigners visiting Turkey during Ramadan to smoke, drink or eat in public. Tourists may find hotels open, which serve regular meals. However, as in the rest of the Muslim world during Ramadan, foreign business people should expect reduced working hours.

Although traditional dress is worn in rural areas, men and women living in urban locations demonstrate a Western influence in their choice of clothing. Women have attained more freedom and acceptance in everyday life since 1934, when they gained the right to vote and the right to divorce, and polygamy was abolished. However, certain traditional values still remain. This is primarily seen in the family structure where patriarchal values prevail, particularly in rural areas. In Turkey, the family comes first. This includes the extended family, which is an important part of the family unit. It is not uncommon for married children to live in their parents' household until they become self-sufficient. Islamic tradition forbids eating pork and drinking alcohol but the consumption of alcohol is common. The main dietary staples are lamb, rice and seafood, and Turkish coffee and/or tea accompanies every meal.

Entertaining guests is an important part of life and Turks are very hospitable. Refusing an invitation would be ill mannered. When invited to a Turkish home, calling ahead and bringing a gift, such as candy, fruit or flowers is customary. Taking off one's shoes upon entering the host's home may be required. It is not recommended to give bad news while visiting a friend or relative in his/her home. Although smoking is not forbidden, it is important to ask others present before doing so.

Negotiation style

Negotiation in Turkey is an art. Establishing relationships and trust is the key to conducting business in the country. This takes time and, therefore, decisions are not made quickly. Bargaining is an expected part of the negotiation ritual. Maintaining personal integrity and refraining from embarrassing one's counterpart is extremely important. Negotiations are fraught with emotion and experience. As a number of Turkish business people have received their degrees in European and American institutions, they are knowledgeable about the various tactics used by their counterparts from those places. Prolonged small talk precedes the negotiation process, as Turks seek to build trust and establish a good relationship before making a deal. Building trust is important because Turks take a long time to trust strangers, that is, those outside of the family and friends.

11.9 Conclusion

Turkey has faced a number of important challenges in recent years. The many economic challenges include enhancing stability by reducing fiscal and trade deficits; ending the boom–bust cycle and achieving moderate, sustainable growth; adopting more prudent policies, such as increasing monetary reserves and improving tax collection; improving economic indicators by reducing inflation, interest rates, and unemployment; and opening the economy to market forces by eliminating government subsidies, increasing privatization, and increasing the competitiveness of local businesses.

Moreover, Turkey has had to cope with political, social, and environmental problems. It has been involved in complex maritime, aerial, and territorial disputes with Greece over Cyprus for more than 40 years, the Hatay question with Syria, and ongoing water disputes with both Syria and Iraq over the development of the Tigris and Euphrates rivers. However, despite these challenges, Turkey remains an attractive market. The new business elite is extremely dynamic. Most foreign business observers agree that Turkey has an outstanding potential to become a very lucrative market.

12
Ukraine

12.1 Basic facts

Situated at the intersection between Central Europe and Russia, Central
Asia and the Middle East, Ukraine is an important emerging market with
substantial potential for growth in both trade and foreign investment.
With its 603,700 sq km, Ukraine is the second largest country in Europe,
slightly larger than France. It shares borders with numerous key Eastern
European countries, including Belarus (891 km) in the north, Russia
(1,576 km) in the northeast and east, Poland (428 km) in the northwest,
Slovakia (90 km) in the west, and Hungary (103 km), Moldova (939 km),
and Romania (531 km) in the southwest. The Black Sea and the Sea of
Azov form the southern coastline (2,782 km) of Ukraine. The landscape
of Ukraine consists mostly of fertile plains and plateaus, the main geographical zones being steppe, wood-steppe and mixed woodlands.
Mountains are found only in the west (the Carpathian Mountains, with
Mount Goverla, 2,061 m) and the far south (the Crimean Peninsula,
with Mount Roman-Cosh, 1,545 m). In most of the country, the climate
is temperate continental with cold winters and warm summers, with hot
spots enjoying a Mediterranean climate on the south Crimean coast.
The average temperature is 67 °F (19 °C) in summer and 21 °F (minus 6 °C)
in winter.

The Ukrainian population consists of 52 million people, that is, 18%
of the population of the former Soviet Union. Native Ukrainians form
73.5% of the total and Russians about 20%. Other ethnic groups with
substantial representation are Belarusians, Moldavians, Poles, Bulgarians,
Armenians, Hungarians, Romanians, and Crimean Tartars. In addition,
seven million Ukrainians are out of the country in the former Soviet
Union and five million live in other countries. The industrial regions in

the east and southeast are the most densely populated, and the urban population makes up 67.9% of the population. The largest cities are Kyiv (Kiev), the capital, (3.2 million inhabitants), Kharkov (2 million), Dnepropetrovsk (1.2 million), Donetsk (1.1 million) and Odessa (1 million), the principal Ukrainian port on the Black Sea. There has been negative population growth since independence, mostly owing to the economic situation and emigration.

The country is divided in 24 administrative units (*oblast*), one autonomous republic (*avtomnaya respublika*) Crimea and two cities with oblast status – Kyiv and Sebastopol. The official language is Ukrainian, an eastern Slavonic language written in the Cyrillic alphabet, but Russian is widely spoken. In areas with significant Russian minorities, for example the Crimea, Russian is also recognized as an official language of correspondence. Other languages spoken include Polish, Hungarian, and Romanian, particularly near the respective borders. The dominant religion is Ukrainian Orthodox (similar to the Russian Orthodox church), followed by Ukrainian Catholic or Uniate (a hybrid of Ukrainian Orthodoxy and Polish Catholicism that is prevalent in the West) and Ukrainian Autocephalous Orthodox.

The education level is high, with a 99% literacy rate and more than 150 universities, 742 institutes of specialized training, and a large range of schools geared to training for specialized industries. Around 70% of adults have a secondary education, and university-level education is open to any national who can pass the admission test. Ukraine is also a leader in science and technology, with studies offered in 80 research institutes. The law guarantees ethnic minorities access to school, cultural facilities and the use of national languages in conducting personal business. The law also guarantees freedom of religion, although religious organizations are required to register with local authorities and with the central government.

Means of communication

Ukraine has 33 television broadcasting stations, several relay stations that carry broadcasts from Russia, 134 AM, 289 FM, and four short-wave radio stations. There are 5,696 newspapers and magazines registered in Ukraine, most of them only for local distribution. The major newspapers are *Holos Ukrayinu*, *Kiyevskiye Vedomosti*, *Uriadovyi Kurier*, *Vseukrainskiye Vedomosti* and *Kiev Post* (in English).

The constitution of Ukraine (Article 34) guarantees the right of freedom of thought and speech, and freedom of expression for everyone. According to data from the Unified State Register of Enterprises and

Organizations of Ukraine, 52.9% of editorial boards and publishing houses are under private ownership, and only 15% of the television and radio companies are under state control. However, most of the printed media use state-owned publishing houses and the distribution system, and broadcasters use state-owned frequencies and air time. President Leonid Kuchma has been slowly eliminating opposition media by shutting down certain hostile newspapers, harassing and investigating opposition television stations, and even threatening journalists. Despite government promises under pressure from the Council of Europe, there have been a growing number of physical attacks on journalists since the last elections in 1998, and these have included 11 murders. Hence the importance of the Internet as a source of 'free' information.

12.2 Historical background

Throughout the first millennium BC, Scythians, Greeks, Sarmatians, Goths and other nomadic peoples settled in Ukraine and created lucrative outposts on trade routes. Later, Eastern Slavic tribes established Kiev as the booming centre of the powerful state of Kievan-Rus, the then largest state in Europe. Prosperity reigned until conflict among the descendants of Volodymyr the Great weakened Kievan-Rus and left it vulnerable. In particular, the Mongols invaded the country and razed Kyiv to the ground in the twelfth century. The following centuries were a succession of changes and shifting borders, the country being regularly annexed and split between Poland, Lithuania and Russia. In 1793, it was reunited as part of the Russian Empire and during 1917–18, three separate Ukrainian republics declared independence. However, by 1921, the Western part of the traditional territory was incorporated into Poland, and the larger, central and eastern areas joined in the formation of the USSR.

Ukrainian nationalism was preserved during the inter-war years, and in January 1929, the Organization of Ukrainian Nationalists (OUN) was officially formed under the leadership of Eugene Konovalets. In response, Stalin decided to make a test case of Ukraine as an example of his ideas about 'harmful' nationalism. He launched terror campaigns, ravaged the intelligentsia, destroyed religious symbols, churches and cathedrals, expropriated foodstuffs and forced collectivization policies in agriculture. In 1932, in a deliberate act of genocide, the Soviets created a grain shortage by increasing the grain procurement quota for Ukraine by 44%. Ukrainian grain, potatoes and beets were collected, stored and guarded by military units while Ukrainian peasants starved in close proximity. To restrict the movement of the peasants searching for food, an internal passport system was introduced. While Moscow feasted, Ukraine went hungry. As a result of these artificial famines, it is now estimated that from five to eight million people living in rural areas died (that is 18.8% of the Ukrainian population). During the purges of 1937–39, millions more Ukrainians were executed or sent to Soviet labour camps.

After the German and Soviet invasions of Poland in 1939, the west Ukrainian regions were also incorporated into the Soviet Union. In 1941, Ukraine – as part of the Soviet Union – was invaded by the Germans, and retaken by Soviet forces in 1944. The fights between the Red Army and the German forces brought further devastation and six million deaths among the population. In total, it is estimated that during the first half of the twentieth century, war, famine and Soviet purges cost the lives of over half the male and a quarter of the female population of Ukraine.

Little changed for Ukraine in the following decades until 1955 to 1964, when Nikita Khrushchev introduced a period of relative liberalization, and Ukrainian communists began to pursue national objectives. In the Gorbachev years of *perestroika*, Ukrainian officials again advanced national goals and Ukraine finally became an independent state on 24 August 1991, spurring on the dissolution of the Soviet Union. The country was a founding member of the Commonwealth of Independent States (CIS). The Communist Party was banned (but revived in 1993). Following free elections held on 1 December 1991, Leonid M. Kravchuk, former chairman of the Ukrainian Supreme Soviet, was elected the first president of independent Ukraine for a five-year term. The initial euphoria of statehood then gave way to a period of economic and social decline. Kravchuk concentrated largely on nation building with less importance given to political and economic reforms. Ukraine, thus, lagged behind other Eastern European economies in the drive towards significant reforms. In the 1994 election, former prime minister Leonid Kuchma replaced Leonid Kravchuk and started working on economic reforms.

12.3 Political structure and climate

Since its independence from the former Soviet Union in 1991, Ukraine has made tremendous strides towards establishing a stable, tolerant and open parliamentary democracy. The first post-Soviet constitution was adopted in June 1996 and codified the fundamental rights of free speech, freedom of the press and assembly, as well as freedom of religion for all Ukrainians. It splits power between the legislative, executive, and judicial branches. The legislative branch is the unicameral parliament, also known as the Supreme Council (*Verkhovna Rada*). It initiates legislation, ratifies international agreements, and approves and controls the budget. It consists of 450 members, 225 of whom are elected by proportional representation via the lists of parties that gained at least 4% of the national votes. The other 225 are filled by representatives of individual single-seat districts for five-year terms.

The executive branch is in the hands of the president (currently Leonid D. Kuchma) and the government. Elected by direct voting for five years and for no more than two terms, the presidency is the pre-eminent post in the country. The president is the commander-in-chief of the armed forces, heads the executive branch and may veto parliament's legislation (although it can override a presidential veto by a two-thirds vote). He or she appoints the prime minister, a first deputy prime minister and three further deputy prime ministers, as well as a cabinet of ministers, all of whom are then subject to approval by the Supreme Council. Other key offices include the National Security and Defence Council (NASDC), the Presidential Administration (PA) and the Council of Regions (CR). The NASDC is made up of the president, prime minister, and key ministers and bears responsibility for developing national policy on domestic and international matters and advising the president. The PA helps to draft presidential edicts and provides policy support for the president. The CR serves as an advisory body and includes chairmen of the Kyiv and Sevastopol municipalities and oblast chairmen.

The judicial branch consists of the Supreme Court, revered as the highest judicial body, the Constitutional Court, which has exclusive jurisdiction over interpretation of the constitution and laws, as well as people's courts and regional courts. The legal system is based on civil law, with a judicial review of legislative acts.

Ukraine has a myriad of political parties with conflicting interests and policy goals. Each party is usually dominated by key personalities, with few trends towards party consolidation. So far, the Communist Party of Ukraine (KPU) dominated parliament and repeatedly attempted to block most of the government's reform plans. Consequently, the president often has to offer concessions to other oligarchic factions in parliament in return for political support at the expense of reform. However, the situation has changed since the March 2002 elections, when only six of the 33 parties and blocs contesting the elections achieved the 4% barrier for representation under the proportional system.

The former prime minister Viktor Yushchenko's centre-right bloc, Our Ukraine, won 23.52% of the votes and 112 seats, followed by the pro-presidential bloc, for a United Ukraine, with 11.98% of the votes and 112 seats (most of which were filled from individual single-seat districts). Another pro-presidential but less loyal force, the Social Democratic Party, altogether won 6.24% of the votes and 23 seats, while the anti-presidential opposition, represented by the Socialist Party of Ukraine (6.93% of the votes, 24 seats) and the pro-reform Yuliya Tymoshenko Bloc (7.21% of the votes, 21 seats), scored well. The Communist Party of Ukraine finished miserably with 20.04% of the votes and 66 seats, half of what they held in the previous parliament. Clearly, the newly elected parliament is the least left-wing of any that has preceded it. Of the six winning parties, only the communists represent a hard-line force opposed to market reform. The others may differ on political questions but speak almost unanimously in favour of reform.

Although these elections should preserve Kuchma's power, his situation is not as enviable as it appears. The president is implicated in a series of scandals ranging from the kidnapping and beheading of a prominent opposition journalist, the assassination of several members of parliament, to an illegal sale of arms to Iraq. The newly elected opposition leaders have, therefore, immediately announced that impeaching Kuchma would be their highest priority in the new parliament. The future will clearly depend on Yushchenko's attitude. So far, he has maintained a neutral stance and serving as a balance between Kuchma and the opposition, apparently keeping in mind the presidential elections due in 2004.

12.4 Economic environment and infrastructure

Macroeconomic tendencies

After independence, the Ukrainian economy declined steadily, with GDP in 1999 no more than 50% of the 1992 level and lower performances than in other newly independent states. The year 2000 brought the first reversal of the negative growth trend. Beating all forecasts, Ukraine's economy grew by 9.1% in 2001 and is expected to post robust growth of about 6% in 2002. Industrial output grew by 14.2%, mainly driven by the 17% growth in processing industries (which represent 72% of industrial output). The continuation of this positive trend is, however, uncertain, since the major obstacle to sustained growth remains the incomplete structural transformation of the economy.

Since end-2000 the NBU has introduced eight consecutive cuts in the discount rate, from 27% to 10.0%. The most important efforts of the Kuchma government have been to bring hyperinflation in 1993 down to a record low 6.1% in 2001. During that year, food prices went up by 7.9%, while prices of non-food items went up only 0.2% and prices of services grew 5.3%. The hryvna, the national currency, has been remarkably stable for two years, and has even appreciated since the beginning of 2001. The government's fiscal discipline has improved markedly, with state budget revenues growing by 7.4% in 2001.

At year-end 2001, total external debt represented US\$ 10 billion (26.7% of GDP) and total debt US\$ 14 billion. All major international rating agencies upgraded Ukraine's sovereign ratings in 2001. In December 2001, Standard and Poor's gave a 'B' to Ukraine's long-term and short-term ratings (both for local and foreign currency) with a 'stable' outlook, ranking the country at the same level as Russia, Brazil, Romania and Bulgaria, and above Turkey. In August 2001 the Ukrainian debt was further boosted when it was included in JP Morgan's Emerging Markets Bond Index Plus.

The IMF has applied pressure to increase reform measures. Its aid came in the form of a Systematic Transformation Facility in 1994, IMF Standby Agreements which functioned for part of 1995–97 and early 1998, and a three-year IMF Extended Fund Facility in September 1998. The country has also received disbursements under major World Bank sectoral loans in areas such as financial sector development, privatization, agriculture and energy.

However, these apparent macroeconomic successes should not hide the fact that poverty has increased considerably. Unemployment rate has risen to 11% despite a declining population, of whom 27% are now believed to be below the poverty line. A large shadow economy persists and is estimated to be as much as one half of actual GDP. More worrying, tuberculosis has re-emerged, several infectious diseases have become more common, and sexually transmitted diseases including HIV/AIDS are spreading rapidly.

Industry

Under the sovietized economy, Ukraine was a major centre for heavy machinery and industrial equipment production (including mining, steel, and chemical equipment), agricultural machinery and large electrical transformers. The industrial sector was built up without competitive forces, with cheap energy costs and full employment. Therefore, restructuring it necessitates painful cuts and the closures of many obsolete plants. Today, the major industries are coal, electric power, ferrous and non-ferrous metals, machinery and transport equipment, chemicals and food processing (in particular sugar). Its natural resources are iron ore, coal, manganese, gas, oil, salt, sulphur, titanium, magnesium, kaolin, nickel, mercury and timber.

Energy

Before independence, Ukraine was one of the world's leading energy producers. With an annual production of 172 TWh, it now ranks no better than 16th and is fourth among the most inefficient energy consumers. Thermal power structures dominate in terms of the total capacity (68%) followed by nuclear (22.8%) and hydro (9.1%).

Despite important proven resources, the Ukrainian oil and gas sectors are currently underdeveloped, through lack of investment. About 80% of oil and gas consumption is imported from Russia and since the traditional Soviet system of exchanging energy for other industrial or agricultural goods is a thing of the past, all transactions are done at (expensive) market prices which results in debt. Efforts between the two countries to restructure this debt have resulted in a Ukrainian promise to construct in southern Ukraine a pipeline that will be used by Russia to export natural gas to Europe. At the same time, Ukraine generates large quantities of electricity through the use of fossil fuel and exports it mostly to Slovakia, Hungary and Poland. Most thermal stations are old and inefficient, and the nuclear power reactors are in poor condition as illustrated by the Chernobyl disaster. To make matters worse, the coal industry is plagued by incessant difficulties, such as shortage of spare parts, unsafe mines, large debts, and strikes over unpaid wages. According to the World Bank, only four of the country's 250 mines are consistently profitable.

Internally, the two major problems are the non-payment of bills by several million consumers and the mandatory free supply of electricity to 35% of Ukrainian families for historical reasons. Externally, the energy debt is high. For gas alone, Ukraine owes more than US$ 3.5 billion to Gazprom, and the company regularly threatens to cut off supplies. Consequently, the government has recently developed an 'Oil and Gas of Ukraine to the Year 2010' programme, with the objective of meeting at least half of the country's oil and gas needs within the next decade and, therefore, significantly reducing its trade imbalance with Russia. The programme resulted in several development projects with companies such as British Petroleum (BP), EuroGas Inc., JKX, Carpatsky Petroleum, and Gazprom with Chornomornaftogaz (the Ukrgazprom subsidiary in the Crimea). The government also began to reduce non-payments and payment of debts in the electricity sector and to develop energy-saving programmes.

Following the World Bank recommendations, the government has introduced a new power-sector model with separate energy generation, transmission and distribution, with the government acting as the overall regulator. Four large state-owned producers still control about 80% of the thermal power sector, but controlling stakes in up to 12 energy-distributing companies will be put up for sale in 2002, and blocking stakes in seven others are to be sold on the stock exchange. There are also significant efforts being made to break up Ukrgazprom, and in so doing, break the monopoly in the gas industry and clear the stage for reform of the gas market.

Ukraine also has a well-developed system of pipelines, with 4,000 km for crude oil, 4,500 km for petroleum products, and 34,400 km for natural gas. However, through lack of investment these infrastructures are now in poor condition and raise considerable environmental and safety concerns. Much of the pipework is in need of anti-corrosive coating to prevent leakage and while 500 km of pipeline needed repair in 1998, sufficient financing was available for just 26 km. It is estimated that up to US$ 1.5 billion is needed to modernize Ukraine's pipelines.

Agriculture

With its arable land characterized by rich, black soil, Ukraine has a high agricultural potential. Most of the country is agricultural land (407,000 sq km), of which 328,830 sq km is tilled. Ukraine was historically known as the 'bread basket' of Europe, with over 25% of total grain output and over 50% of sugar beet production of the former Soviet Union. However, lack of reform has meant that production has declined steadily since independence.

Despite the independent, individualistic farming tradition of private ownership of land prior to the Soviet years, opposition to private land ownership remains strong in parliament and government circles, for fear of foreign ownership and dominance in the agricultural sector. A good sign for the future is the fact that 2% of Ukrainian land that is privately owned yields the majority of the country's grain, sugar beet, vegetables, sunflower seeds, fruit, meat, eggs and milk. Today, agriculture and forestry represent 12% of GDP and, along with food, beverages and agricultural products, 11.4% of exports. The food industry also holds promise as one of the most lucrative sectors yet to be developed.

Financial sector

The National Bank of Ukraine (NBU) is a governmental body. It controls the money supply, fixes the exchange rate of the hryvna and transfers funds from and into foreign currencies. Its major role according to the Constitution is to stabilize the currency. Its chairman is appointed by parliament upon the proposal of the president.

Supervised by the NBU, the Ukrainian banking system is still fragmented (more than 210 banks with total assets of only US$ 12 billion) and strongly undercapitalized (the minimum capital for a bank is US$ 1.3 million). The five largest players (Ukrayina Bank, Prominvestbank, UkrSotsBank, UkrEximBank and Oschad Savings Bank) dominate the market, while smaller banks are unwilling to provide financing other than short-term loans at high interest rates, and remain fragile essentially because of former bad loans. Nevertheless, the banking system is developing and gradually strengthening. In 1998, it adopted the international accounting standards (IAS). A Banks and Banking Law and a Deposit Insurance Law are under preparation. Although not yet widely available, credit cards and automatic teller machines have begun to appear. Foreign licensed banks are entitled to operate in the same capacity as domestic banks. Credit Lyonnais was the first to enter Ukraine in 1994, and was followed by numerous others. Citibank is still the only US bank represented in Kyiv.

The largest stock exchange is the Ukrainian Stock Exchange (USE), which is regulated by the Commission for Securities and the Stock Market, a structure similar to the SEC. Most stocks are purchased directly from the State privatization Fund through USE facilities. In addition a computerized OTC trading system, PFTS, has been launched and is intended to become a self-regulatory organization similar to the NASDAQ. The Ukrainian equity market, as measured by the KP-Dragon index, has a market capitalization of US$ 0.4 billion, a monthly volume of US$ 19.2 million and an annual turnover of 56%. In 2001, the Ukrainian equity market lost 42.6% of its value after posting an impressive 58.7% gain in 2000. Most blue-chips are utilities, mining companies or oil and gas related. Market valuation is generally low, by international standards.

Telecommunications

In 1991, when Ukraine gained independence, the telecommunication systems were outdated, inefficient, and unreliable. Since then, telecommunications in Ukraine have improved, but they still lag behind many other countries in Central and Eastern Europe. With 18 fixed phones and 0.1 mobile phone per 100 people, the tele-density is low. A major reason is that the Communications Law prohibits foreign shareholders from holding more than 49% of a telecommunication service, whatever the extent of their investment. This has considerably reduced the capital-intensive development of the telecom market. Two companies, Ukrtelecom and Utel, dominate national and long-distance services. Ukrtelecom is a state-owned company created in 1993 by the merger of several departments from the Ministry of Communications. It has a monopoly on all transmission facilities and administers the national fixed-line infrastructure. Its services are still unsatisfactory both for business and personal use. Utel is an international joint venture created in 1992. It has developed communication networks (including ISDN lines), installed digital long-distance telephone exchanges and now provides Western standard telecommunications. Industry experts regularly discuss the likelihood that Ukrtelecom will be privatized, which would change the structure of the telecom market.

Ukraine still has one of the lowest percentages of mobile phone subscribers in Europe. Several problems can explain this. First, the attribution of frequency licences has been slow, since the 900 MHz band was used by military and civil aviation. Second, government policy was inconsistent, unclear, and non-transparent for the tendering process, with exorbitant fees requested and rules changed to favour local competitors. Third, the mobile phone rate structure is prohibitive with respect to the average wage. Finally, the same 49% rule applies to foreign investors. In addition, mobile phone service providers cannot access fixed line switches or use public networks without the agreement of Ukrtelecom (which generally demands in return a free 9% ownership of the provider). Nonetheless, because of the lack of fixed telephones in the country, mobile telecommunications in the country now show great potential. Eight independent mobile networks (covering only a limited region) are being built. Many firms are competing on the market, generally with a foreign manufacturer providing an open equipment credit line or becoming a shareholder in the operating firm. This competition could ultimately benefit the consumer, but not in the near future.

The Ukrainian computer market is one of the most dynamic sectors. While home use of PCs is still limited due to high prices, the professional sector is increasingly reliant on computers. In addition, state agencies and enterprises have to replace outdated technology. All the major computer hardware manufacturers have a market presence in Ukraine. However, the market for Internet services remains young and limited. An important barrier is the Cyrillic alphabet and a poor knowledge of English. Many individuals use the Latin alphabet to spell Ukrainian or Russian texts 'as it sounds'.

Transportation

Ukraine has 172,565 km of highways (including 163,937 km of paved roads, and 1,875 km of expressways), 23,350 km of railways (8,600 km electrified), and 4,400 km of navigable waterways. The most popular and efficient freight transport mode is road haulage. However, it is expensive and costed by the kilometre rather than by weight, due to poor road conditions and high security costs. In particular, intercity travel at night and in winter can be hazardous. Rail shipment is less costly in some cases, but it is often slow and sometimes unreliable. The major waterways are the Dnieper River, the Dunai and Pivdenni Bug. Ukraine's major ports and harbours are Berdyansk, Illichivsk, Izmayil, Kerch, Kherson, Kyiv, Mariupol, Mykolayiv, Odessa, and Reni. The largest airports are Kyiv, Simferopol, Donetsk, Odessa, Lviv and Kharkiv.

In addition, over 2,000 km of petroleum pipelines and 7,800 km of natural gas pipeline pass through its territory, including Soiuz (natural gas from the Urals to Europe), Urengj-Uzhhorod (natural gas from Western Siberia to Europe) and Druzhba (oil from Western Siberia to Europe). As the main transit route for Russian natural gas shipments to Europe, transit fees are a major source of revenue for Ukraine.

12.5 Legal environment and regulations

Crime and corruption

Corruption, bribery and organized crime are a constant problem throughout Ukraine. Corruption is common (if not the norm) among officials from government and regulatory agencies seeking payment for routine authorizations. These people view small bribes as a necessary supplement to their paltry salaries, and refusing to pay simply delays the requested authorisation forever. The word 'blat' translates literally to 'access' or 'connections' and can take the form of small presents (e.g. cigarettes or candy) to grease the wheels of everyday transactions. The word *vzyatka* translates to 'bribe' and generally means a bigger payment. Local representatives can be effective in dealing with corruption, as they are less likely to be a target – or at least, the amounts would be less. This stresses the importance of a careful selection of a local partner in any business venture.

The Mafia presence in Ukraine is also well established. Organized crime's main activities include money laundering, drug and arms trafficking, tax and stock fraud, protection rackets, illegal commodity trade, and the sex trade. Due to rising street crime, weak law enforcement, and the emergence of a strong business mafia, caution is recommended.

Judicial system, dispute settlement and bankruptcy procedures

Ukraine's legal system can be tactfully described as being in the midst of evolution. Although it is based on civil law and judicial review of legislative acts, its contradictions pose substantial difficulties for foreign investors, particularly regarding their rights and the protection of their investment. The major problem is the numerous sources of 'legislative acts': laws and resolutions are voted by parliament, decrees, edicts and orders having the force of law are issued by the president; and the Council of Ministers has the power to adopt resolutions and issue instructions on implementing its legislative acts. Other problems are the inconsistent translations. The lack of a codification system and/or cross-referencing to other legislative acts in the original Ukrainian text, complicates the process of identifying which legislative acts supersede, modify, amend or supplement the prior legislation. This is still a heritage of the Soviet era, when the only place where legislative acts were published was in the official government press and when there were no law libraries or other repositories or statute books where a lawyer could have access to this legislation.

Like Ukraine's legal system in general, the judicial system suffers from several problems. In particular, the judiciary is still quite weak, corrupt, and prone to political and other influences. As an illustration, a former prime minister, during his term in office, announced that the government would stop paying the salary of judges issuing decisions against the tax authorities. Significant improvements have occurred in recent years, creating a more conducive environment for unambiguous business activity, but much remains to be done. As a rule, the chances of getting a fair trial at the higher levels of the system are better, so it is advisable to move as quickly as possible through the appeal stages towards higher central courts.

Ukraine is a member of the 1958 New York Convention on international arbitration and recently acceded to the Convention on the Settlement of Investment Disputes Between States and Nationals of Other States (the ICSID Convention). However, its courts in practice often refuse to hear the recognition and enforcement claims, sending the claimants to the Ministry of Justice, which sends the claims back to the court, and so on and so forth. Therefore, most foreign investors avoid taking disputes to court and prefer quasi-judicial mechanisms aimed at an out-of-court settlement (akin to mediation). For example, president Kuchma has created a Chamber of Independent Experts that consists of both Ukrainian and foreign legal experts and is designed to serve as a non-binding arbitration forum. This chamber is supposed to provide impartial opinions on disputes brought before it. Although the implementation of its decisions is not mandatory, the government authorities usually pay serious attention to them, and they are usually either implemented voluntarily or trigger a settlement satisfactory to foreign investors.

Current bankruptcy law provides for the liquidation of enterprises, but a revised law is in preparation and, if enacted, will be one of the most progressive bankruptcy laws in the newly independent states.

Taxation, accounting, and auditing rules

Tax issues still present one of the major obstacles to the emergence of a favourable commercial environment in Ukraine. It had already established a full fledged State Tax Administration by mid-1996, but the tax system is far from coherent and is in an almost constant state of flux, often without advance notice and sometimes retroactively. To make matters worse, fines imposed by the Ukrainian state tax authority are among the highest in the world, and the authorities have the power to freeze, without prior judicial proceedings, the bank account of any entity believed to be in tax debt.

At the corporate level, taxes are very high. The average profit tax is around 30%, withholding taxes are 15% on royalties and interests and 30% on dividends and capital gains. At the personal level, the latest Ukrainian tax laws extend equal treatment to both Ukrainian and foreign citizens residing in Ukraine (i.e. more than 183 days a year). The tax rate, based on minimum monthly salaries, increases progressively and quickly reaches the maximum overall tax rate of 50%. Moreover, to ensure that they are paying their taxes on their worldwide income, Ukraine residents are not allowed to maintain foreign currency abroad. For these reasons many foreigners choose to ignore the tax provisions altogether or use creative solutions to avoid taxation. A new tax code is expected to be approved at the end of 2002.

Except for the banking sector, which converted to international accounting standards (IAS) in 1998, one should also be aware that accounting, tax-reporting and tax-payment practices do not conform to international standards. All companies (except banks, but including representative offices of foreign firms) must operate in Ukrainian currency and according to Ukrainian accounting rules, whereas most foreign companies use double accounting. It might therefore be necessary to obtain the services of experienced international accountants, since most local accountants are not familiar with IAS.

Laws on establishing and conducting business

In September 1991, the Ukrainian parliament passed legislation specifying restrictions and regulations on the organization of businesses (known as 'economic associations' in Ukraine). Accordingly, foreign investors operating in Ukraine must register a business structure within one month.

Various forms of business organizations available to foreigners

Currently, four major forms of business structures are available: a representative office, a 100% wholly owned subsidiary, a joint-stock company (JSC) or a limited liability company (LLC). The optimal choice depends on the ownership and length of the investment. A representative office is considered a separate subdivision of a foreign business entity. It can carry out most activities on behalf of the company, and is treated similarly to an independent legal entity for regulatory and taxation purposes, but it is not a legal entity and cannot, therefore, sign any agreement. The 100% wholly owned subsidiary is recommended if the company intends to carry out manufacturing or other significant local commercial activities. In a JSC, which can be can be created as a closed company (shares are not sold publicly) or as an open company (shares can be sold to the public), at least two shareholders are liable to the extent of their capital contributions. Finally, in an LLC, the authorized capital is divided into one to fifty parts, where the size and rights of these parts are set down in the constituting documents. The financial liability of the company's founders is limited to the extent of their capital contribution.

There are also additional responsibility companies (ARC), in which the participants are responsible for the association's debts and the limits of individual responsibility are set forth in the constituent documents. Finally, there are also complete associations, where the participants carry joint responsibility for the association's commitments regarding all its property, regardless of percentages of ownership.

Restrictions on foreign investments

Ukrainian law stipulates that foreign participation in corporate enterprises should not exceed 49% of the capital. This percentage can even be reduced to 30% in some 'strategic' areas (e.g. telecommunications, radio, television, etc.). However, the provision does not regulate profit distribution, which can reflect the actual investment made by shareholders. In addition, the law requires the approval by the anti-monopoly committee in establishing legal entities, mergers, and acquisitions. This process can be long and costly.

It must also be noted that although foreign entities may own property in Ukraine and may use these properties for commercial and leasing purposes, ownership of land is a different story. The land code of Ukraine, adopted in 1992, stipulates that legal entities, foreign or domestic, with the exception of Ukrainian agricultural companies, are prohibited from owning land.

Investment incentives

Tax breaks are no longer provided although a number of state guarantees, the most important being unhindered and immediate repatriation of profits, have been granted. As a rule, trusts do not provide investment incentives in Ukraine. As an example, in 1997, a new law abolished all five-year taxation exemptions given to companies with foreign investment registered before 1995. Foreign investors who filed lawsuits in the Ukrainian Constitutional Court are still waiting for a ruling.

Protection of property rights

In theory, Ukraine has several laws on its books protecting copyrights, design, and intellectual property. It is also a member of several organizations and international agreements, including the Universal Copyright Convention and the World Intellectual Property Organization (WIPO). In practice, intellectual property rights have been and continue to be a thorny issue, since copyright piracy in Ukraine is widespread. As an illustration, illegal software represents about 40% of the software used by the government, 30% of large corporate customers, and almost 100% of small and medium businesses. On 1 May 1998, Ukraine was even placed on the Special 301 Watch List owing to its lack of enforcement of copyright piracy legislation.

Entry requirements

A valid passport and a visa are required for all persons entering in the country. A transit visa may also be necessary for certain nationals. Visas can be obtained in advance from any Ukrainian embassy or consulate general upon presentation of a letter of invitation from a person, company, or organization in Ukraine. Travelling within the country is unrestricted, but foreigners must register with local Ukrainian authorities upon arrival. This formality is usually taken care of either by the hotel or host businesses. Foreigners may also be asked to present their passport and visa upon demand by local police. Due to the large market for stolen passports, it is recommended to carry photocopies.

Under current customs regulations travellers may bring up to US$ 10,000 into Ukraine without special permission; larger amounts require a written statement by the traveller. Changing US dollars into Ukrainian hryvna or other currency is legal only at banks, currency exchange desks in hotels, and at licensed exchange booths. In addition, travellers should retain their customs forms, as they will be required to present them upon departure. Any undeclared items are subject to confiscation. Travellers are also required to purchase Ukrainian medical insurance at their point of entry, even though they may already be covered by their insurance.

12.6 Business environment

Privatization

Privatization in Ukraine officially started in 1992, with the establishment of the State Property Fund. Since then, privatization has proceeded quite slowly due to considerable resistance from political factions, enterprise management, and local bureaucracy, despite the personal involvement of president Kuchma. Small-scale privatization was a large success, with several thousand enterprises (representing 62% of Ukraine's industrial production and 50% of all industrial employment) privatized. But much remains to be done for medium and large-scale enterprises (including UkrTelekom, the state telephone monopoly) and in agriculture (land and grain elevators).

The State Property Fund may use several means to privatize assets. These include commercial bids (the highest bidder clinches the deal), non-commercial bids (the buyer with the best strategy according to the bidding commission clinches the deal), cash auctions (assets are sold to the highest bidder) or management and employee buy-outs. The latter technique remains the most popular form of privatization, with the majority of shares in medium and large enterprises held by employees and the public. However, this situation creates problems because it diffuses ownership and there is a lack of a secondary market to publicly trade shares and encourage further investment. Moreover, to reduce unemployment and social tensions, the government often retains up to 25% ownership in privatized enterprises and may block restructuring. It should be noted that all Ukrainian citizens have received privatization certificates for a value of 500 hryvna. They can use them to invest directly in management and employee subscriptions, to bid in specialized certificate auctions, or put them in an investment company that participates in auctions on their behalf. In addition, holders of savings bank accounts have received compensation certificates (similar to privatization certificates) for losses due to hyperinflation.

The 1999 privatization Programme called for the privatization of 455 medium and large-scale enterprises, 5,500 small enterprises, and 402 unfinished construction sites. The privatization process for over 400 grain elevators had also started with the sale of at least 70% of over 350 elevators. Land privatization continues to move slowly and several enterprises will remain in the hands of the government for strategic reasons. In the energy sector, Ukrainian legislation stipulates that all thermal power generation companies and regional powers distribution companies must be privatized. Oil and gas remains in the hands of the government for the time being. The Ukrainian telecommunications industry, monopolized by Ukrtelekom, the state-owned giant, desperately needs financing. Fierce opposition in parliament has often delayed its privatization, but Ukrainian government officials have announced plans to sell 25% of Ukrtelekom shares for US$ 0.7–1 billion and to delegate the management of the company to strategic investors.

Foreign direct investment (FDI)

Ukraine comes bottom of the list of attractiveness to investors and ranks among the lowest in the region for foreign direct investment (FDI). The reasons for this are essentially historical. Since its independence, Ukraine has made known publicly its desire for FDI (about US$ 40 billion over the next four years). It established the National Agency of Ukraine for Development and European Integration (NAUREI) to promote the country as an investment opportunity and voted the Investment Activity Law (1992) and the Foreign Investment Law (1996), which guaranteed registered foreign investors equal treatment with domestic investors, and even possible special privileges in certain government-designated priority sectors. However, these laws were subsequently revised to remove certain tax breaks previously awarded to foreign investors and to ensure equal tax treatments for foreign and domestic investors. Consequently, the government has not managed to establish a climate of confidence to effectively encourage business and investment. At the end of 2000, cumulative FDI in Ukraine amounted to US$ 4 billion, which is very low in comparison with foreign investment in neighbouring countries, such as Poland (US$ 30 million) and Hungary (US$ 20 billion).

In July 2001, sectors that attracted the most FDI were the food industry (20.1%), the domestic wholesale/retail trade (18.8%), engineering and metallurgy (9.0%) and the financial sector (6.4%). The United States is the largest foreign investor (16.4% of the total, with companies such as Coca-Cola, PepsiCo, McDonald's, Philip Morris and RJ Reynolds), followed by Cyprus (9.6%), the Netherlands (9.4%), Russia (8.1%), the United Kingdom (7.7%) and Germany (6.2%).

Free economic and trade areas

At present, several free-trade zones (FTZ) or free experimental economic zones (FEZ) are operational in Ukraine: Azov and Donetsk (in the Donetsk oblast, until 2058), Zakarpattya (western Ukraine, until 2029), Slavutych (close to Chernobyl area, until 2009), Truskavets and Yavoriv (in the Lviv oblast, until 2019). Companies investing in FTZs are eligible for a wide range of benefits, including various tax breaks, no quotas, no licences, no VAT, no import duties, no custom tariffs on import to and export from the free zone, reduced 20% business profit tax, no Chernobyl tax, etc. In addition, the government guarantees full compensation of losses in case of the liquidation of the zone.

Ukraine is not a member of the Commonwealth of Independent States' customs union, but it has signed free trade agreements with each of the former Soviet republics (except Kyrgyzstan and Tajikistan) and intends to become a full member of the Central European Free Trade Agreement (CEFTA), the first step towards becoming a member of the World Trade Organization (WTO). Ukraine has signed bilateral investment agreements with various countries, including the United States (1996). Accordingly, the Overseas Private Investment Corporation (OPIC) risk insurance and direct financing programmes are also available to US investors in Ukraine.

Foreign trade opportunities

As the economic situation improves and the ageing population infrastructure is slowly rejuvenated, many windows of opportunity should open for investors, entrepreneurs, and business people who see potential in Ukraine. Hot sectors include energy, building materials, consumer goods, technology and information, healthcare, the chemical industry, tourism services and agribusiness.

Major trade partners

Ukraine's export volume grew by 8% and peaked at US$ 21.1 billion in 2001, while imports grew by 12.5% and amounted to US$ 20.5 billion. The trade balance was positive and chalked up US$ 0.6 billion. The major trading partners were Russia (20.7% export, 47.6% import), the EU

(17% export, 23% import), China (6.3% export), Turkey (5.8% export) and the US (4% export, 3% import).

Value added tax (VAT)

The value added tax (VAT) rate is currently at 20% based on the customs value of the invoice, and is generally payable at the time of customs clearance by the importer. For manufacturing and commercial firms, one should be aware that VAT-reporting and VAT-paying practices do not conform to international practices. VAT is paid on a quarterly basis, and companies have to pay VAT even if they did not receive payment from their customer.

Tariff system

Ukraine maintains several duties, tariffs and regulations. Although the average weighted tariff rate is 7.02%, import duties range from 0 to 200%, and excise taxes range from 10 to 300%. In addition, several non-tariff barriers take the form of non-transparent standards, expensive import licences, and lengthy certification procedures. It is, therefore, advisable to contact a local representative for the most up-to-date customs and duties information.

Market structure

With over 50 million people, Ukraine may well become one of Europe's important markets. The market has historically been a large, but since 1991 (when Ukraine opened up to imports), it has dwindled to one-fourth of its previous size. Ukrainian consumers can be divided in two categories. On the one hand, there is a strong consumer enthusiasm for Western brand names, particularly American. On the other hand, there is a conviction that familiar and home-made products and brands are better and much more reliable. The first attitude is far greater among the younger generation, while the second is particularly apparent among the older segment of the population, who have experienced dissatisfaction with dubious origin, low-quality, cheap imported goods from Turkey, China, the Middle East, and the former Soviet-bloc countries. Therefore, success in the Ukrainian market can only be attained if several conditions are met. First, broad promotional advertising (television, newspaper, commercial radio, etc.) is necessary to acquaint the average Ukrainian customer with unfamiliar brand names. Although it is not mandatory (except for some specific products), a customer's confidence in a particular foreign product will be greatly increased by a description in Ukrainian. Second, companies should pay due attention to sales services and customer support, and emphasize quality over packaging. Generally, they should include some form of warranty or after sales maintenance guarantee. Third, since dealing with many small consumers is simply inexpedient, and the major cities are not the only hub of trade (with about only 13% of the population in the three largest), Western companies often fare better if they market their goods through Ukrainian distributors or dealers rather than directly. It is noteworthy that a good pricing policy should account for the regional and age differences, as well as for the education level among target end-users. In particular, offering a flexible credit policy is necessary for small-scale businesses.

Using local partners

One of the key factors in the success of a foreign company in Ukraine is the choice of a local agent or distributor with good connections and a 'large Rolodex'. He will provide valuable insights and commercial intelligence, avoid problems and hassles with state structures and deal with corruption issues. Numerous companies will attempt to approach foreigners (typically, outside the customs area at the airport or at a hotel) to propose these kinds of services. In many cases, these people have no contacts whatsoever. A better starting point to find a local partner is the US embassy's commercial service programmes, or a trustworthy foreign recommendation. As a means to encourage investment, the Ukrainian government has established NAUDEI, the National Agency of Ukraine for Development and European Integration. The main task of the agency, comprised of the State Credit and Investment Company and the Agency for Technical Assistance Co-ordination, is to promote investment opportunities in Ukraine. It provides potential investors with information about Ukrainian companies and the legal environment. Investors may use the NAUDEI database as one source of information when looking for a potential Ukrainian partner. That said, available state statistics are often unreliable. It is advisable to treat local surveys and 'experts' with caution. In any case, one should closely examine potential partners, but remember that obtaining information is hard and often not reliable, since it is not a practice in Ukraine for banks to provide information on the financial status of their clients, and there is no nationwide service for registering enterprises of doubtful solvency. Usually, specialized companies offer a better service. It is worth remembering that the former Communist Party is still a very efficient networking organization, and that the old boy network remains intact.

12.7 Culture, business customs, practices and etiquette

Culture

Despite successive partitioning, external control and important pressures from foreign governments, Ukrainians have made an important effort to preserve their cultural traditions and customs. Ukrainian literature began to flourish in the nineteenth century. It is exemplified in the works of Taras Shevchenko, Ivan Franko, Vasyl Stefanyk and others. The nineteenth century was also marked by the foundation of the Ukrainian National Theatre (by Les Kurbas) and the Ukrainian School of Monumental Painting by Mykhalo Boitchuk. Party controls and official Russification were also obstacles in the Soviet period, but the 1920s and the 1960s were times of considerable cultural creativity. Since the late 1980s, there has been a cultural revival, especially through the medium of the Ukrainian language. Independence in Ukraine was a tangible impulse to develop Ukrainian music and ballet, which has achieved a high level of perfection. Vaslav Nijinsky and Serge Lifar are great ballet dancers of world renown. Victoria Lucyanets, Anatoly Kocherga, Svetlana Dobronravova, and Mykhailo Didyk, soloists of the National Opera of Ukraine, have performed in many countries of Europe. Today, there are 34 operas and 24 ballets on the repertory of the Kyiv Opera and Ballet Theatre, which makes it one of the biggest repertoires in the world. In addition, the country boasts more than 136 theatres, 314 museums and 24,000 public libraries.

Business customs

At the beginning of a meeting, shaking hands and exchanging business cards is common practice. It is a good idea to have one side of them printed in Cyrillic. Men should wait for a woman to extend her hand before offering theirs. Gloves should be removed before shaking hands, and handshakes should never take place across the threshold of a door out of superstition (it is a sign of bad luck and forecasts a quarrel). When they meet, Ukrainians often simply state their name instead of exchanging such niceties as 'How do you do?'. It is appropriate to respond in kind. They attach great importance to ceremony, corporate titles and respect for elders when conducting business. As an example, in a meeting it is frequent to have chairs around the table for important persons and chairs along the walls for junior people. Therefore, you should always watch your host's team to know where to go and remain standing until your host invites you to sit. If a translator is needed, always test their abilities and qualifications before the meeting.

Negotiations in Ukraine are an exercise in 'power politics' and can easily become very contentious. Therefore, it is imperative to arrive at the meeting armed with clearly established goals. Ukrainians often use time as a strategy – meetings tend to be very long, and may be postponed or cancelled without notice, or the wrong people show up. Westerners should arrive on time for all meetings, as tardiness would be taken as a sign of disrespect. However, high-level Ukrainian managers are likely to arrive late as a means of demonstrating their status.

Negotiations often start with a very general discussion, but other eventualities may occur later on, including shouting and displays of temper. In the latter case, either respond in kind or ignore the behaviour and wait for negotiations to begin again. Ultimatums should be avoided as they are seen as threats. Beware too of compromise, which is often interpreted as a sign of weakness. If the negotiation reaches an impasse, do not attempt to force decisions. It is best to continue the meeting assuming that the problem will be solved later. During meetings, you should not slump in the chair or put your hands in your pockets. Crossing your legs at the ankle is also seen as a sign of assertiveness or hostility. Each meeting usually ends with the signing of a (unenforceable) protocol or letter of intent that summarizes the discussion and intentions of each party. They will be accepted or rejected. It is only after a series of meetings that the contract or official agreement will be signed. It is worth noting that most firms will require some sort of official seal or letterhead in addition to the signature.

Ukrainians are also famous for their hospitality. Most business dinners take place in restaurants, but business should not be discussed at the dinner table. Guests must not drink any alcohol until there is a toast. The host will generally give the first toast. Remember that guests should remain silent during a toast, even though it may last several minutes. They should also prepare a toast of their own, as they may have to make one ('peace' and 'co-operation' are good topics). Remember that refusing a drink without a good reason (for instance, being on medication or allergic) is offensive for Ukrainians. Remember too that there is zero tolerance of drinking and driving in Ukraine.

A home invitation should be seen as a special honour. It is customary to bring small gifts (flowers for the hostess, a bottle of cognac or whisky for the host, and small presents for the children) and to remove your shoes when entering the home. An invitation to your host to visit your company is a very good way to build closer contacts.

Finally, one should never forget that Ukrainians are very proud of their independent status, their heritage and traditions. One point of contention for them is to be lumped together as 'Slavs' or worse as Russians. This is considered an insult. Likewise, do not refer to the country as 'The Ukraine'. Upon independence, Ukraine shed the disparaging article in front of the country's name to forget their subordinate role as the provincial bread-basket for Russia and then the Soviet Union. Attitudes about female inferiority are still firmly entrenched and surprisingly widespread in Ukraine. Consequently, some Ukrainian men will never take a woman leader seriously. Similar sentiments prevail against coloured people, especially Asians. Remember too that some Ukrainians, particularly the elderly population, have lived their entire lives or the majority of it under the Soviet system and are terrified by the changes taking place. They tend to dislike foreigners and accuse them of being responsible for all the ills of capitalism (e.g. proliferation of poverty, alcoholism, prostitution, homelessness, pornography, lawlessness, and the rising power of the Mafia). For similar motives, Russians may feel unwelcome, particularly in Western Ukraine. However, most Ukrainians, and especially the younger generation, are interested in foreigners and welcome them.

12.8 Conclusion

Located at the crossroads of Eastern Europe, Central Asia, Russia and the Middle East, Ukraine was one of the key industrial and agricultural components of the former USSR. Due to its ample human, technical, and natural resources, its has great potential to become one of the best medium-term prospects for development, provided necessary economic reforms are achieved. Unfortunately, as of today, a combination of political, ideological, institutional and legislative obstacles have prevented Ukraine from achieving its economic transition and attracting a large level of foreign direct investments. The country still has a long road ahead to develop a true free market economy and independent industry. Its development and success hinge on its government's ability to stabilize both its political and economic environment, implement thorny economic reforms, clarify its legal and regulatory mechanisms and fight corruption. Privatization, for Ukrainian citizens as well as foreign investors, could be a key variable in shaping Ukraine's success or failure in implementing market reforms.

Many foreign companies are waiting for signs of further improvement in business conditions before entering the market. Others are pressing ahead and contributing to the improvement of these conditions, taking a major role in providing capital investments and the know-how needed to modernize and restructure the economy. Their overwhelming sentiment regarding Ukraine and the reform effort is that progress, albeit arduous, will most definitely occur.

Useful Contacts and Addresses

Belarus

Administration of the President
of the Republic
ul. K. Marksa, 38
220016 Minsk
Tel: (+375 17) 222 60 06
Fax: (+375 17) 226 06 10
www.president.gov.by

Belarusian Chamber of Commerce
and Industry
Masherova Ave., 14
220035 Minsk
Tel: (+375 17) 226 91 27
Fax: (+375 17) 226 98 60
www.cci.by

Belarusan Union of Businessmen
Internationalnaya str., 13
220050 Minsk
Tel: (+375 17) 227 16 47
Fax: (+375 17) 227 15 96

Council of Ministers of the
Republic of Belarus
Dom Pravitel'stva
220010 Minsk
Tel: (+375 17) 222 61 05
Fax: (+375 17) 222 66 65

Council of the Republic of the
National Assembly
ul. Krasnoarmeyskaya, 4
220016 Minsk
Tel: (+375 17) 222 66 94
Fax: (+375 17) 222 66 94

Free Economic Zone 'Brest'
Kommunisticheskaya str., 23
224005 Brest
Tel: (+375 16) 222 16 07
     (+375 16) 220 46 31

Fax: (+375 16) 220 08 83
www.fezbrest.com

Free Economic Zone 'Gomel-Raton'
Feduninski str., 17
246044 Gomel
Tel: (+375 23) 256 32 34
Fax: (+375 23) 257 92 91
www.gomelraton.com

Free Economic Zone 'Minsk'
Office 606
Stankevicha str., 3
220050 Minsk
Tel/Fax: (+375 17) 226 48 74
E-mail: invest@nsys.by

Ministry of Agriculture and
Foodstuffs
Kirova str., 15
220050 Minsk
Tel: (+375 17) 227 81 04
Fax: (+375 17) 227 42 96
mshp.minsk.by

Ministry of Architecture and
Construction
Myasnikova, 39
220048 Minsk
Tel: (+375 17) 227 26 42
Fax: (+375 17) 220 74 24

Ministry of Communication
Skoriny Ave., 10
220050 Minsk
Tel: (+375 17) 227 21 57
Fax: (+375 17) 227 21 57

Ministry of Culture
pr. Macherova, 11
220004 Minsk
Tel: (+375 17) 223 75 74
Fax: (+375 17) 223 58 25

Ministry of Economy
Stankevich str., 14
220050 Minsk
Tel: (+375 17) 222 60 48
Fax: (+375 17) 220 37 77
www.main.gov.by/index.htm

Ministry of Education
ul. Sovetskaya, 9
220010 Minsk
Tel: (+375 17) 227 47 36
Fax: (+375 17) 220 84 83

Ministry of Enterpreneurship and
   Investment
ul. Myasnikova, 39
220048 Minsk
Tel: (+375 17) 220 16 23
Fax: (+375 17) 227 22 40

Ministry of Finance
Sovetskaya str., 7
220010 Minsk
Tel: (+375 17) 222 61 37
Fax: (+375 17) 222 45 93
ncpi.gov.by/minfin

Ministry of Foreign Affairs
Lenin str., 19
220030 Minsk
Tel: (+375 17) 227 29 22
Fax: (+375 17) 227 45 21
www.mfa.gov.by

Ministry of Industry
Partisansky Ave., 4, 2 Bild
220033 Minsk
Tel: (+375 17) 224 87 84
Fax: (+375 17) 224 87 84
www.niievm.minsk.by/minprom

Ministry of Justice
Kollectornaya str., 10
220048 Minsk
Tel: (+375 17) 220 97 55
Fax: (+375 17) 220 97 55
ncpi.gov.by/minjust

Ministry of Natural Resources and
   Environmental Protection
Kollectornaya str., 10
220048 Minsk
Tel: (+375 17) 220 66 91
Fax: (+375 17) 220 55 83
www.president.gov.by/minpriroda

Ministry of Sport and Tourism
ul. Kirova 8, korp. 2
220600 Minsk
Tel: (+375 17) 227 72 37
Fax: (+375 17) 227 76 22

Ministry of Statistics and Analysis
Partizanskij Ave., 12
220070 Minsk
Tel: (+375 17) 249 42 78
Fax: (+375 17) 249 22 04
www.president.gov.by/minstat

Ministry of Trade
Kirov str., 8/1
220050 Minsk
Tel: (+375 17) 227 61 21
Fax: (+375 17) 227 24 80

Ministry of Transport and
   Communications
ul. Chicherina, 21
220029 Minsk
Tel: (+375 17) 234 11 52
Fax: (+375 17) 232 83 91

Ministry on State Property Control
   and Privatization
ul. Myasnikova, 39
220097 Minsk
Tel: (+375 17) 276 81 78
Fax: (+375 17) 220 65 47

National Bank of the Republic of
   Belarus
F. Skorina Ave., 20
220008 Minsk
Tel: (+375 17) 219 23 03
Fax: (+375 17) 227 48 79
www.nbrb.by

National Center of Legal Information
Berson str., 1a
220050 Minsk
Tel: (+375 17) 222 70 64
Fax: (+375 17) 222 70 64
ncpi.gov.by

State Committee on Energy-Saving
and Inspection
ul. K. Marksa, 14
220677 Minsk
Tel: (+375 17) 229 84 96
Fax: (+375 17) 227 19 57

State Committee on Patents
pr. F. Skoriny, 66
220072 Minsk
Tel: (+375 17) 284 20 53
Fax: (+375 17) 284 06 68
www.belgospatent.org/english

State Committee on
Standardization, Metrology
and Certification
Starovilenskiy trakt, 93
220053 Minsk
Tel: (+375 17) 237 52 13
Fax: (+375 17) 237 25 88

State Institute for Standardization and
Certification
Meleja str., 3
220013 Minsk
Tel: (+375 17) 262 52 80
Fax: (+375 17) 262 15 20
www.belgiss.org.by

State Customs Committee
ul. Kommunisticheskaya, 11
220029 Minsk
Tel: (+375 17) 284 74 85
Fax: (+375 17) 284 68 93

World Bank Group
Gertsena str., 2a
220030 Minsk
Tel: (+375 17) 226 52 84
Fax: (+375 17) 211 03 14

Croatia

Central Bureau of Statistics
Ilica, 3
P.O. Box 671
10000 Zagreb
Tel: (+385 1) 48 06 154
Fax: (+385 1) 48 06 148
www.dzs.hr

Croatian Bank for Reconstruction
and Development
Strossmayerov trg, 9
10000 Zagreb
Tel: (+385 1) 45 91 666
Fax: (+385 1) 45 91 721
www.hbor.hr

Croatian Chamber of Economy
Rooseveltov trg, 2
10000 Zagreb
Tel: (+385 1) 45 61 555
Fax: (+385 1) 48 28 380
www.hgk.hr

Croatian Investment Promotion
Agency (CIPA)
Avenija Dubrovnik, 15
10000 Zagreb
Tel: (+385 1) 65 54 560
Fax: (+385 1) 65 54 563
www.hr/hapu

Croatian Privatization Fund
Ivana Lučića, 6
10000 Zagreb
Tel: (+385 1) 45 96 111
Fax: (+385 1) 61 15 568
www.hfp.hr

International Finance Corporation
J.F. Kennedya trg, 6b
10000 Zagreb
Tel: (+385 1) 23 57 236
Fax: (+385 1) 23 57 233
www.ifc.hr

Ministry for European Integration
Ulica Grada Vukovara, 62
10000 Zagreb

Tel: (+385 1) 45 69 335
Fax: (+385 1) 63 03 183
www.mei.hr

Ministry for Handicraft, Small and
  Medium-sized Enterprises
Ksaver, 200
10000 Zagreb
Tel: (+385 1) 46 98 300
Fax: (+385 1) 46 98 308
www.momsp.hr

Ministry for Trades, Small and
  Medium Businesses
Ksaver, 200
10000 Zagreb
Tel: (+385 1) 46 98 300
Fax: (+385 1) 46 98 308
www.momsp.hr

Ministry of Agriculture and
  Forestry
Ulica Grada Vukovara, 78
10000 Zagreb
Tel: (+385 1) 61 06 111
Fax: (+385 1) 61 09 201
www.mps.hr

Ministry of Culture
Burze trg, 6
10000 Zagreb
Tel: (+385 1) 46 10 477
Fax: (+385 1) 46 10 489
www.min-kulture.hr

Ministry of Defence
Kralja Petra Kresimira IV trg, 1
10000 Zagreb
Tel: (+385 1) 45 67 111
Fax: (+385 1) 45 51 105
www.morh.hr

Ministry of Economy
Ulica Grada Vukovara, 78
10000 Zagreb
Tel: (+385 1) 61 06 111
Fax: (+385 1) 61 09 110
www.mingo.hr

Ministry of Environmental Protection
  and Regional Planning
Ulica Republike Austrije, 20
10000 Zagreb
Tel: (+385 1) 37 82 143
Fax: (+385 1) 37 72 555
www.mzopu.hr

Ministry of Finance
Ulica Matije Petra Katanciceva, 5
10000 Zagreb
Tel: (+385 1) 45 91 333
Fax: (+385 1) 49 22 583
www.mfin.hr

Ministry of Foreign Affairs
Nikole Subica Zrinskog trg, 78
10000 Zagreb
Tel: (+385 1) 45 69 964
Fax: (+385 1) 49 20 149
www.mvp.hr

Ministry of Health
Ksaver, 200a
10000 Zagreb
Tel: (+385 1) 46 07 555
Fax: (+385 1) 46 77 076
www.tel.hr/mzrh

Ministry of Interior
Savska Cesta, 39
10000 Zagreb
Tel: (+385 1) 61 22 111
Fax: (+385 1) 61 22 452
www.mup.hr

Ministry of Justice, Administration
  and Local Self-Administration
Ulica Republike Austrije, 14
10000 Zagreb
Tel: (+385 1) 37 10 666
Fax: (+385 1) 37 10 772
www.zatvor-zg.hr

Ministry of Labour and Social Welfare
Prisavlje, 14
10000 Zagreb
Tel: (+385 1) 61 69 111
Fax: (+385 1) 61 69 206
www.mrss.hr

Ministry of Maritime Affairs,
Transportation and
Communications
Prisavlje, 14
10000 Zagreb
Tel: (+385 1) 61 69 111
Fax: (+385 1) 61 96 473

Ministry of Public Works,
Reconstruction and Construction
Ulica Vladimira Nazorova, 61
10000 Zagreb
Tel: (+385 1) 37 84 500
Fax: (+385 1) 37 84 598
www.momsp.hr

Ministry of Science and Technology
Josipa Jurja Strossmayerov trg, 4
10000 Zagreb
Tel: (+385 1) 45 94 444
Fax: (+385 1) 45 94 469
www.mzt.hr

Ministry of Tourism
Ksaver, 200
10000 Zagreb
Tel: (+385 1) 46 98 300
Fax: (+385 1) 46 98 308
www.momsp.hr

National Bank of Croatia
Hrvatskih Velikana trg, 3
10002 Zagreb
Tel: (+385 1) 45 64 555
Fax: (+385 1) 45 50 726
www.hnb.hr

Office of the President of the Republic
Pantovčak, 241
10000 Zagreb
Tel: (+385 1) 456 51 09
Fax: (+385 1) 456 52 08
www.predsjednik.hr

State Bureau of Intellectual Property
Ulica grada Vukovara, 78
10000 Zagreb
Tel: (+385 1) 61 06 111
Fax: (+385 1) 61 12 017
www.dziv.hr

State Office for Standardization and
Metrology
Ulica grada Vukovara, 78
10000 Zagreb
Tel: (+385 1) 610 63 20
Fax: (+385 1) 610 93 20
www.dznm.hr

World Bank
J.F. Kennedya trg, 6b/3
10000 Zagreb
Tel: (+385 1) 238 72 22
Fax: (+385 1) 238 72 00
www.worldbank.hr

Zagreb Stock Exchange
Ksaver, 200
10000 Zagreb
Tel: (+385 1) 46 77 925
Fax: (+385 1) 46 77 680
www.zse.hr

Czech Republic

American Chamber of Commerce in
the Czech Republic
Dušní, 10
CZ-11000 Prague 1
Tel: (+420 2) 2232 9430
Fax: (+420 2) 2232 9433
www.amcham.cz

Association for Foreign Investment
Štěpánská, 15
CZ-12000 Prague 2
Tel: (+420 2) 9634 2504
Fax: (+420 2) 9634 2502
www.afi.cz

Association of Direct Marketing
Domazlicka, 3
CZ-13000 Prague
Tel: (+420 2) 6121 6030
Fax: (+420 2) 6121 6031
www.admaz.cz

Association of Innovative
Entrepreneurship CR
Novotného lávka, 5

CZ-11668 Prague 1
Tel: (+420 2) 2108 2275
www.aipcr.cz

Association of Realtors
Na Chodovci, 2880/3
CZ-14100 Prague 4
Tel: (+420 2) 7276 2953
Fax: (+420 2) 7276 6401
www.arkcms.cz

Brno Trade Fairs and Exhibitions
Výstaviště, 1
CZ-64700 Brno
Tel: (+420 5) 4115 1111
Fax: (+420 5) 4115 3070
www.bvv.cz

Confederation of Industry
Mikulandská, 135/7
CZ-11361 Prague 1
Tel: (+420 2) 2493 4088
Fax: (+420 2) 2493 4597
www.spcr.cz

Czech Agrarian Chamber
Department of International Relations
Štěpánská, 63
CZ-11210 Prague
Tel: (+420 2) 2421 5946
Fax: (+420 2) 2421 3944
www.agrocr.cz

Czech Agricultural and Food
Inspection
Department of International Relations
Kvetná, 15
CZ-60200 Brno
Tel: (+420 5) 4354 0111
Fax: (+420 5) 4354 0202
www.czpi.cz

Czech Customs Office
Budějovická, 7
CZ-14096 Prague
Tel: (+420 2) 6133 1111
Fax: (+420 2) 6133 2000
www.cs.mfcr.cz

Czech National Bank
Na Příkopě, 28
CZ-11503 Prague 1
Tel: (+420 2) 2441 1111
Fax: (+420 2) 2421 8522
www.cnb.cz

Czech Securities Commission
P.O. Box 208
Washingtonova, 7
CZ-11121 Prague 1
Tel: (+420 2) 2109 6112
Fax: (+420 2) 2109 6110
www.sec.cz

Czech Statistical Office
Sokolovska, 142
CZ-18604 Prague 8
Tel: (+420 2) 7405 2451
Fax: (+420 2) 7405 2457
www.czso.cz

Czech Trade Promotion Agency
Dittrichova, 21
P.O. Box 76
CZ-12801 Prague 2
Tel: (+420 2) 2490 7500
Fax: (+420 2) 2490 7503
www.czechtrade.cz

Czech Venture Capital Association
c/o Fond Rizikoveho Kapitalu
Na Šťáhlavce, 2
CZ-16000 Prague 6
Tel: (+420 2) 3332 6340
Fax: (+420 2) 3332 6295
www.cvca.cz

Czechinvest National Promotional
Agency
Stepanska, 15
CZ-12000 Prague 2
Tel: (+420 2) 9634 2500
Fax: (+420 2) 9634 2502
www.czechinvest.com

Economic Chamber
Seifertova, 22
CZ-13000 Prague 3
Tel: (+420 2) 2409 6111

Fax: (+420 2) 2409 6222
www.hkcr.cz/en

Export Guarantee and Insurance
  Corporation
Vodickova, 34/701
CZ-11121 Prague 1
Tel: (+420 2) 2284 1111
Fax: (+420 2) 2284 4110
www.egap.cz

General Customs Directorate
Budějovická, 7
CZ-14096 Prague 4
Tel: (+420 2) 6133 1111
Fax: (+420 2) 6133 2000
www.cs.mfcr.cz

Industrial Property Office
Antonína Cermáka, 2a
CZ-16068 Prague 6
Tel: (+420 2) 2038 3111
Fax: (+420 2) 2432 4718
www.upv.cz

International Finance Corporation
  Office
Husova, 5
CZ-11000 Prague
Tel: (+420 2) 2440 1402
Fax: (+420 2) 2440 1410
www.worldbank.cz/1ifc.htm

Ministry of Agriculture
Těšnov, 17
CZ-11705 Prague 1
Tel: (+420 2) 2181 1111
Fax: (+420 2) 2481 0478
www.mze.cz

Ministry of Finance
Letenská, 15
CZ-11810 Prague 1
Tel: (+420 2) 5704 1111
Fax: (+420 2) 5704 2788
www.mfcr.cz

Ministry of Foreign Affairs
Loretánské Nám., 5
CZ-11800 Prague 1

Tel: (+420 2) 2418 1111
www.mfa.cz

Ministry of Industry and Trade
Na Františku, 32
CZ-11015 Prague 1
Tel: (+420 2) 2485 1111
Fax: (+420 2) 2231 1970
www.mpo.cz

Ministry of Justice & Commercial
  Register
Vyšehradská, 16
CZ-12810 Prague 2
Tel: (+420 2) 2199 7111
www.justice.cz

Ministry of the Environment
Vrsovicka, 65
CZ-11000 Prague 10
Tel: (+420 2) 6712 1111
www.env.cz

Ministry for Regional
  Development
Staromestske Nam., 6
CZ-11015 Prague 1
Tel: (+420 2) 2486 1111
Fax: (+420 2) 2486 1333
www.mmr.cz

Ministry of Transport and
  Communication
P.O. Box 9
Nab. Ludvika Svobody, 12/22
CZ-11015 Prague 1
Tel: (+420 2) 5143 1111
Fax: (+420 2) 5143 1184
www.mdcr.cz

National Property Fund
Rašínovo Nábřeží, 42
CZ-12800 Prague 2
Tel: (+420 2) 2499 1111
Fax: (+420 2) 2499 1379
www.fnm.cz

Prague Stock Exchange
Rybna, 14
CZ-11005 Prague 1

Tel: (+420 2) 2183 1111
Fax: (+420 2) 2183 3040
www.pse.cz

Revitalization Agency
Janovského, 438/2
CZ-17006 Prague 7
Tel: (+420 2) 2014 1111
Fax: (+420 2) 3337 2033
www.czka.cz

Estonia

American Chamber of Commerce
Estonia
Tallinn Business Center
Harju 6, 234a
10130 Tallinn
Tel: (+372) 631 0522
Fax: (+372) 631 0521
www.acce.ee

Bank of Estonia
Estonia bld., 13
15095 Tallinn
Tel: (+372) 668 0719
Fax: (+372) 668 0954
www.ee/epbe/en

BMF Baltic Media Facts
Ahtri, 12
10151 Tallinn
Tel: (+372) 626 8400
Fax: (+372) 626 8401
www.bmf.ee

Consumer Protection Board
Kiriku 4
15071 Tallinn
Tel: (+372) 620 1700
Fax: (+372) 620 1701
www.consumer.ee

Estonian Chamber of Commerce
and Industry
Toomkoli, 17
10130 Tallinn
Tel: (+372) 646 0244
Fax: (+372) 646 0245
www.koda.ee

Estonian Investment Agency
Roosikrantsi, 11
10119 Tallinn
Tel: (+372) 6271 9420
Fax: (+372) 627 9427
www.eia.ee

Estonian Legal Translation Centre
Tõnismägi, 8
10119 Tallinn
Tel: (+372) 693 5100
Fax: (+372) 646 1075
www.legaltext.ee

Estonian Patent Office
Toompuiestee, 7
15041 Tallinn
Tel: (+372) 627 7900
Fax: (+372) 645 1342
www.epa.ee

Estonian Regional Development
Agency
Roosikrantsi, 11
10119 Tallinn
Tel: (+372) 627 9720
Fax: (+372) 627 9777
www.erda.ee

Estonian Trade Council
Liimi, 1503
10621 Tallinn
Tel: (+372) 656 3299
Fax: (+372) 656 3923
www.etc.ee

Estonian Trade Promotion Agency
Roosikrantsi, 11
10119 Tallinn
Tel: (+372) 627 9440
Fax: (+372) 627 9427
www.export.ee

Ministry of Agriculture
Lai, 39–41
15056 Tallinn
Tel: (+372) 625 6101
Fax: (+372) 625 6200
www.agri.ee

Ministry of Economic Affairs
Harju tn., 11
15072 Tallinn
Tel: (+372) 625 6342
Fax: (+372) 631 3660
www.mineco.ee

Ministry of Finance
Suur Ameerika, 1
15006 Tallinn
Tel: (+372) 611 3558
Fax: (+372) 696 6810
www.fin.ee

Ministry of Foreign Affairs
Islandi väljak 1
15049 Tallinn
Tel: (+372) 631 7000
Fax: (+372) 631 7099
www.vm.ee

Ministry of Justice
Lõkke, 4
19081 Tallinn
Tel: (+372) 611 3843
Fax: (+372) 646 0165
www.eer.ee

Ministry of Transport and
Communications
Viru tn., 9
15081 Tallinn
Tel. (+372) 639 7659
Fax: (+372) 639 7606
www.tsm.ee

National Customs Board
Tolliamet, Lõkke, 5
15175 Tallinn
Tel: (+372) 696 7722
Fax: (+372) 696 7727
www.customs.ee

National Standards Board
Aru, 10
10317 Tallinn
Tel: (+372) 605 5050
Fax: (+372) 605 5070
www.evs.ee

Office of the President
Weizenbergi, 39
15050 Tallinn
Tel: (+372) 631 6202
Fax: (+372) 631 6250
www.president.ee

Public Procurement Office
Kiriku, 2–4
10130 Tallinn
Tel: (+372) 620 1811
Fax: (+372) 631 1602
www.rha.gov.ee

Statistical Office of Estonia
Endla, 15
15174 Tallinn
Tel: (+372) 625 9300
Fax: (+372) 625 9370
www.stat.ee

Hungary

American Chamber of Commerce in
Hungary
Deák Ferenc útca 10/5
H-1052 Budapest
Tel: (+36 1) 266 9880
Fax: (+36 1) 266 9888
www.amcham.hu

Association for Direct Marketing
Bajza útca 31
H-1062 Budapest
Tel: (+36 1) 413 6397
Fax: (+36 1) 342 0536
www.dmsz.net/ns

Budapest Court of Registry
Nádor útca 28
H-1051 Budapest
Tel: (+36 1) 131 0177
Fax: (+36 1) 111 1216

Budapest Stock Exchange
Deák Ferenc útca 5
H-1052 Budapest
Tel: (+36 1) 429 6700
Fax: (+36 1) 429 6800
www.bse.hu

Central Statistical Office
Keleti Károly útca 57
H-1024 Budapest
Tel: (+36 1) 345 6000
Fax: (+36 1) 345 6378
www.ksh.hu

Chamber of Commerce and
Industry
Krisztina körút 99
H-1016 Budapest
Tel: (+36 1) 488 2000
Fax: (+36 1) 488 2000
www.bkik.hu

Chamber of Small and Medium
Entrepreneurs
Krisztina körút 99
H-1016 Budapest
Tel: (+36 1) 156 8281

Court of Arbitration
Kossuth L. tér 6–8
H-1051 Budapest
Tel: (+36 1) 474 5156
Fax: (+36 1) 474 5158
www.bkik.hu

Customs and Finance
Headquarters
Szent István tér 11/B
H-1051 Budapest
Tel: (+36 1) 132 4314
Fax: (+36 1) 132 3414

Government Debt Management
Agency
Csalogány útca 911
H-1027 Budapest
Tel: (+36 1) 488 9300
Fax: (+36 1) 488 9405
www.allampapir.hu

Hungarian Customs Headquarters
Mester útca 7
H-1095 Budapest
Tel: (+36 1) 218 0036
Fax: (+36 1) 218 2000

Hungarian Financial Supervisory
Authorities
Krisztina körút 39
H-1013 Budapest
Tel: (+36 1) 489 9100
Fax: (+36 1) 489 9102
www.pszaf.hu

Hungarian Investment and Trade
Development Agency
Alkotmány útca 3
H-1054 Budapest
Tel: (+36 1) 472 8100
Fax: (+36 1) 472 8101
www.itd.hu

Hungarian Privatization and State
Holding Company
Pozsonyi útca 56
H-1133 Budapest
Tel: (+36 1) 237 4400
Fax: (+36 1) 237 4100
www.apvrt.hu

Hungarian Venture Capital
Association
Nádor útca 32
H-1051 Budapest
Tel: (+36 1) 475 0924
Fax: (+36 1) 475 0925
www.hvca.hu

Hungexpo (information on
trade fairs)
P.O. Box 44
H-1441 Budapest
Tel: (+36 1) 263 6000
Fax: (+36 1) 263 6098
www.hungexpo.hu

International Finance
Corporation
Daewoo Bank Building
Bajcsy Zsilinszky útca 42–46/5
H-1054 Budapest
Tel: (+36 1) 374 9590
Fax: (+36 1) 374 9597
www.worldbank.hu/1ifc.html

Ministry of Agriculture and
  Regional Policy
Kossuth L. tér 11
H-1055 Budapest
Tel: (+36 1) 301 4000
Fax: (+36 1) 302 0408
www.fvm.hu

Ministry of Defence
Balaton útca 7/11
H-1055 Budapest
Tel: (+36 1) 332 2500
Fax: (+36 1) 311 0182
www.h-m.hu

Ministry of Economic Affairs
Honvéd útca 13–15
H-1055 Budapest
Tel: (+36 1) 374 2700
Fax: (+36 1) 374 2925
www.gm.hu

Ministry of Finance
József Nádor tér 2/4
H-1051 Budapest
Tel: (+36 1) 318 2066
www.meh.hu

Ministry of Foreign Affairs
Bem rakpart 47
H-1027 Budapest
Tel: (+36 1) 458 1000
Fax: (+36 1) 212 5918
www.kum.hu

Ministry of Home Affairs
József A. útca 2/4
H-1051 Budapest
Tel: (36 1) 331 3700
www.b-m.hu

Ministry of Justice
Kossuth L. tér 4
H-1055 Budapest
Tel: (+36 1) 268 3000
www.im.hu

Ministry of Transport,
  Communications and Water
  Management

Dob útca 75–81
H-1077 Budapest
Tel: (+36 1) 461 3300
www.khvm.hu

National Bank of Hungary
Szabadság tér 8–9
H-1850 Budapest
Tel: (+36 1) 302 3000
Fax: (+36 1) 332 3913
www.mnb.hu

National Committee for
  Technological Development (OMFB)
Szervita tér 8
H-1052 Budapest
Tel: (+36 1) 117 5900
Fax: (+36 1) 118 7998
www.omfb.hu

National Industrial Association
  (OKISZ)
Thököly útca 58–60
H-1146 Budapest
Tel: (+36 1) 141 5150

Office of the President of the
  Republic
Kossuth L. tér 3–5
H-1055 Budapest
Tel: (+36 1) 268 4000

Prime Minister's Office
Kossuth L. tér 1–3
H-1055 Budapest
Tel: (+36 1) 268 3000
www.meh.hu

Privatization and State Holding
  Company
Pozsonyi útca 56
H-1133 Budapest
Tel: (+36 1) 237 4400
Fax: (+36 1) 237 4100

Regional Environmental Center
Miklós tér 1
H-1035 Budapest
Tel: (+36 1) 168 6284
Fax: (+36 1) 168 7851

Soros Foundation
Bolyai útca 14
H-1023 Budapest
Tel: (+36 1) 315 0303
Tel: (+36 1) 315 0201
www.soros.hu

State Audit Office
Apáczai Csere János útca 10
H-1364 Budapest
Tel: (+36 1) 484 9100
Fax: (+36 1) 338 4710
www.asz.gov.hu

State Property Agency (SPA)
Pagony útca 18
H-1124 Budapest
Tel/Fax: (+36 1) 129 2650

Tax and Financial Control
  Administration
Széchenyi útca 2
H-1054 Budapest
Tel: (+36 1) 428 5100
www.apeh.hu

World Bank
Bajcsy-Zsilinszky
  útca 42–46/5
H-1054 Budapest
Tel: (+36 1) 374 9500
Fax: (+36 1) 374 9597
www.worldbank.hu

Latvia

American Chamber of Commerce in
  Latvia
Torna iela 4, IIa-301
LV-1050 Riga
Tel: (+371) 721 2204
Fax: (+371) 782 0090
www.amchamlatvia.lv

Bank of Latvia
Kr. Valdemāra iela 2a
LV-1050 Riga
Tel: (+371) 702 2300
Fax: (+371) 702 2420
www.bank.lv

Central Statistical Bureau of Latvia
Lāčplēša iela 1
LV-1301 Riga
Tel: (+371) 736 6850
Fax: (+371) 783 0137
www.csb.lv

European Bank for Reconstruction
  and Development
Kalku 15/4
LV-1050 Riga
Tel: (+371) 722 5068
Fax: (+371) 783 0301

International Finance
  Corporation
Smilsu iela 1/4, 5th floor
LV-1050 Riga
Tel: (+371) 722 0744
Fax: (+371) 782 8058

International Monetary Fund
Smilsu iela 1, Room 475
LV-1919 Riga
Tel: (+371) 709 5650
Fax: (+371) 782 0269
www.imf.org/external/country/lv

Latvian Chamber of Commerce
  and Industry
Brīvības bulvāris 21, 4th floor
LV-1849 Riga
Tel: (+371) 722 5595
Fax: (+371) 782 0092
sun.lcc.org.lv

Association of Latvian Commercial
  Banks
Pērses iela 9–11
LV-1001 Riga
Tel: (+371) 728 4528
Fax: (+371) 782 8170
www.bankasoc.lv

Latvian Customs Department
Kr. Valdemāra iela 1a
LV-1841 Riga
Tel: (+371) 732 3858
Fax: (+371) 732 2440

Latvian Development Agency
Perses iela 2
LV-1010 Riga
Tel: (+371) 703 9400
Fax: (+371) 703 9401
www.lda.gov.lv

Latvian National Certification
Centre
Klijanu iela 7
LV-1039 Riga
Tel: (+371) 737 5667
Fax: (+371) 737 5464

Latvian Parliament (Saeima)
Jekaba iela 11
LV-1811 Riga
Tel: (+371) 708 111
Fax: (+371) 783 0333
www.saeima.lv

Latvian Privatization Agenvcy
Kr. Valdemāra iela 31
LV-1010 Riga
Tel: (+371) 702 1358
Fax: (+371) 783 0363
www.lpa.bkc.lv

Latvian Traders' Association
(Henriks Danusevics, Chairman)
Gertrudes 36
LV-1011 Riga
Tel: (+371) 721 7372
Fax: (+371) 782 1010
www.lta.lv

Ministry of Agriculture
Republikas laukums 2
LV-1981 Riga
Tel: (+371) 702 7010
Fax: (+371) 702 7250
www.zm.gov.lv

Ministry of Economy
Brīvības bulvāris 55
LV-1010 Riga
Tel: (+371) 701 3101
Fax: (+371) 728 0882
www.lem.gov.lv

Ministry of Environmental Protection
and Regional Development
Peldu 25
LV-1494 Riga
Tel: (+371) 702 6418
Fax: (+371) 782 0442
www.varam.gov.lv

Ministry of Finance
Smilsu iela 1
LV-1919 Riga
Tel: (+371) 722 6672
Fax: (+371) 709 5503
www.fm.gov.lv

Ministry of Foreign Affairs
Brīvības bulvāris 36
LV-1395 Riga
Tel: (+371) 701 6210
Fax: (+371) 782 8121
www.mfa.gov.lv

Ministry of Interior
Raina bulvāris 6
LV-1050 Riga
Tel: (+371) 721 9212
Fax: (+371) 721 3142
www.iem.gov.lv

Ministry of Justice
Brīvības bulvāris 36
LV-1536 Riga
Tel: (+371) 703 6801
Fax: (+371) 728 5575
www.tm.gov.lv

Ministry of Transport
Gogola 3
LV-1743 Riga
Tel: (+371) 722 6922
Fax: (+371) 721 7180
www.sam.gov.lv

Register of Enterprises
Perses iela 2
LV-1011 Riga
Tel: (+371) 242 509
Fax: (+371) 284 353
www.lursoft.lv

Translation and Terminology Centre
Kr. Valdemāra iela 37
LV-1010 Riga
Tel: (+371) 733 1814
Fax: (+371) 733 6038
www.ttc.lv

World Bank Latvia Office
Smilsu iela 8, 5th Floor
LV-1162 Riga
Tel: (+371) 722 0744
Fax: (+371) 781 4245
www.worldbank.org.lv

Lithuania

Administrative Disputes Commission
Vilniaus str., 27
LT-2001 Vilnius
Tel: (+370 2) 684 050
Fax: (+370 2) 684 051
www.vagk.lt/eng

American Chamber of Commerce
Lukiskiu str., 5, Room 204
LT-2600 Vilnius
Tel: (+370 2) 611 181
Fax: (+370 5) 212 6128

Association of Lithuanian
  Chambers of Commerce and
  Industry
J. Tumo-Vaižganto g. 9/1-63a
LT-2001 Vilnius
Tel: (+370 22) 612 102
Fax: (+370 22) 612 112
www.chambers.lt

Association of Lithuanian
  Entrepreneurs
A. Jaksto str., 9
LT-2600 Vilnius
Tel: (+370 2) 614 963
Fax: (+370 2) 220 448

Bank of Lithuania
Gedimino pr. 6
LT-2001 Vilnius
Tel: (+370 22) 680 029

Fax: (+370 5) 212 1501
www.lbank.lt

Commercial Court of the Republic
  of Lithuania
Gedimino pr. 39/1
LT-2640 Vilnius
Tel: (+370 2) 622 843
Fax: (+370 2) 619 927

Confederation of Lithuanian
  Industrialists
LPK A.Vienuolio g. 8
LT-2000 Vilnius
Tel: (+370 2) 225 217
Fax: (+370 2) 225 209
www.lpk.lt

Customs Department
Jaksto 1/25
LT-2600 Vilnius
Tel: (+370 2) 226 415
Fax: (+370 2) 224 948
www.cust.lt

Department of Statistics
Gedimino pr. 29
LT-2746 Vilnius
Tel: (+370 2) 364 822
Fax: (+370 2) 364 845
www.std.lt

European Committee under the
  Government of Lithuania
Gedimino pr. 56
LT-2685 Vilnius
Tel: (+370 2) 661 700
Fax: (+370 2) 496 178
www.euro.lt

International Finance Corporation
Vilniaus str., 28
LT-2600 Vilnius
Tel: (+370 2) 226 803
Fax: (+370 2) 226 829

Lithuanian Development Agency
Sv. Jono str., 3
LT-2001 Vilnius
Tel: (+370 2) 627 438

Fax: (+370 5) 212 0160
www.lda.lt

Lithuanian Development Agency
for Small and Medium-sized
Enterpriese
Žygimantųstr., 11/5
LT-2001 Vilnius
Tel: (+370 2) 627 978
Fax: (+370 5) 212 2926
www.svv.lt

Lithuanian Standardization Board
Kosciuskos str., 30
LT-2600 Vilnius
Tel: (+370 2) 226 252
Fax: (+370 2) 226 252
www.lsd.lt

Lithuanian State Property Fund
Vilniaus str., 16
LT-2600 Vilnius
Tel: (+370 2) 684 999
Fax: (+370 2) 684 997
www.vtf.lt

Ministry of Agriculture
Gedimino pr. 19
LT-2025 Vilnius
Tel: (+370 2) 391 001
Fax: (+370 2) 224 440
www.zum.lt

Ministry of Economy
Gedimino pr. 38/2
LT-2600 Vilnius
Tel: (+370 2) 622 412
Fax: (+370 2) 623 974
www.ekm.lt

Ministry of Finance
J. Tumo Vaizganto 8a/2
LT-2600 Vilnius
Tel: (+370 2) 390 000
Fax: (+370 2) 791 481
www.finmin.lt

Ministry of Transport and
Communications
Gedimino pr. 17

LT-2679 Vilnius
Tel: (+370 2) 393 911
Fax: (+370 2) 124 335
www.transp.lt

National Stock Exchange
of Lithuania
Ukmerges str., 41
LT-2661 Vilnius
Tel: (+370 2) 723 871
Fax: (+370 2) 721 847
www.nse.lt

State Competition and Consumer
Protection Office
Vienuolio str., 8
LT-2600 Vilnius
Tel: (+370 2) 212 6492
Fax: (+370 2) 212 6492
www.konkuren.lt

State Patent Bureau
Kalvariju 3
LT-2600 Vilnius
Tel: (+370 2) 780 250
Fax: (+370 2) 750 723
www.vpb.lt

State Property Fund
Vilniaus str., 16
LT-2600 Vilnius
Tel: (+370 2) 684 999
Fax: (+370 2) 684 997
www.vtf.lt

State Tax Inspection under the
Ministry of Finance
Vasario 16-osios g. 15
LT-2600 Vilnius
Tel: (+370 5) 687 802
Fax: (+370 2) 212 5604
www.vmi.lt

State Veterinary Service
Siesiku str., 19
LT-2010 Vilnius
Tel: (+370 2) 404 361
Fax: (+370 2) 404 362
www.vet.lt

Tourism Department
Vilniaus str., 4/35
LT-2600 Vilnius
Tel: (+370 2) 622 610
Fax: (+370 2) 226 819
www.tourism.lt

World Bank
Business Center 2000
Jogailos g. 4
LT-2001 Vilnius
Tel: (+370 5) 210 7680
Fax: (+370 2) 210 7681
www.worldbank.lt

Poland

Agency for Restructuring and
  Modernization of Agriculture
Al. Jana Pawła II 70
PL-00175 Warsaw
Tel: (+4822) 8602950
Fax: (+4822) 8602980
www.arimr.gov.pl

American Chamber of Commerce in
  Poland (AmCham)
Warsaw Financial Center, 13th Floor
ul. Emilii Plater 53
PL-001163 Warsaw
Tel: (+4822) 520 59 99
Fax: (+4822) 520 99 98
www.amcham.com.pl

Association for Direct Marketing
  (SMB)
ul. Lucka 2/4/6
PL-00845 Warsaw
Tel: (+4822) 654 68 33
Fax: (+4822) 654 55 33
www.smb.pl

Business Centre Club
Palac Lubomirskich
Plac Zelaznej Bramy 2
PL-00136 Warsaw
Tel: (+4822) 625 30 37
Fax: (+4822) 621 84 20
www.bcc.org.pl

Central Statistical Office
Al. Niepodleglości 208
PL-00925 Warsaw
Tel: (+4822) 608 30 00
Fax: (+4822) 608 30 01
www.stat.gov.pl

Customs Head Office
ul. Swietokrzyska 12
PL-00916 Warsaw
Tel: (+4822) 694 31 94
www.guc.gov.pl

European Bank for Reconstruction
  and Development
Warsaw Financial Center, 13th Floor
ul. Emilii Plater 53
PL-00113 Warsaw
Tel: (+4822) 520 57 00
Fax: (+4822) 520 58 00

International Finance Corporation
Warsaw Financial Center, 9th Floor
ul. Emilii Plater 53
PL-00193 Warsaw
Tel: (+4822) 520 61 00
Fax: (+4822) 520 61 01

Ministry of Agriculture and Rural
  Development
ul. Wspolna 30
PL-00930 Warsaw
Tel: (+4822) 623 10 00
Fax: (+4822) 623 27 50
www.minrol.gov.pl

Ministry of Economy
Pl. Trzech Krzyzy 5
PL-00950 Warsaw
Tel: (+4822) 693 50 00
Fax: (+4822) 628 68 08
www.mg.gov.pl

Ministry of Environment
ul. Wawelska 52/54
PL-00922 Warsaw
Tel: (+4822) 579 29 00
Fax: (+4822) 579 22 24
www.mos.gov.pl

Ministry of Finance
ul. Swietokrzyska 12
PL-00916 Warsaw
Tel: (+4822) 694 55 55
www.mofnet.gov.pl

Ministry of Foreign Affairs
Al. J. Ch. Szucha 23
PL-00580 Warsaw
Tel: (+4822) 523 90 00
Fax: (+4822) 629 86 35
www.msz.gov.pl

Ministry of Health
ul. Miodowa 15
PL-00952 Warsaw
Tel: (+4822) 831 23 24
Fax: (+4822) 831 12 12
www.mzios.gov.pl

Ministry of Justice
Al. Ujazdowskie 11
PL-00950 Warsaw
Tel: (+4822) 521 28 88
www.ms.gov.pl

Ministry of State Treasury
ul. Krucza 36
PL-00522 Warsaw
Tel: (+4822) 665 80 00
Fax: (+4822) 628 08 72
www.msp.gov.pl

Ministry of Transportation and
   Maritime Economy
ul. Chalubinskiego 4/6
PL-00928 Warsaw
Tel: (+4822) 621 56 76
Fax: (+4822) 830 02 61
www.mtigm.gov.pl

National Bank of Poland
Świętokrzyska 11/21
PL-00919 Warsaw
Tel: (+4822) 653 10 00
Fax: (+4822) 620 85 18
www.nbp.pl

National Chamber of Commerce
   of Poland

ul. Trebacka 4
PL-00074 Warsaw
Tel: (+4822) 630 96 00
Fax: (+4822) 827 46 73
www.kig.pl

Patent Office of Republic
   of Poland
Al. Niepodleglości 188/192
PL-00950 Warsaw
Tel: (+4822) 825 80 01
Fax: (+4822) 825 05 81
www.uprp.pl

Polish Agency For Foreign
   Investment
Al. Roz 2
PL-00559 Warsaw
Tel: (+4822) 334 98 00
Fax: (+4822) 334 99 99
www.paiz.gov.pl

Polish Bank Associations
ul. Smolna 10a
PL-00375 Warsaw
Tel: (+4822) 828 14 09
Fax: (+4822) 828 14 06
www.zbp.pl

Polish Center for Testing and
   Certification
ul. Klobucka 23a
PL-02699 Warsaw
Tel: (+4822) 857 99 16
Fax: (+4822) 647 12 22
www.pcbc.gov.pl

Polish Chamber of Information
   Technology and
   Telecommunications
ul. Nowogrodzka 31, Room 204
PL-00503 Warsaw
Tel: (+4822) 628 22 60
Fax: (+4822) 628 55 36
www.piit.org.pl

Polish Chamber of Tourism
ul. Astronomow 3/411
PL-01415 Warsaw
Tel: (+4822) 836 99 71

Fax: (+4822) 836 99 73
www.pit.org.pl

Polish Securities and Exchange
Commission
pl. Powstańców Warszawy 1
PL-00950 Warsaw
Tel: (+4822) 556 08 00
Fax: (+4822) 826 81 00

World Bank
Warsaw Financial Center, 9th Floor
ul. Emilii Plater 53
PL-001163 Warsaw
Tel: (+4822) 520 80 00
Fax: (+4822) 520 80 01
www.worldbank.org.pl

Slovakia

American Chamber of Commerce in
the Slovak Republic
Hotel Danube, Rybne Namestie 1
SK-813 38 Bratislava
Tel: (+421 7) 5934 0508
Fax: (+421 7) 5934 0556
www.amcham.sk

Antimonopoly Office
Drieňová 24
SK-826 03 Bratislava 29
Tel: (+421 7) 4333 7305
Fax: (+421 7) 4333 3572
www.antimon.gov.sk

Association for Direct Marketing
Galvaniho 10
SK-821 04 Bratislava
Tel: (+421 7) 5063 3693
Fax: (+421 7) 5063 3693
www.adima.sk

Attorney Generalship
Župné nám. 13
SK-812 85 Bratislava 1
Tel: (+421 7) 5935 3111
Fax: (+421 7) 5441 2333
www.genpro.gov.sk

Constitutional Court
Hlavna 72
P.O. Box E35
SK-042 65 Kosice 1
Tel: (+421 95) 622 7671
www.concourt.sk

Customs Directorate
Mierova 23
SK-821 05 Bratislava
Tel: (+421 7) 4827 3172
Fax: (+421 7) 4329 3281

Financial Market Authority
Radlinského Ul
SK-813 18 Bratislava
Tel: (+421 7) 5726 2110
www.uft.sk

Ministry of Administration and
Privatization of National Property
Drienova 24, P.O. Box 76
SK-820 09 Bratislava 29
Tel: (+421 7) 4333 1090
Fax: (+421 7) 4333 3335
www.privatiz.gov.sk

Ministry of Agriculture
Dobrovičova 12
SK-812 66 Bratislava 1
Tel: (+421 7) 5926 6111
Fax: (+421 7) 5296 8510
www.mpsr.sk

Ministry of Construction and
Regional Development
Spitalska 8
SK-816 44 Bratislava 1
Tel: (+421 7) 5975 1111
Fax: (+421 7) 5293 1203
www.build.gov.sk

Ministry of Culture
Nám. SNP č. 33
SK-813 31 Bratislava 1
Tel: (+421 7) 5939 1155
Fax: (+421 7) 5441 9671
www.culture.gov.sk

Ministry of Defence
Kutuzovova 8
SK-832 47 Bratislava 3
Tel: (+421 7) 254 500
Fax: (+421 7) 258 904
www.mod.gov.sk

Ministry of Economy
Mierova 19
SK-827 15 Bratislava 212
Tel: (+421 7) 4854 1111
Fax: (+421 7) 4333 7827
www.economy.gov.sk

Ministry of Education
Stromova 1
SK-813 30 Bratislava 1
Tel: (+421 7) 5937 4111
www.education.gov.sk

Ministry of Environment
Nam. L. Stura 1
SK-812 35 Bratislava 1
Tel: (+421 7) 5956 1111
Fax: (+421 7) 5956 2438
www.lifeenv.gov.sk

Ministry of Finance
Stefanovicova 5
SK-813 08 Bratislava
Tel: (+421 7) 357 1111
Fax: (+421 7) 398 042
www.finance.gov.sk

Ministry of Foreign Affairs
Hlboká 2
SK-833 36 Bratislava 37
Tel: (+421 7) 5978 1111
Fax: (+421 7) 5978 2213
www.foreign.gov.sk

Ministry of Health
Limbova 2, P.O. Box 52
SK-813 05 Bratislava 3
Tel: (+421 7) 376 161
Fax: (+421 7) 377 934
www.health.gov.sk

Ministry of Interior
Pribinova 2

SK-812 72 Bratislava 1
Tel: (+421 7) 526 1111
Fax: (+421 7) 325 292
www.minv.sk

Ministry of Justice
Zupne Nam. 13
SK-813 11 Bratislava 1
Tel: (+421 7) 535 3111
www.justice.gov.sk

Ministry of Management and
    Privatization of National Property
Drienova 24
SK-820 09 Bratislava
Tel: (+421 7) 4333 1090
Fax: (+421 7) 4333 3335
www.privatiz.gov.sk

Ministry of Transportation, Post
    and Telecommunication
Slobody Nam. 6
SK-810 05 Bratislava 1
Tel: (+421 7) 5949 4111
Fax: (+421 7) 5249 4794
www.telecom.gov.sk

Ministry of Work, Social Affairs
    and Family
Spitalska 4
SK-816 43 Bratislava 1
Tel: (+421 7) 5975 1111
www.employment.gov.sk

National Agency for Development of
    Small and Medium Enterprises
Prievozska 30
SK-821 05 Bratislava
Tel: (+421 7) 5341 7328
Fax: (+421 7) 5341 7339
www.nadsme.sk

National Bank of Slovakia
Sturova 2
SK-813 25 Bratislava 1
Tel: (+421 7) 5953 1111
www.nbs.sk

National Council
Mudronova 1

SK-812 80 Bratislava 1
Tel: (+421 7) 5934 1111
www.nrsr.sk

National Property Fund
Drienova 27
SK-821 01 Bratislava 2
Tel: (+421 7) 4827 1111
Fax: (+421 7) 4827 1289
www.natfund.gov.sk

News Agency of the
Slovak Republic
Pribinova 23
SK-819 28 Bratislava 111
Tel: (+421 7) 5921 0152
Fax: (+421 7) 5296 2468
www.tasr.sk

Office of International Ownership
Svermova 43
SK-974 05 Banska Bystrica
Tel: (+421 8) 8430 0111
Fax: (+421 8) 8413 2563
www.indprop.gov.sk

Office of Standards, Metrology and
Testing
Stefanovicova 3
P.O. Box 76
SK-810 05 Bratislava 15
Tel: (+421 7) 5249 6847/5249 8030
www.normoff.gov.sk

Office of the President
Stefanikova 2
P.O. Box 128
SK-810 00 Bratislava 1
Tel: (+421 7) 5720 1147
www.prezident.sk

Slovak Export Information Centre
Incheba Building, 15th Floor
Viedenská cesta 5
SK-85220 Bratislava
Tel: (+421 7) 6241 1367
Fax: (+421 7) 6241 1390

Statistical Office
Mileticova 3

SK-824 67 Bratislava 26
Tel: (+421 7) 5023 6111
www.statistics.sk

Supreme Court
Zupne Nam. 13
SK-814 90 Bratislava 1
Tel: (+421 7) 5935 3111
Fax: (+421 7) 5441 1535
www.justice.gov.sk/nssr

Supreme Inspection Office
Priemyselna 2
SK-824 73 Bratislava 26
Tel: (+421 7) 5542 3069
Fax: (+421 7) 5542 4628
www.controll.gov.sk

Telecommunications Office
Továrenská 7
P.O. Box 18
SK-81006 Bratislava 16
Tel: (+421 7) 5788 1111
Fax: (+421 7) 5293 2096
www.teleoff.gov.sk

Slovenia

Agency of the Republic of Slovenia
for Payments
Supervision and Information
Tržaška cesta 16
SI-1000 Ljubljana
Tel: (+386 1) 477 41 00
Fax: (+386 1) 425 97 70
www.sdk.si

Agency of the Republic of
Slovenia for Restructuring
and Privatization
Kotnikova 28
SI-1000 Ljubljana
Tel: (+386 1) 131 21 22
Fax: (+386 1) 131 60 11
www.arspip.si/ang

Agency of the Republic of Slovenia
for the Audit of the Ownership
Transformation of Companies

Dunajska 22
SI-1000 Ljubljana
Tel: (+386 1) 434 33 44
Fax: (+386 1) 300 84 55
www.gov.si/arlpp

American Chamber of Commerce in
    Slovenia
Topniska 14
SI-1000 Ljubljana
Tel: (+386 1) 130 92 20
Fax: (+386 1) 130 92 25
www.am-cham.si

Association of Slovenian Banks
Subiceva 2
SI-1000 Ljubljana
Tel: (+386 1) 251 21 80
Fax: (+386 1) 425 21 06
www.zbsgiz.si

Bank of Slovenia
Slovenska 35
SI-1505 Ljubljana
Tel: (+386 1) 471 90 00
Fax: (+386 1) 251 55 16
www.bsi.si

Chamber of Commerce and
    Industry of Slovenia
Dimičeva 13
SI-1504 Ljubljana
Tel: (+386 1) 589 80 00
Fax: (+386 1) 589 81 00
www.gzs.si

Customs Administration of the
    Republic of Slovenia
Šmartinska 55
SI-1523 Ljubljana
Tel: (+386 1) 478 38 00
Fax: (+386 1) 478 39 00
www.sigov.si/mf/angl/curs/
    welcome.htm

Institute of Macroeconomic
    Analysis and Development
Gregorčičeva 27
SI-1000 Ljubljana

Tel: (+386 1) 178 21 12
Fax: (+386 1) 178 20 70
www.sigov.si/zmar/imad.html

Ljubljana Stock Exchange
Slovenska cesta 56
SI-1000 Ljubljana
Tel: (+386 1) 471 02 11
Fax: (+386 1) 471 02 13
www.ljse.si

Metrology Institute of the
    Republic of Slovenia
Šmartinska 140
SI-1000 Ljubljana
Tel: (+386 1) 478 30 47
Fax: (+386 1) 478 30 96
www.usm.mzt.si

Ministry of Agriculture, Forestry
    and Food
Parmova 33
SI-1000 Ljubljana
Tel: (+386 1) 436 22 92
Fax: (+386 1) 436 33 43
www.sigov.si/mkgp

Ministry of the Economy
Kotnikova 5
SI-1000 Ljubljana
Tel: (+386 1) 478 36 21
Fax: (+386 1) 478 35 22
www2.gov.si/mg/mgslo.nsf

Ministry of the Environment, Spatial
    Planning and Energy
Dunajska cesta 48
SI-1000 Ljubljana
Tel: (+386 1) 478 74 00
Fax: (+386 1) 478 74 27
www.sigov.si/mop

Ministry of Finance
Župančičeva 3
SI-1502 Ljubljana
Tel: (+386 1) 478 52 11
Fax: (+386 1) 478 56 55
www.sigov.si/mf

Ministry of Foreign Affairs
Prešernova cesta 25
SI-1000 Ljubljana
Tel: (+386 1) 478 20 00
fax: (+386 1) 478 23 40
www.sigov.si/mzz

Ministry of Information Society
Langusova 4
SI-1508 Ljubljana
Tel: (+386 1) 478 80 00
Fax: (+386 1) 478 83 75
www2.gov.si/mid/mideng.nsf

Ministry of the Interior
Štefanova 2
SI-1501 Ljubljana
Tel: (+386 1) 472 51 11
Fax: (+386 1) 251 43 30
www.mnz.si

Ministry of Justice
Župančičeva 3
SI-1000 Ljubljana
Tel: (+386 1) 369 52 00
Fax: (+386 1) 369 55 19
www.gov.si/mp

Ministry of Transport
Langusova 4,
SI-1000 Ljubljana
Tel: (+386 1) 478 80 00
Fax: (+386 1) 478 81 39
www.sigov.si/mpz

Office of the Prime Minister
Gregorčičeva 20
SI-1000 Ljubljana
Tel: (+386 1) 478 10 00
Fax: (+386 1) 478 16 07
www.gov.si/pv/indexang.html

Office of the Public Prosecutor
of the Republic of Slovenia
Dunajska 22
SI-1000 Ljubljana
Tel: (+386 1) 232 03 96
Fax: (+386 1) 431 03 81

Slovenian Intellectual Property
Office
Kotnikova 6
P.O. Box 206
SI-1000 Ljubljana
Tel: (+386 1) 478 31 00
Fax: (+386 1) 478 31 10
www.uilsipo.si

Slovenian Tourist Board
Dunajska 156
SI-1001 Ljubljana
Tel: (+386 1) 589 18 40
Fax: (+386 1) 589 18 41
www.tourist-board.si

Small Business Development
Centre
Dunajska 156
SI-1001 Ljubljana
Tel: (+386 1) 189 18 70
Fax: (+386 1) 188 11 78
www.pcmg.si

Tax Administration
Šmartinska 55
SI-1523 Ljubljana
Tel: (+386 1) 478 27 80
Fax: (+386 1) 478 27 52
www.gov.si/durs

Trade and Investment Promotion
Office (TIPO)
Kotnikova 28
SI-1000 Ljubljana
Tel: (+386 1) 178 35 57
Fax: (+386 1) 178 35 99
www.investslovenia.org

Turkey

Ankara Chamber of Commerce
Sehit Tegmen Kalmaz Caddesi 30
TR-06050 Ulus, Ankara
Tel: (+90 312) 310 48 10
Fax: (+90 312) 310 84 36
www.atonet.org.tr

Ankara Chamber of Industry
Ataturk Bulvari 193/4
TR-06680 Kavaklidere, Ankara
Tel: (+90 312) 417 12 00
Fax: (+90 312) 417 20 60

Association for Foreign Capital
   Coordination
Koza Is Merkezi B Blok/Kat 1
TR-80700 Besiktas, Istanbul
Tel: (+90 212) 272 50 94
Fax: (+90 212) 274 66 64

Central Bank of Turkey
İstiklal Caddesi 10 Ulus
TR-06100 Ankara
www.tcmb.gov.tr

Foreign Economic Relations Board
Kurulu Istiklal Caddesi 286/9
TR-80050 Odakule Beyoglu,
   Istanbul
Tel: (+90 212) 243 41 80
Fax: (+90 212) 243 41 84

General Directorate of Free Trade
   Zones
Eskisehir Karayolu Inonu Bulvari
TR-06510 Emek, Ankara
Tel: (+90 312) 212 82 61
Fax: (+90 312) 212 89 06

International Finance Corporation
Yildiz Posta Caddesi 17/5
TR-80280 Esentepe, Istanbul
Tel: (+90 212) 212 65 35
Fax: (+90 212) 212 91 65

Istanbul Chamber of Commerce
Ragip Gumuspala Caddesi 84
TR-34378 Eminonu, Istanbul
Tel: (+90 212) 511 41 50
Fax: (+90 212) 526 21 97

Istanbul Chamber of Industry
Mesrutiyet Caddesi 118
TR-80050 Tepebasi, Istanbul
Tel: (+90 212) 252 29 00
Fax: (+90 212) 249 39 63

Istanbul Stock Exchange
TR-80860 İstinye, Istanbul
Tel: (+90 212) 298 21 00
Fax: (+90 212) 298 25 00
www.ise.org

Ministry of Agriculture and Rural Affairs
Milli Müdafaa Caddesi 20
TR-06100 Kızılay, Ankara
Tel: (+90 312) 424 05 80
Fax: (+90 312) 425 44 95
www.tcmb.gov.tr

Ministry of Energy and Natural
   Resources
İnönü Bulvari, 27
Bahçelievler Ankara
Tel: (+90 312) 212 69 15
www.enerji.gov.tr

Ministry of Finance
www.maliye.gov.tr

Ministry of Foreign Affairs
TR-06100 Balgat, Ankara
Tel: (+90 312) 292 10 00
www.mfa.gov.tr

Ministry of Industry and
   Commerce
Eskisehir Yolu 7. Km.
Eski Citosan Binasi
Ankara
Tel: (+90 312) 286 03 65
Fax: (+90 312) 285 63 11

Ministry of Justice
Adalet Bakanlığı PK
TR-06659 Kızılay, Ankara
Tel: (+90 312) 417 77 70
www.adalet.gov.tr

Patent Institute (Türk Patent Enstitüsü)
Necatibey Caddesi 49
TR-06440 Ankara
Tel: (+90 312) 232 54 25
www.turkpatent.gov.tr

State Institute of Statistics (SIS)
Necatibey Caddesi 49

TR-06440 Bakanliklar, Ankara
Tel: (+90 312) 417 64 40
Fax: (+90 312) 425 33 87
www.die.gov.tr

Turkish American Business Association
American Chamber of Commerce
Barbaros Bulvari Eser, Apt. No. 48
K.5 D.16
TR-80700 Balmumcu, Istanbul
Tel: (+90 212) 274 28 24
Fax: (+90 212) 275 93 16
www.taba.org.tr

Turkish Competition Authority
(Rekabet Kurumu)
Bilkent Plaza B3 Blok pk
TR-06530 Bilkent, Ankara
Tel: (+90 312) 266 69 69
Fax: (+90 312) 266 79 20
www.rekabet.gov.tr

Turkish Industrialists' and
  Businessmens' Association
Mesrutiyet Caddesi 74
TR-80050 Tepebasi, Istanbul
Tel: (+90 212) 249 19 29
Fax: (+90 212) 249 13 50

Turkish Standards Institute
Necatýbey Caddesi 112
TR-06100 Bakanliklar, Ankara
Tel: (+90 312) 417 83 30
www.tse.org.tr

Undersecretariat for Foreign Trade
Eskisehir Karayolu Inonu Bulvari
TR-06510 Emek, Ankara
Tel: (+90 312) 342 39 00
Fax: (+90 312) 342 40 01
www.foreigntrade.gov.tr

Union of Chambers of Commerce,
  Industry, Maritime Commerce
  and Commodity Exchanges of
  Turkey (TOBB)
Ataturk Bulvari 149
TR-06640 Bakanliklar, Ankara
Tel: (+90 312) 418 33 60
Fax: (+90 312) 418 32 68

World Bank Office
Ugur Mumcu Caddesi 88, 2nd Floor
TR-06700 Gaziosmanpasa, Ankara
Tel: (+90 312) 446 38 24
Fax: (+90 312) 446 24 42
www.worldbank.org.tr

Ukraine

American Chamber of Commerce
  in Ukraine
42–44 Shovkovychna Vul., 2nd Floor
01004 Kiev
Tel: (+38 044) 490 5800
Fax: (+38 044) 490 5801
www.amcham.kiev.ua

Business Incubator Development
  Program in Ukraine
Usaid Project
13, Triohsvyatytelska Vul.
01011 Kiev
Tel: (+38 044) 229 2480
Fax: (+38 044) 229 4320
itri.loyola.edu/bid

Chamber of Commerce and
  Industry (CCI) of Ukraine
33, Velyka Zhytomyrska Vul.
01601 Kiev
Tel: (+38 044) 212 2911
Fax: (+38 044) 212 3353
www.ucciorg.ua

Eurasia Foundation – Regional
  Office For Ukraine, Moldova
  and Belarus
26, Lesi Ukrainky Vul., Suite 506
01133 Kiev
Tel/Fax: (+38 044) 295 1065
E-mail: eurasia@eurasia.kiev.ua

European Bank for Reconstruction
  and Development (EBRD)
27/23, Sophyivska Vul.
01001 Kiev
Tel: (+38 044) 464 0132
Fax: (+38 044) 464 0813
www.ebrd.com

European Business Association
20, Esplanadna str., 11th Floor
01023 Kiev
Tel: (+38 044) 229 7777
Fax: (+38 044) 227 0626
www.eba.com.ua

Harvard Institute For International
 Development
10b, Khreshchatyk Vul.,
 7th Floor
01001 Kiev
Tel: (+38 044) 229 5467
Fax: (+38 044) 228 1349
www/harvard.kiev.ua

International Finance
 Corporation
4, Bohomoltsa Vul., 5th Floor
01024 Kiev
Tel: (+38 044) 293 0662
Fax: (+38 044) 490 5830
www.ifc.org

International Monetary Fund
24/7, Institutska Vul., Suites
 6 and 8
01008 Kiev
Tel: (+38 044) 247 7007
Fax: (+38 044) 247 7005
www.un.kiev.ua/imf

International Union of Ukrainian
 Businessmen
2-v, Pyrohova Vul.
01030 Kiev
Tel: (+38 044) 228 3308
Fax: (+38 022) 228 8384

Ministry of Agricultural Complex
24, Khreshchatyk Vul.
01001 Kiev
Tel: (+38 044) 226 3466
Fax: (+38 044) 229 8545

Ministry of Defence
6, Povitroflotskuy Prospect
03168 Kiev
Tel: (+38 044) 226 2656
Fax: (+38 044) 226 2015

Ministry of Economics
12/2, Hrushevskoho Vul.
01008 Kiev
Tel: (+38 044) 226 2315
Fax: (+38 044) 226 3181
www.me.gov.ua

Ministry of Environment and
 Natural Resources
5, Khreshchatyk Vul.
01601 Kiev
Tel: (+38 044) 226 2428
Fax: (+38 044) 229 8383

Ministry of Finance
12/2, Hrushevskoho Vul.
01008 Kiev
Tel: (+38 044) 293 5363
Fax: (+38 044) 293 8243

Ministry of Foreign Affairs
1, Mykhailivska Ploscha
01018 Kiev
Tel: (+38 044) 212 8286
Fax: (+38 044) 226 3169
www.mfa.gov.ua

Ministry of Fuel and Energy
4, Bohdana
 Khmelnytskoho Vul.
01001 Kiev
Tel: (+380 44) 226 2273
Fax: (+380 44) 228 2131

Ministry of Health
7, Hrushevsky str.,
01021 Kiev
Tel: (+38 044) 253 2472
Fax: (+38 044) 253 8162
www.moz.gov.ua

Ministry of Industrial Policy
3, Surykova Vul.
03035 Kiev
Tel: (+38 044) 245 4778
Fax: (+38 044) 246 3214
www.industry.gov.ua

Ministry of Justice
13, Horodetskoho Vul.

01001 Kiev
Tel: (+38 044) 228 3723
www.minjust.gov.ua

Ministry of Transportation
7–9, Shchorsa Vul.
03150 Kiev
Tel: (+38 044) 226 2204
Fax: (+38 044) 268 1041
www.mintrans.kiev.ua

National Bank of Ukraine (NBU)
9, Instytutska Vul.
01008 Kiev
Tel: (+38 044) 293 0180
Fax: (+38 044) 293 1698
www.bank.gov.ua

Presidential Administration
11, Bankova Vul.
01220 Kiev
Tel: (+38 044) 291 5333
Fax: (+38 044) 291 6161

State Committee for Youth Policy,
   Sport and Tourism
36, Yaroslaviv Val str.,
01034 Kiev
Tel: (+38 044) 220 0366
Fax: (+38 044) 220 1294
www.utis.com.ua

State Committee of Statistics
3, Shota Rustaveli Vul.
01023 Kiev
Tel: (+38 044) 227 2433
Fax: (+38 044) 227 4266

State Property Fund
50r, Shevchenko Vul.
212-0841 Kiev
Tel: (+38 044) 295 1274
Fax: (+38 044) 295 1274
www.spfu.kiev.ua

State Tax Administration
   of Ukraine
8, Lvivska Ploshcha
04655 Kiev

Tel: (+38 044) 212 2691
Fax: (+38 044) 212 0841
www.sta.gov.ua

Ukrainian Union of
   Industrialists
   and Entrepreneurs
34, Khreshchatyk Vul.
01001 Kiev
Tel: (+38 044) 224 8346
Fax: (+38 044) 226 3152

Union of Small, Medium and
   Privatized Enterprises
16, Shevchenko Vul.
252601 Kiev
Tel/Fax: (+38 044) 224 1219

World Bank
2, Lysenka Vul.
01032 Kiev
Tel: (+38 044) 490 6672
Fax: (+38 044) 490 6672
www.worldbank.org.ua

Websites

Central and East European Business
   Directory
<www.ceebd.co.uk/ceebd/
   business.htm>

CIA World Factbook
<www.odci.gov/cia/publications/fact
   book/index.html>

CountryWatch
<www.countrywatch.com>

Economist Intelligence Unit
<www.eiu.org>

European Bank for Reconstruction and
   Development (EBRD)
<www.ebrd.org/english/index.htm>

International Business Resources on
   the WWW
<Ciber.bus.msu.edu/busres.htm>

ISI Emerging Markets
<site.securities.com>

Library of Congress
Country Studies
<lcweb2.loc.gov/frd/cs/
cshome.html >

Organization for Economic
Co-operation
and Development (OECD)
<www.oecd.org>

School of Slavonic and East European
Studies, University College London
<www.ssees.ac.uk/general.htm>

Stat-USA
<www.stat-usa.gov>

United States Department of State
<www.state.gov>

World Bank
<www.worldbank.org>

Bibliography

Adam, J. (1994), 'Transition to a Market Economy in Poland', *Cambridge Journal of Economics*, 18, December, 607–18.

Allison, C. and D. Ringold (1996), 'Labor Markets in Transition in Central and Eastern Europe: 1989–1995', Social Challenges of Transition Series (New York: World Bank/Oxford University Press).

Aslund, A. (2001), 'The Myth of Output Collapse after Communism', Carnegie Endowment for International Peace Working Paper No. 18 (March).

Bakos, G. (1994), 'Hungarian Transition After Three Years', *Europe-Asia Studies*, 46(7), 1189–1214.

Baldassarri, M., L. Paganetto and E.S. Phelps (eds) (1993), *Privatization Processes in Eastern Europe: Theoretical Foundations and Empirical Results* (New York: St Martin's Press (now Palgrave Macmillan) in association with Rivista di Politica Economica, SIPI, Rome, and CEIS, University Tor Vergata, Rome).

Batt, J. (1988), *Economic Reform and Political Change in Eastern Europe: A Comparison of the Czechoslovak and Hungarian Experiences* (New York: St Martin's Press (now Palgrave Macmillan)).

Bell, J. (1995), 'Beyond the Limits', *Central European*, March, 32–4.

Berry, R. (1994), 'Hungary: The Political Economy of Change, 1990–1994', *Coexistence: A Review of East–West and Development Issues*, 31, December, 325–39.

Blagnys, G. (1991), 'Economy – Baltic States: New Year Promises Optimistic Outlook', Global Information Network Interpress Service, 9 January.

Brown, K. (2001), 'Europe Reinvented – Transfer of State Assets', *Financial Times*, 26 January.

Bunce, V. (1999), 'The Political Economy of Post-Socialism', *Slavic Review*, 58(4), 756–93.

Comerford, M. (1995), 'IBM Slates Major Plant in Hungary', *Budapest Sun*, 2–8 February, p. 5.

Dallago, B., G. Ajani and B. Grancelli (eds) (1992), *Privatization and Entrepreneurship in Post-socialist Countries: Economy, Law, and Society* (New York: St Martin's Press (now Palgrave Macmillan)).

Divila, E. and Z. Sokol (1994), 'Transformation of the Agricultural Sector: Conceptual Questions of Forming New Enterpreneurial Entities in Czech Agriculture', *Eastern European Economics: A Journal of Translations*, 32, September–October, 51–64.

Earle, J.S., et al. (1994), *Small Privatization: The Transformation of Retail Trade and Consumer Services in the Czech Republic, Hungary, and Poland* (Budapest/New York: Central European University Press).

Earle, J.S., R. Frydman and A. Rapaczynski (eds) (1993), *Privatization in the Transition to a Market Economy: Studies of Preconditions and Policies in Eastern Europe* (New York: St Martin's Press (now Palgrave Macmillan)).

European Bank for Reconstruction and Development (1999), *Transition Report 1999* (London: EBRD, November).

European Bank for Reconstruction and Development (2000), *Transition Report 2000* (London: EBRD, November).

European Bank for Reconstruction and Development (2001), *Transition Report Update* (London: EBRD, April).

Freedom House (2001), *Freedom in the World 2000–2001* (New York: Freedom House, May).

Frydman, R. and A. Rapaczynski (1994), *Privatization in Eastern Europe: Is the State Withering Away?* (Budapest/New York: Central European University Press).

Frydman, R., *et al.* (1993), *The Privatization Process in Central Europe: Economic Environment, Legal and Ownership Structure, Institutions for State Regulation, Overview of Privatization Programs, Initial Transformation of Enterprises* (Budapest/ New York: Central European University Press).

Fuller, F., *et al.* (2002), 'Accession of the Czech Republic, Hungary and Poland to the European Union: Impacts on Agricultural Markets', World Economy, 25(3), 407–28.

Hellman, J., G. Jones and D. Kaufmann (2000), 'Seize the State, Seize the Day: State Capture, Corruption, and Influence in Transition', World Bank Policy Research Working Paper 2444 (World Bank Institute and EBRD, September).

Hellman, J., *et al.* (2000), 'Measuring Governance and State Capture: The Role of Bureaucrats and Firms in Shaping the Business Environment', World Bank Working Paper 2312.

Henderson, K. (1994), 'Czechoslovakia: Cutting the Gordian Knot', *Coexistence: A Review of East–West and Development Issues*, 31, December, 309–24.

Hoffmann, L. and F. Mollers (eds) (2001), *Ukraine on the Road to Europe* (Germany: Physica-Verlag).

International Monetary Fund (2001), *World Economic Outlook* (Washington, DC: IMF, May).

Janos, A.C. (1997), *The Political Economy of Ethnic Conflict: The Dissolution of Czechoslovakia and Yugoslavia* (Washington, DC: National Council for Eurasian and East European Research).

Johnson, S., D. Kaufmann and A. Shleifer (1997), 'Politics and Entrepreneurship in Transition Economies', Working Paper Series No. 57 (University of Michigan: William Davidson Institute).

Jones, C. (1995), 'A New Central Europe', *The Banker*, April, 23–6.

Kasch-Haroutounian, M. and S. Price (2001), 'Volatility in the Transition Markets of Central Europe', Applied Economics, 33(1), January, 93–105.

Katz, B.S. and L. Rittenberg (eds) (1992), *The Economic Transformation in Eastern Europe: Views from Within* (Westport, CT: Praeger).

Kideckel, D.A. (ed.) (1995), *East European Communities: The Struggles for Balance in Turbulent Times* (Boulder, CO: Westview Press).

Kopits, G. (1994), 'Hungary: Midway in the Transition', *Eastern European Economics*, 32(6), November–December, 29–55.

Liargovas, P. and D. Chionis (2001), 'Economic Integration between the European Union and the Transition Economies of Central European Initiative Countries', *Post-Communist Economies*, 13(1), 57–70.

Liberati, P. (2001), 'Poverty and Monetary Transfers in Belarus: Some Options for Gradual Reforms', *Economics of Transition*, 9(1), 175–203.

Newbery, D.M. (1994), 'Restructuring and Privatizing Electric Utilities in Eastern Europe', *Economics of Transition*, 2, September, 291–316.

Piazolo, D. (2000), 'EU Integration of Transition Countries: Overlap of Requisites and the Remaining Tasks. Intereconomics', *Review of International Trade and Development*, 35(6), November–December, 264–273.

Repse, E. (2000), Latvia: Focus on Country Development, *Finance and Development*, 37(3), September, 17–19.

Rondinelli, D. (ed.) (1994), *Privatization and Economic Reform in Central Europe: The Changing Business Climate* (Westport, CT: Quorum).

Schneider, F. and D. Enste (2000), 'Shadow Economies: Size, Causes, and Consequences', *Journal of Economic Literature*, 38, March.

Stevens, C. (1994), 'Hungary: Oh, To Be Beautiful Again', *Global Finance*, 8, November, 87–8, 91–2, 95–6.

Svejnar, Jan (ed.) (1995), *The Czech Republic and Economic Transition in Eastern Europe* (San Diego, CA: Academic Press).

Transparency International (2000), *Corruption Perceptions Index* (September).

United Nations Children's Fund (2000), *State of the World's Children 2001* (New York: UNICEF, December).

United Nations Development Programme (2000), *Human Development Report 2000* (New York: Oxford University Press/UNDP).

United Nations Economic Commission for Europe. Economic Survey of Europe 2000. Geneva. No. 2/3 (December 2000).

United States Agency for International Development/Europe & Eurasia Bureau (1998), *Monitoring Country Progress in Central and Eastern Europe and Eurasia*, Appendix II: Transition Paths (Washington, DC: USAID, No. 4 , October).

United States Agency for International Development, Europe & Eurasia Bureau (1999), *From Transition to Partnership: A Strategic Framework for USAID Programs in Europe and Eurasia* (Washington, DC: USAID, December).

United States Agency for International Development, Europe & Eurasia Bureau (1999), *Transition With a Human Face: Broadening the Benefits of Economic and Political Reform in Central and Eastern Europe and the New Independent States* (Washington, DC: USAID, August).

United States Agency for International Development/Europe & Eurasia Bureau (2000), *Monitoring Country Progress in Central and Eastern Europe and Eurasia* (Washington, DC: USAID, No. 6, May).

United States Bureau of the Census (1995), *Populations at Risk in CEE: Labor Markets*, prepared for USAID/E&E/PCS (Washington, DC: US Department of Commerce, No. 2, February).

Weber, R. and G. Taube (2000), 'Estonia Moves toward EU Accession', *Finance and Development*, 37(3), September, 28–31.

Winiecki, J. (2000), 'Solving Foreign Trade Puzzles in Post-Communist Transition', *Post-Communist Economies*, 12(3), September, 261–78.

World Bank (2000), *Making Transition Work for Everyone: Poverty and Inequality in Europe and Central Asia* (New York: Oxford University Press).

World Bank (2001), *Global Economic Prospects and the Developing Countries 2001* (New York: Oxford University Press).

World Bank (2001), *World Development Indicators 2001* (New York: Oxford University Press).

Zizmond, E. (1994), 'Economic Developments in Slovenia', *Eastern European Economics: A Journal of Translations*, 32, November–December, 75–99.

Index